Acknowledgements

There are many people in both India and Britain whose energy, encouragement and advice has been invaluable in the compilation of these teachings. Special thanks go to Dr Karan Singh and Mr R. P. Malaviya of the Ramayan Vidyapeeth in New Delhi, Dr K. D. Tripathi and Dr B. Mishra of the Sanskrit Learning and Theology Department in Benares Hindu University, and Dr Kapila Vatsyayan of the Indira Institute of Arts, New Delhi.

I would also like to express my deep gratitude to Dr Maya Goyle and her family in Benares for their unlimited hospitality and the insights they willingly gave into their own culture; and to the Panchmatia family in Manchester who showed that their culture's warmth and generosity survives in any climate.

Many thanks also to the team at the International Consultancy of Religion, Education and Culture: Martin Palmer for his editorial work, Pallavi Mavani and Joanna Edwards for their many hours of transcribing tapes, Joanne O'Brien, Barbara Cousins and Liz Breuilly for their endless patience in the face of what seemed, at times, an endless project.

Contents

Code and Details of Contributors

Swami A. Parthasarathy   (Parth.)
Vedanta Academy, Bombay

with

Nila Pancholi   (Panch.)
M.A. Sanskrit Literature

Swami Bhavyananda   (Bhav.)
Ramakrishna Mission, UK

Bhakti Charu Swami and Ranchor Das   (Char./Das.)
International Society of Krishna Consciousness

Dr Frank Chandra   (Chand.)
World Congress of Faiths

Anuradha Roma Choudhury   (Choud.)
M.A. Sanskrit Literature

Dr B. K. Matilal   (Mat.)
Spalding Professor of Eastern Religions, Oxford University

A Note on Translation

These readings, in almost all cases, have been translated by the commentator from the original Sanskrit. In the case of the Hare Krishna movement the translation given is that of Swami Prabbhupadas (see Bibliography).

The commentaries have been drawn from the writings and lectures of the contributors noted on p. ix. They are usually atributed to one source but, where no note has been given, two or more contributors have agreed an interpretation. The diversity of interpretations in this text reflects the diversity of Hindu thought (see Introduction).

Preface

The term 'Hindu' was first used by the medieval Muslim invaders to describe the dwellers of the Indus valley. But the culture we now know as Hinduism and which the Indians call Sanatana Dharma – Eternal Law – predates that label by thousands of years. It is more than a religion in the doctrinal sense that the West understands religion. One can believe in any god or no god and still be a Hindu. It is a way of life, a state of mind.

It is very difficult to find any viewpoint which is not incorporated in the vast body of knowledge of this culture which is, in fact, many cultures combined. Therefore, in taking on this book, we have not presumed to cover its beliefs totally but merely to give some idea of its enormous wealth and diversity.

At its heart it is neither strange nor exotic but uncannily familiar. It is a sublimely simple and extravagantly complex system of systems which seems, at times, to say everything the West has ever said or is likely to say about anything. We must ask ourselves: why is it that so many great thinkers have admitted their debt to the Upanishads or discovered theories that unwittingly echo the ideas of those books written thousands of years earlier?

The answer lies to some extent in a gentle piece of advice given by one of our eminent advisers in New Delhi when we began research for the book. Having been presented with a list of Hindu concepts, to which she was asked to put her mind, she then, in the course of discussion, gave an analogy of the world as the lens through which we see Truth. The West has broken up the lens the better to understand it, laying out the pieces each as a seperate discipline of 'knowledge'. While the West has taken a long time reshuffling its pieces and learning the ins and outs of every piece, Hindu researchers in the form of the great spiritual masters have used the lens in one piece to look directly at the ultimate Truth.

Despite their pride in the wisdom of their culture, Hindus would be the first to say that the ultimate Truth cannot be found merely by reading a book on it. It lies within the soul of every human being. Nevertheless, we hope our readers might catch a glimpse of Truth through this book as they might catch sight of a long-lost friend across a crowded street thousands of miles from home.

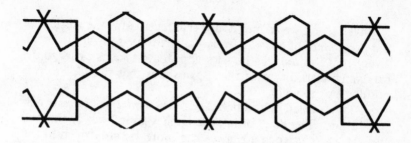

Introduction

Access to the Vedas is the greatest privilege this century may claim over all previous centuries ... In the whole world there is no study so beneficial and so elevating as that of the Upanishads. It has been the solace of my life and it will be the solace of my death.

Schopenhauer

In the last century the 3000-year-old Vedas were translated into European languages, sending a tremor through the libraries of the Western world. Modern thinkers who read these ancient books were, and still are, humbled by the realization that wisdom we so proudly claim as the triumph of twentieth-century Western progress is, indeed, very ancient.

A system which is in some respects almost identical with that thought out by Spinoza and the profoundest thinkers of modern Europe. Indeed, if you will pardon the anachronism, the Hindus were Spinozas more than two thousand years before the existence of Spinoza and Darwinians ... many centuries before the doctrines of evolution had been accepted by the Huxleys of our time and before any word like Evolution existed in any language in the world.

Professor Monier-Williams

Pre-empting Darwin and Spinoza was only the tip of the iceberg. The recently rediscovered sixteen aphorisms of Vedic mathematics provide the formulae for the mental compution of complex equations in all branches of mathematics. A culture which was, and is, essentially oral could calculate a square root without putting pen to paper or fingers to calculator.

Examples abound in all the arts and sciences, from psychology to physics, and we cannot doubt that, even now, the wisdom of the great seers of ancient India has yet to be fully appreciated. Every move in modern physics appears to take us closer to the fundamental theorem of the Upanishads that the Universe is nothing but thought itself.

Sir James Dean in his book, *Mysterious Universe*, comes to this conclusion: 'The river of knowledge has gone back upon itself and the more science advances the more we are driven to the conclusion that the whole of the universe appears to be a great thought rather than a great machine.'

This wisdom of the ancient rishis came to them through means foreign to our modern Western process of investigation which grabs the material world by the throat and turns it inside out. The rishis took the human soul by the heart and turned it inside out. Through tremendous discipline of body, mind and intellect they came to terms with a Reality Western science has long pursued.

The increasing convergence of thought from these two very different approaches is, in itself, witness to the rishis' claim that this entire material Universe is One all-pervading spiritual Reality. If this is so then certainly whatever road of investigation one takes, whether material or spiritual, the answer should, ultimately, be the same.

It would be misleading, however, to ascribe to the Vedas or later scriptures a single immutable philosophy. As with Western science and philosophy we see development through a chain of inspired thinkers.

THE SRUTI – *The Revealed Scriptures*

Historical Background

The dating of the Vedas remains hazy with a divergence of opinion of about 2500 years. Even if we take the latest dates simply as a hypothetical starting point we are still talking about scriptures which are over 3000 years old.

On this calculation the Vedic period begins around 1500 BCE* with the arrival of an Aryan race of herders, probably from

---

* The terms CE and BCE replace AD and BC.

central or northern Asia, who swept down to the plains of the Punjab and into the Indus Valley before gradually infiltrating south in a process which continues today. With them they brought the Sanskrit language, the priestly class of the brahmins and a theology reminiscent of the Semitic beliefs which were to shape Western culture. Varuna, one of the gods attributed to the Aryans who appears in the early Vedas, is male, a punitive ruler of heaven and hell. In contrast, the village religions which these Aryan invaders encountered were agricultural and therefore inclined to express their spirituality in terms of fertility goddesses. God, the mother, has remained a constant in Indian worship, especially in the south where Aryan influence is least and the worship of the goddess Shakti remains dominant. It is likely that the pre-Aryan cultures of India believed in the transmigration of souls; this belief has remained a constant in all permutations of Hindu thought but does not appear to have been part of Aryan theology. The meditating yogi is also ascribed to indigenous culture and re-emerged significantly at the time of the Upanishads and then again with the growing tradition of Shiva devotion (Shaivism).

The development of Vedic culture was, from the start, an absorption process of, on the one hand, the Aryan culture and, on the other, the many local cults of the indigenous population. Who was absorbing whom is arguable. The gods, priests and principles of both are apparent in what was to become identified as the rich and varied Hindu culture. This tolerance for all-comers has been the strength and genius of Hinduism and the explanation for its resilient vitality in the face of all social challenges and upheavals.

The caste system which developed and solidified during the Vedic period from 1500 to 500 BCE partly reflected a division between the indigenous peoples and the Aryans in which the Aryan brahmin was of the highest order, with warriors next in priority and ordinary tribesmen as traders and labourers. The assimilation of non-Aryan priests into the brahmin caste was, however, a part of the mutual cultural absorption. Religion was inevitably used to uphold and bolster the brahmin-ruled caste system but reaction to this was to become a significant catalyst for the evolution and, at times, revolution of a religion which, along with Judaism, is a 'grandparent' religion of the world.

In truth we understand little of Hinduism's early philosophy other than what has been conjectured from its first scriptural records, the Vedas, which reflect the central role of animal sacrifice.

The Vedas

The first series of Vedas are the Samhitas, the liturgies which accompanied the sacrificial rites of the Aryan brahmins. They include hymns for prayer and chanting during the sacrifical rites as well as sacrificial formulae. Sacrifice has remained a cornerstone of Hinduism but the interpretation of its significance evolved through the growing body of scriptures into a remarkable social and cosmological system which may or may not have been what was understood by the Vedic brahmins.

The Samhitas, dated as late as 1000 BCE, were followed by the Brahmanas, the Aranyakas and, finally, the Upanishads. The Brahmanas, dated by Western scholars at around 800 BCE, give practical advice on sacrifical and other rites and general rules of conduct. The Aranyakas, meaning 'forest-dwellers', are the first of the great teachings arising from the practice of renouncing the world to take up study and meditation in the forests. The Aranyakas are the immediate predecessors of the Upanishads and display the same hallmark of deep metaphysics. Western scholarship's estimates date the Aranyakas and Upanishads at between 700 and 300 BCE.

It is likely that ageing brahmins retired to the forests as a natural extension of their priestly experience and there, along with members of the warrior and, occasionally, the lower castes, took up the lifestyle of meditation and physical austerity which marked this new phase. The Aranyakas have been described as a reaction by disgruntled brahmins and non-brahmins to the limitations of Brahmanas rituals and the increasing power of the Brahmins. There may well be truth in this, given the revolutionary nature of the Aranyakas.

Nevertheless, elegant metaphysical knots had hoisted the hymns in the last book of the Rig Veda to greater heights, so these new texts should be viewed less as a complete break than a continuation, however controversial, of the spiritual research begun through the channels of ritualized religion.

Although officially part of the Vedas, the Upanishads and

Aranyakas are so distinctive that they tend to be designated as the 'Upanishads' while the term 'Vedas' is used to refer to the earlier sacrificial hymns and instructions. Therefore, in talking about the Vedas we shall only be referring to that part of them which forms the early collection. The Aranyakas and Upanishads will be dealt with separately.

There are four Vedas: Rig Veda, Yajurveda, Samaveda and Atharvaveda.

Rig Veda

As the original collection of sacred songs to which other collections were added, the Rig Veda is the seminal work. It consists of ten books or mandalas of hymns whose primary concern is peace, prosperity and liberation to a better world.

On the whole, the hymns are invocations of specific gods as personifications of the powers of the Universe. The names, functions and prominence of the gods in these Vedas change considerably by the time of the Upanishads as more local cults are embraced and spiritual exploration takes some dramatic turns. Varuna, who enjoyed relative prominence in the Vedas without any particular affinity to an aspect of nature, is a casualty of these developments, becoming a water god of little importance.

Indra, traditionally the god of the sky and rain and ruler of the physical world, is, with almost a quarter of the hymns devoted to him, the most frequently invoked god. Second in frequency of appearance is Agni. As god of fire, Agni is also the messenger god, taking the offerings of the priests to the gods and bringing the gods to the sacrifice. Although no longer such dominant figures, both these gods remain important in the Hindu pantheon.

In general, the tenth and final book of the Rig Veda is proclaimed as the beginning of monotheism when all the many gods are acknowledged as manifestations of the One Reality. In a famous verse (see p. 128) the Rig Veda declares that Mithra, Varuna, Agni, etc., are the One Reality. In an equally famous hymn (see p. 126) it describes the One which comes before all the gods, 'when existence and non-existence was not', when 'that One, breathless, breathed by its own nature'.

Whether this was an underlying attitude of the indigenous or

Aryan culture now asserting itself or a philosophical turning point for all concerned is a matter for debate, but certainly the notion of one universal god is out in the open by the end of the late Vedic period and profoundly expounded in the last books of the Vedas, the Upanishads (see below).

In the tenth book of the Rig Veda sacrifice is also given a deep symbolism beyond the barter system of offerings to the gods in exchange for a peaceful and bountiful world. Hymn no. 129 narrates the sacrifice of the Immortal Being to create the material world (see p. 29). Thus sacrifice is identified as the order of the Universe. Without it there is no Universe.

The Yajurveda

The Yajurveda is divided into two parts: Shukla meaning white and Krishna meaning black. It consists mainly of sacrificial formulae in both prose and verse to be chanted at a sacrifice. Sacrificial rites involved two priests, one to perform the physical actions and the other to chant the sacred hymns.

The Samaveda

The Samaveda is composed of many verses from the Rig Veda set to music for singing during sacrificial rituals. Sound was, and is, the essential medium of spiritual communication in Hinduism, both between teacher and student and between humanity and God.

Out of over 1500 mantras in the Samaveda there are only seventy-five which are original. The rest are from the Rig Veda. Much praise is devoted to the sacred soma juice, an intoxicating drink which was used in rituals to attain a state of spiritual elevation. Soma itself was heralded as god while also elevating the imbiber to this state. We see in this relationship an under-standing of Divinity which has remained essential to Hinduism. Nature *is* the gods, rather than being ruled *by* the gods. There is a latent Divinity in everything.

The Atharvaveda

The compilation of the Atharvaveda is dated after the other three Vedas, although its subject matter is believed to pre-date the arrival of the Aryans. Atharvaveda literally means 'fire-priest knowledge' and it is in this Veda that we find the practical arts and sciences. It is full of charms and medicinal secrets while also taking in the wider context, praising and explaining the nature of life and time.

The Upa-Vedas

The five Upa-Vedas are subordinate Vedas, taking up where the Atharvaveda left off to deal with the various aspects of the material world.

Ayur-Veda deals with the science of medicine, both preventative and curative, embracing anatomy, physiology, hygiene and surgery.

Dhanur-Veda deals with military sciences such as archery and charioteering.

Gandharva-Veda deals with the performance arts of music and dance.

Sthaptya-Veda takes in mathematics as well as its practical applications in the visual arts and sciences: engineering and architecture, sculpture and painting.

The Aranyakas and Upanishads

The Upanishads, including the Aranyakas, are the final chapter of the Vedas and are known as Vedanta, the 'end of knowledge' (*veda* = knowledge; *anta* = end). They are revered by Hindus as the highest expression of Truth revealed by the great sages of ancient times who acquired this knowledge through realization of God within themselves. The Upanishads are the aspect of the Vedas which has maintained the Vedas' unshakable authority and power for thousands of years.

They turn inward from the contemplation and praise of the external world (which characterizes the Vedic hymns) and travel into the very depths of the soul to find here the same gods and goddesses ruling the internal landscape. Beyond these deities lies identification with the Supreme Consciousness, Brahman. This identification is God-realization or Self-realization.

The Upanishads are most noted in the development of Hindu philosophy for the identification of the Brahman, the all-pervading spirit which maintains the Universe, with the Atman, the eternal spirit which maintains each individual. Brahman-

Atman is understood as the motionless, changeless Infinite
Reality which is veiled by Its own creative power, maya. Maya
perpetuates the illusory, ever-changing, ever-active, pluralistic
world of our daily experience. Why? The implied answer is that
anything which is Infinite must include both Truth and Untruth
and, in regard to this, we are presently 'on the wrong side of the
tracks'.

These concepts, which lie beyond the grasp of our dualistic
this-or-that, is-or-isn't thought processes, are expressed in
appropriately paradoxical, poetic language.

Although there are verses in the Upanishads which say point-
blank that the Brahman is the Atman (see p. 145) there is,
nevertheless debate in both West and East as to how
unequivocally and consistently the Upanishads uphold this
monistic view as opposed to the dualistic view of a personal God
whose identity is separate from our own. Certainly, there is no
avoiding the fact that the Upanishads do say it and mean it again
and again, no matter how equivocal or catholic the translation.
The four great aphorisms of the Upanishads, known as the
Mahavakyas (commandments or statements), are: 'Consciousness is Brahman', 'That Thou art', 'The Self is Brahman' and 'I
am Brahman'.

The sticking point is whether every Upanishad unfailingly
denies the possibility of an omniscient but separate and personal
God. The argument becomes intense around the Bhagavad Gita
(see below) which can more obviously be cited to substantiate the
dualistic view. But it is important to understand the ease with
which the Hindu mind slips between the notion of an external
God to be worshipped and a God that is each one of us. Within
the commentaries of our contributors you will see this diversity
of view and the rationale which lies behind it.

The Upanishads are also noted for their definition of the world
as nothing but names, forms and activities. This illusion, we are
told, is sustained by setting ourselves up as subjects experiencing
the 'objective' world which, in reality, we create as we go along.
The dualism of subject and object, experiencer and experienced,
dissolves as soon as we recognize the unity of all things. The
individual essence is one with the universal essence. The
macrocosm is a projection of the microcosm.

Twentieth-century 'discoveries' in some subtler schools of

philosophy and science – semiology, structuralism, Jungian psychology, new physics and so on – are pre-empted by the Upanishads in defining the problem, if not in the conclusion they have currently reached. In all their delvings into the nature of Reality, Western thinkers, until recently, dismissed dreams as the last place to look, but these provided the Upanishadic sages with a rich vein of metaphysical gold which continues to be tapped. The great analogy for which the Upanishads are renowned is that of the waker-dreamer-deep sleeper. This beginningless, endless Universe is the dream of Brahman. We are the dreaming figures in that world which is constantly in the process of being dreamt up. It is uncreated and created at every moment in the same sense that the dream world is uncreated and created by the dreamer at every moment until he or she wakes – at which point the dream world dissolves.

Dominant also in the cosmological scheme is the legacy of the earlier Vedas – sacrifice. As a principle of living it is presented repeatedly as a means of soaking up every aspect of existence. In the Brhadaranyaka Upanishad there are passages which speak of the Vedic sacrificial horse, equating it with the various aspects of time, space and causation. Later in the same Upanishad the act of ritual sacrifice is equated with the various configurations of life in which there is a symbolic fire, fuel, trough, offering and sparks. This 'obsession' with equating everything with everything has tended to irritate or amuse Westerners but is, in truth, fundamental to the notion of a pluralistic world which is also a single unity, only differentiated by rearrangements of form.

The power of sacrifice, as both a potent force for ruling the external world and a state of mind to which one should aspire, has remained the key to Indian culture. Hindus of all persuasions, from the strict rationalism of the Advaiti Vedanta school to the devotional acceptance of the bhakti cults, testify that the *yagna* (sacrifice) ceremony does bring rain in time of drought. As an attitude of giving one's all to the world, sacrifice is cited by Indians as both a reason for India's spiritual potency and resilience and for its material downfall at the hands of invaders who were not so bound by this principle.

What may seem to us fascinating theories and mind puzzlers are, as far as the Hindu culture is concerned, a declaration of the Truth, just as the works of Newton and Einstein are our culture's declaration of the Truth even if the majority of Westerners only have a very incomplete understanding of their theories.

Just as Darwin's *On the Origin of Species* does not form part of popular reading or educational study in the West, the Upanishads, despite their unchallenged authority and wisdom, are not widely read by Hindus. It is the epics, especially the Bhagavad Gita (see below), which express in popular form the wisdom of the Upanishads; the Gita is beloved and known by all Hindus, more often through hearing and chanting it than through reading it.

Before turning to the Upanishads a teacher will first direct a student to the Bhagavad Gita as a foundation and, indeed, a comprehensive guide to living and spiritual understanding. The Upanishads are taught later when the student is further along the path to spiritual enlightenment. The ultimate Truth expressed, as much as it can be, in the Upanishads will only take root in the most highly tuned and receptive mind.

The student–teacher dialogue is the modus operandi of the Upanishads and it is this dialogue which has passed on Vedic knowledge for thousands of years. *Upa-ni-shad* (literally, 'near-below-sit') indicates the student–teacher relationship and the three attitudes necessary for attaining the Truth: receptivity, devotion and introspection.

These three qualities were a condition for the original teaching. The God-realized rishis (seers) living in the forests and Himalayas were sought out by spiritual aspirants and asked all the imponderables about life, its source and its purpose. They taught only those who had already prepared themselves through devotional study and had shown a dedication to God-realization during a probationary year. The Prasnopanishad (see pp. 161–2) begins with five students approaching a guru, all of them well established in devotional practices and study, yet the guru sends them away for another year of discipline, abstinence and spiritual reflection before he will answer their questions.

One can never be over-prepared for the Upanishads but one can easily be under-prepared. Swami Parthasarathy, whose brilliant commentaries on Hindu texts have inspired audiences around the world, devotes nine hours of lectures to a single short Upanishad, such as the Kenopanishad, and this is merely an introduction to a text which, in dedicated study, would be afforded six months' attention.

Of over 200 Upanishads there are between ten and thirteen which are considered the classical Upanishads: Aitareya, Kausitaki, Taittirya, Brhadaranyaka, Chandogya, Kena, Katha, Shvetashvatara, Isavasya, Mundaka, Prasna, Maitrayaniya and Mandukya.

THE SMRITI – *The Remembered Texts*

Historical Background

The Upanishads see the last of the srutis – the 'heard' texts – and the beginning of the smriti – the 'remembered' texts. These are of human rather than divine inspiration.

As with the srutis, the dating of these texts varies considerably; they tend, however, to be dated by Western scholars from two or three centuries before the Common Era (CE) to two or three centuries after it started.

By the beginning of the Common Era there were six classifications of orthodox thought recognized by the brahmins as roads to salvation. The heterodox schools included Buddhism and Jainism which had flouted Brahmin authority but which, nevertheless, continued to affect, and be affected by, the orthodox schools. Of these, Vedanta most concerns us, being recognized today as the high philosophy of Hinduism. Vedanta accepts the authority of the Vedas but emphasizes the Upanishads and the essential Oneness of all existence. The other five schools variously proclaim Vedic rituals; logic; an atomized universe of soul, mind, time and space; a dualistic, atheistic Universe in which the spirit is entangled in matter; and a dualistic world in which physical discipline and meditation on an immortal god lead to repatriation in the spiritual realm. In practical terms, these elements are not clearly segregated into schools but form part of a general pool of Hindu thought which informs its multitude of cults and traditions to varying degrees.

Vedanta is the most influential school today and was enshrined first in the Brahma-sutras, commentaries on the

Upanishads dated somewhere between the second century BCE and the first century CE, and then in the commentaries by the three great saints, Sankaracharya, Ramanuja and Madhva.

As important as the 'six schools' are the bhakti (devotional) cults whose beginnings are dated from somewhere shortly before the Common Era to early within it. These cults, based on devotion through prayer and chanting to a particular god, arose largely in response to a social system which disenfranchized many men and all women from religious education and activity. Flanked by brahminism on one side and Buddhism's atheistic response to caste-dominated religion on the other, the majority of the population were inclined to bhakti. Indeed, devotion to local gods always existed as the 'little tradition' of local cults which brahminism accommodated into its 'greater tradition' of Vedic culture. Bhakti does not deny the Vedas. On the contrary, it points to the devotional hymns of the Vedas as confirmation of bhakti as the true path to God.

The three major deities – with already established followings – who became the objects of this devotional form of faith were Shiva, Vishnu and, in the south of India, the goddess Shakti (also known as Durga) who, like Shiva, has her roots in a pre-Vedic religion.

During the Gupta dynasty's rule in India from 320 to 650 CE, retrospectively acclaimed as the golden age of Hinduism, these three cults consolidated as the three major traditions, absorbing other gods, heroes and great sages into their personalities through the development in religious thought of avataras – divine incarnations. Vishnu, who pulled the two most beloved personalities of Hindu scriptures, Rama and Krishna, into his orbit, is particularly associated with this concept, having ten official avataras as well as innumerable extras.

Today, although they will worship many gods on an occasional basis, Hindu families will identify themselves as Vaishnavites (Vishnu worshippers), Shaivites (Shiva worshippers) or Shakti worshippers.

Now, as always, the Vedas are not the common reading of the masses. They are the background on which the great stories and epics of the gods, in particular Vishnu and Shiva, are played out.

The Puranas

The Puranas began in the post-Vedic period as the popularized teachings of the higher Truth and continued to accumulate through the Middle Ages. They catered to women and the lower castes who were denied access to education. Each is a mixture of history, philosophy and mythology beginning with the creation of the world; each includes material which pre-dates the Vedic period. There is also a substantial amount of astrology, geography, medicine, anatomy and military arts threaded through the dialogues between sage and disciple.

There are eighteen principal Puranas (Mahapuranas) and eighteen lesser Puranas (Upapuranas). The principal Puranas are divided into three groups which are ostensibly devoted to either Brahma, Shiva or Vishnu, who had emerged above all the lesser gods as the three manifestations of the Absolute Reality, Brahman. Shiva and Vishnu, however, appear most consistently in all three groups, reflecting the strong followings these two gods had acquired by the Middle Ages through the growth of bhakti.

The Epics

The two great epics of Hindu culture, whose significance and prominence cannot be underestimated, are the Ramayana and the Mahabharata. These epics and their divine protagonists, Rama and Krishna, both incarnations of the god Vishnu, have left no corner of Hindu life uninfluenced. Revered as historical and moral teachings, they are the endless subject of performance and visual arts, festivals and worship and the standard topic of evening narrations by trained story-tellers. The images of their characters are everywhere, in shops, offices, institutions, taxis, homes, etc. Their characters provide role models for all occasions. They encompass within their verses social, psychological, political, natural and spiritual laws as information and guidelines for correct living and spiritual development. It would be virtually impossible to find any Hindu in India or a South-East Asian Hindu country who was old enough to speak but could not give an elaborate account of these two epics.

The Ramayana

The Ramayana is a 24,000-verse poem written by the sage Valmiki. Western scholarship dates its nucleus at anywhere from 500 to 200 BCE with revisions and additions up to 200 CE.

Although considered a historical tale, its importance is as an exposition of the highest ideals of Hindu culture.

The Ramayana tells the story of Sri Rama, born at a time when the people of India were oppressed by Ravana, the demon king of Sri Lanka. Ravana's reign of terror was so comprehensive that even the gods were oppressed; they sent down the god Vishnu in his seventh incarnation to deal with the matter.

The finer details of the story have Vishnu spread between four sons but, in principle, Rama was Vishnu incarnate, while his wife Sita was Vishnu's consort Lakshmi incarnate. Rama represents the ideal man in all situations, as husband, son, disciple, friend, brother, king, warrior, citizen, while Sita represents the ideal woman as wife and queen.

On the eve of his coronation, Rama is exiled for fourteen years because of a promise which his father had made to his step-mother. Accompanied by Sita and his half-brother Lakshmana, he goes into the forest to live for a while in peaceful seclusion. Ravana, having heard of the threesome, persuaded his uncle to transform himself into a golden deer which, with Sita's unwitting aid, lures Rama and Lakshmana away. The deer is killed and its true identity revealed but, in the meantime, Ravana, disguised as a beggar, abducts Sita. Realizing the trick, the two brothers immediately set off in pursuit. With the help of the monkey god, Hanuman, and his monkey army they track down Sita in Sri Lanka. A bridge is built across to the island where Sita waits patiently in seclusion, performing austerities and refusing the advances of Ravana.

In a final great battle Ravana is killed and Sita restored to her husband. Their fourteen years of exile over, Rama, Sita and Lakshmana are able to return to their kingdom of Ayodhya although Sita then undergoes a trial by fire because of unjust imputations of infidelity. All ends happily with Rama being reunited with Sita and ruling Ayodhya as a perfect king, bringing peace and happiness to all his people. Such ideal administration is known as Rama-rajya and is what Mahatma Gandhi preached and worked for throughout his lifetime.

The Mahabharata

With 100,000 verses, the Mahabharata is the longest poem ever written and about seven times as long as the combined *Iliad* and *Odyssey*. There is a saying in India, 'What is not in this epic is not in India.' It is a huge reservoir of philosophy, rituals and mythology, woven around the tale of two warring families, the Pandavas and the Kauravas. The god Vishnu is present in his incarnation as the Pandava charioteer Krishna.

Western scholarship dates the epic at anywhere from the fourth century BCE to the fourth century CE. Tradition says that the Mahabharata was written by the rishi Vyasa who compiled the Vedas. It is said he dictated the poem to Lord Ganesha, the elephant-headed god of success. Ganesha agreed to undertake the transcription on the condition that Vyasa should complete the entire dictation from start to finish without pausing. Vyasa accepted the condition on another condition that Ganesha should not write anything down until he grasped the meaning of what was dictated, thereby giving the rishi a chance to compose more verses while Ganesha tried to fathom the deeper meanings of the verses. The story covers the lead-up to a battle, the battle and its aftermath with numerous subsidiary stories woven in to elaborate and substantiate the moral teachings.

As with the Ramayana the Mahabharata is concerned with dharma which translates as universal law, righteousness, duty and true nature.

No one should leave the path of dharma on any account – neither by temptation nor by fear nor by greed nor for life. Because pleasure and pain are both transitory, dharma is permanent and follows the soul in all directions.

Mahabharata: Asvamedha Parva 43:14

The circumstances of the Mahabharata are such that we are witness, in the unfolding plot, to every conceivable challenge to a person's ability to remain righteous – true to dharma. To start with, the warring families, the Pandavas and the Kauravas, are cousins. The kingdom of the five sons of Pandu is usurped by the 100 sons of the blind king Dhiritarashtra. Despite their rightful claim the Pandavas offer to give it up in exchange for a token payment of five villages. This offer receives a sneering

refusal from Duryodhana, the oldest Kaurava, who informs the
Pandavas they won't be receiving so much as a pinprick of land.
As charioteer and lifelong friend of the Pandavas, Krishna
makes one last bid for peace, but the Kauravas are hell-bent on
their course of action and so the two armies line up on the
battlefield of Kurukshetra in the Punjab. This is the point at
which Arjuna, the third son of Pandu, loses his nerve and has to
be talked onto the battlefield by Krishna. Their exchange was
recorded as the eighteen chapters of the Bhagavad Gita, after
which Arjuna goes on to fight. The Kaurava army is annihilated
and the Pandavas reclaim their kingdom.

The Bhagavad Gita

The Bhagavad Gita, meaning 'the Song of the Lord', is a 700-
verse poem which occurs in the middle of the Mahabharata. It is
the most popular, well-known Hindu scripture, drawing
extensively on the Upanishads, at times verbatim. But, unlike
the Upanishads, the Bhagavad Gita is not so much a declaration
of metaphysical Truth as a comprehensive code of living.

The context is the imminent battle on the field of
Kurukshetra. The Gita opens as the bugles blow to herald the
start of the battle. Arjuna asks Lord Krishna, who is incarnated
as his charioteer, to drive him between the two armies so that he
can assess the strength of the enemy. At the sight of his own
kinsmen, teachers and friends lined up against one another and
the realization of the inevitable carnage, Arjuna is overwhelmed
with emotion. He falls to his knees in despair, declaring that a
battle won at the expense of the blood of his own relatives and
teachers is not a battle worth fighting. 'I will not fight,' he tells
Krishna. But Krishna does not support Arjuna in his moral
stance. He urges Arjuna to fight on the grounds of a higher
morality. The battle is righteous and it is Arjuna's personal fate
and duty (*swa-dharma*) to fight. The discussion develops into a
full-scale exposition on the nature of existence, the law of karma
(action) and the various paths by which one can rise above
bondage to karma. In the course of the teaching Krishna, at
Arjuna's request, reveals himself in his absolute divine state.
Arjuna sees before him the entire Universe in time and space.
His vision is both beautiful and horrific and Arjuna opts for the

return of Krishna in his less intimidating form as Vishnu, the four-armed god of sustenance.

By the end of the Bhagavad Gita Krishna's teaching has rehabilitated Arjuna from a state of grief-stricken, fearful confusion to that of steady-minded purpose. He goes on to fight and win the battle. Krishna's deep insights into human psychology withstand the rigours of time as only genuine wisdom can do. The battlefield is, of course (as stated in the first verse of the Gita), the battlefield of life and the challenge Arjuna faces, in which duty and morality, fear and grief become hopelessly entangled, is the challenge which we all face constantly.

The Gita is particularly notable for two developments in Hindu philosophy. It emphasizes the social nature of human existence and enjoins active participation in society, rather than retirement to the forests, as the path to liberation. All the great teachings of the rishis are to be put into action but without physically pulling out of worldly life. It is not renunciation *of* action that the Bhagavad Gita teaches, but renunciation *in* action. The concept of sacrifice is fully developed as a state of mind in which one gives up the fruits of all action. Physical possession is harmless provided there is no mental bondage to this wealth, power or fame. How to retain the spirit of renunciation while acting in the world is the theme of the Bhagavad Gita.

This is its great success. It recognizes that the vast majority of humanity is actively committed to worldly affairs and a long way from meditation and spiritual study. Not only does the Gita say, 'Act in the world,' but it also says, 'You must act in the world but in a manner which will ensure your own spiritual and material well-being.' It provides those techniques for skilful, dynamic and successful living which will bring internal peace and spiritual elevation.

The second important development in Hindu philosophy, expressed in the Gita, is the role of bhakti (devotional) yoga. Krishna, having revealed Himself as the ultimate Reality, tells Arjuna that the most direct route to liberation is to 'surrender unto Me'. This is the point at which interpretation of the Gita goes off in two different directions with the middle ground being well covered by the general Hindu population.

On the one hand, there is the Advaita Vedantist school, based on the Upanishads to which Krishna himself refers. Vedanta argues that, when Krishna says 'Me', he is speaking of the Supreme Self which is in each one of us as much as it is in Him. Having revealed Himself as everyone and everything, all that is and will be, Krishna can hardly be referring to a separate personal God. Krishna is telling us to become Self-realized like Himself, so that we also are the 'Me' in everything – the all-pervading subject of an objectless world. The point, therefore, is to surrender all thoughts and actions to this realization.

At the other extreme is the bhakti (devotional) approach which accepts Krishna's words at face value, of surrendering to the god Krishna as the Supreme God of gods, who, while embracing all existence, is nevertheless a separate and personal God. Liberation is 'return to Krishna' but it does not involve becoming One with Him. Individual identity is retained even in the state of Absolute Bliss.

Straddling these two views is the approach of modified Vedanta which, while acknowledging that the final goal is to become One with Divinity, upholds devotion to a personal God as the easiest and most effective route.

As an expression of the full spectrum of modern Hinduism – and indeed of possible approaches to God – you will find all three approaches within our commentaries.

The Dharmashastras

The eighteen Dharmashastras are the books of the religious law which supplement and explain the Vedas. They are general guidebooks to social living and outline individual, family and national duties. They are smriti (remembered) texts and are often referred to as such. The Manusmriti is the foremost among the Dharmashastras and is dated from the first two centuries of the Common Era. It gives details on the duties of the four castes as they had evolved by that time, explaining the basics of political administration and the vows and observances to be followed as expiation for committing certain sins. Manu is the legendary first man who was, according to the Mahabharata, appointed by Lord Brahma, the creator god, to run the affairs of humanity. His smriti has remained the authority on moral law throughout the subsequent centuries.

The Manusmriti is significant, not least because of its role in confirming the caste system as a religious principle and the brahmins as advisers to the kings.

Medieval Writings and Commentaries

Historical Background

The three strands of Vedanta which embrace the full spectrum of Hindu philosophy were best encapsulated by three great Hindu saints: Sankara, Ramanuja and Madhva. Between them they expounded the arguments for Advaita Vedanta (non-dualism), Vishishtadvaita Vedanta (qualified non-dualism) and Dvaita Vedanta (dualism).

Sankara (788–820 CE) was a brahmin who converted to the doctrine of Advaita Vedanta (non-dualism), bringing with him many of the yogic principles of Shaivism, his own family tradition. He is hailed as the single-handed revivalist of the teachings of the Upanishads at a time when the personalized gods of the bhakti cults were enjoying increasing popularity.

He reasserted, in no uncertain terms, the proposition that every individual is one with the all-pervading and indivisible Reality and that the only obstacle to realization of this is maya. As the quality which creates the illusion of plurality, maya is the root of all sin and suffering. It is the senses which first fall prey to maya, taking the rest of the material self with them. So it is the senses which must first be controlled as the means of transcending the illusory world of maya and realizing the Eternal Self.

The eleventh-century saint, Ramanuja, was a student of Advaita Vedanta who turned toward Vaishnavism and then took up the task of reconciling the concept of a single all-pervading Reality with that of devotional practice to a separate God. He developed a system known as Vishishtadvaita (qualified non-dualism) in which Brahman, the one Reality, has three qualities: the individual soul, the insensient world and the Supreme Soul. The individual soul and insensient world are lesser parts of the Supreme Soul and totally controlled by it. Release for the individual soul arises from its recognizing itself as part of the Supreme Soul rather than as part of the material world. The path to this release is a combination of religious practice and knowledge which culminates in bhakti, interpretated by Ramanuja as contemplation on the Supreme Soul.

Madhva was a saint of the twelfth to thirteenth centuries who refuted Sankara's concept of maya and of the Oneness of all souls. He supported Ramanuja's general theory but took it one stage further toward full-scale Dvaita Vedanta (dualism) and bhakti principles. He disputed the notion that the individual soul and insentient matter were parts of God, arguing that they were totally separate.

Whilst Ramanuja tends to be revered and cited by both the dualists and the non-dualists, Sankara and Madhva are respected but given no authority by their respective theological opponents.

The bhakti cults of de-ritualized devotion to a personal god were, and are, particularly fervent in the south of India which, significantly, has been least affected by the Aryan invaders and the Vedic culture they inspired. The point was to turn daily existence into an act of worship rather than to allocate worship to priestly activities and ritual sacrifices or to yogic meditation and austerity.

Bhakti, however, was also encouraged in the north through the influence of the Muslim Turkish invaders who cascaded into Northern India in the eleventh century. In their wake came Sufi missionaries who adopted a policy of building Muhammad into the avatara (divine incarnation) system. But Advaita Vedanta was also able to draw sustenance from Islam by concentrating on its concept of one absolute omniscient God. Hinduism of all persuasions took its usual approach of soaking up the new. The partial success of this is apparent in the confusion surrounding a number of saints as to whether they are Muslim Hindus or Hindu Muslims.

The Atmabodha

The Atmabodha (knowledge of the Self) was written by the seventh- and eighth-century saint, Sankara (see above). Sankara's literary works include devotional songs, commentaries on the scriptures, and prose and poetry illuminating scriptural concepts. The Atmabodha falls into this last category. It has been largely overshadowed by Sankara's commentaries which have had an enormous influence on modern interpreters. The

Atmabodha, however, is a powerful commentary in its own right, providing a vivid gallery of metaphoric images with which to grasp some of the profounder metaphysics of the sacred texts.

The Bhajans – Devotional Songs

The tradition of devotional songs developed with the bhakti cults, coming into its own in the seventh century in the Tamil region of South India where the growth of bhakti was most vigorous.

The collections of hymns composed by the bhakti saints now form a major part of the bhakti scriptures. A life of composing and singing bhajans continued as a traditional saintly existence throughout the medieval and modern period. While identified as love songs to personal gods, bhajans are by no means the sole province of bhakti cults. Committed non-dualists, such as Sankara, also expressed their devotion through these songs. Bhajans remain an important part of daily life, being sung in the streets and homes of India as well as on the radio.

Modern Saints and Commentators

Historical Background

The Hindu culture's expansive personality met an even greater challenge than Islam in European Christianity which arrived in the sixteenth century in the form of Portuguese traders and Catholic missionaries, to be followed by the Dutch, French and, finally and most importantly, the British. It was not so much the Christian missionaries as Christian liberal values, arriving via British education and government administration, which had such a resounding influence.

After being severely undermined initially by Western influence, Hinduism found a more constructive critique of its culture, not on the basis of measuring up to Christian values but, rather, of valuing its own Vedic tradition. Idolatry, child-marriage, self-immolation by widows and untouchability were recognized as corruptions of the ancient culture which advocated none of these. Love and service to all human beings (and, indeed, to all beings) as Divinity incarnate was pulled out of the Hindu treasure trove and dusted off. Having regained its equanimity and pride in its own spiritual prowess, Hindu theology developed a new activity, with some prompting from its Muslim and Christian brethren, which said 'preach'.

Although inspired by outside examples, its preaching was notably Hindu in approach, taking its cue from its own ancient tradition of universalism. Unmatched in its experience of the major world faiths as well as in its myriad of local faiths, Hinduism declared that the many faiths were but different paths to the same spiritual goal.

India of the nineteenth and twentieth centuries produced a vanguard of brilliant individuals who went westward or stayed on home ground and fought for their country's economic and cultural independence in a characteristically Hindu spirit of universalism. All of them without fail, not least the Nobel-prizewinning poet Rabindranath Thakur (Tagore) and his friend Mohendas (Mahatma) Gandhi, who became the spiritual leader of India, turned to the ancient Indian scriptures for their inspiration.

Sri Ramakrishna (1836–86)

The modern Hindu attitude that all religions are one is embodied in the nineteenth-century saint, Ramakrishna, whose disciple, Vivekananda, established the Ramakrishna Mission, now an active welfare organization in India and abroad.

Sri Ramakrishna was a Bengali brahmin whose spiritual search led him quickly into priesthood at a Kali (Shakti) temple near Calcutta. He was a Hindu holy man of his time, having followed in his spiritual travels the various paths of Hinduism as well as Christianity and Islam. His conclusion was, 'I have found that it is the same God toward whom all are directing their steps.'

Ramakrishna's enormous breadth of understanding was reflected in his spiritual practices and sayings which swung, without any sense of self-contradiction, between total immersion in an impersonal Absolute and worshipping as a devout child of the Divine. But he did declare that, of the three paths to eternal release – work, knowledge and devotional love (bhakti) – the latter was the easiest and the path of our time.

Sri Ramakrishna was also typical, as a Hindu saint, in the effortlessness of his renown. Indians recognized purity of soul and flocked from all over India to hear his parables and be inspired by his deep faith.

Concerned by the news of Ramakrishna's religious ecstasies, his mother and brother arranged for him to marry but, typically, Ramakrishna took his new wife as a spiritual partner, worshipping her as Kali incarnate. Sri Sarada Devi continues to be venerated as the Holy Mother by devotees of Ramakrishna.

Swami Vivekananda

As the first Hindu swami to go West and penetrate the Western wall of self-satisfied Christianity, Swami Vivekananda was the national and international voice of his spiritual master Ramakrishna.

He was a boisterous, flamboyant youth of an upper-caste family who was both an athlete and a scholar. The university-educated rationalist was on the point of dismissing God as a necessary invention of humanity when he encountered Sri Ramakrishna. He asked the holy man if he had seen God. Ramakrishna replied that not only had he seen God but he could show God to him.

Vivekananda trained with Ramakrishna for five years until the saint's death. Not yet twenty-three, he took on his guru's cause of universal love and service. He established a math (monastery) and then wandered the length and breadth of India, studying her soul and her problems at first hand and forming solutions for her regeneration. This pilgrimage was one of the landmarks of his life and a source of inspiration in his call to India to revitalize her ancient spirit.

In 1893 Vivekananda left by steamer for America to attend the Parliament of Religions in Chicago to which he had not been invited.

Having enrolled with some difficulty, he went on to impress and fascinate the 'Sisters and Brothers of America' with a rallying call for harmony and universalism. He stayed for months in America, lecturing and teaching, then he went to England and Europe, becoming a bridge of understanding between the Orient and the Occident.

Vivekananda returned to his homeland in 1897 to honour and acclaim. Nationalism and universalism were placed shoulder to shoulder in his call to India. He reminded his compatriots of the national ideal of renunciation and of their privilege in belonging to the oldest and most spiritual culture in the world.

In the year of his return from the West, Vivekananda also established the Ramakrishna Mission, an enduring symbol of the newly awakened India; the Mission continues today in its international work of service to humanity and universal education.

Swami Rama Tirtha (1873–1906)

Rama Tirtha was another Indian holy man whose impact in the West was as important as that in his own land. Born into a poor Brahmin family of the Punjab, Tirtha Rama, as he was first called, proved a brilliant student. At his own insistence he gained an English education at Lahore where stories abound of his spiritual passion and his fanatical dedication to study, in particular, to his favourite subject, mathematics.

His short life was one of inspired teaching of non-dualist Vedanta, drawing on both his intellectual and spiritual genius. Long periods were spent in the Himalayas where he became Self-realized, having thrown himself in desperation into the dangerous currents of the Ganges.

Rama Tirtha met Vivekananda in 1897 and he also travelled, going first to Japan where he declared, 'Rama has nothing to teach these people. They are all Vedantins. They are all Ramas. How cheerful, how happy, how quiet, how industrious. This is all that Rama calls life.' He later went to America where he spent two years lecturing on the universal principles of the 'common path'. As a Self-realized man he always began his lectures by addressing his audience as 'My Own Dear Self'. He was not the showman that Vivekananda was, but his indisputable sincerity, joyful personality and the intellectual brillance of his teaching had enormous impact.

He drowned in the Ganges after many months of meditating. His final words to his disciple, Narayana, forewarned him of the event; 'Ram's body soon becomes inactive. Never shall he leave his dear Ganga's bosom... Have no griefs, no worries, no sorrows. Feel Ram with you, within you. He is your body. He is your mind. He is your all in all. He is your own self...'

Swami Prabhupada and the Hare Krishna Movement

Another major advance from East to West began with Swami Bhaktivedanta Prabhupada. He was a devotee of one of the great figures in the bhakti movement, Sri Caitanya, a fifteenth-century Bengali who founded the Krishna-bhakti sect which continues to day as a widespread Vaisnava (Vishnu-worshipping) sect in the north-east of the continent. To his devotees Caitanya is the dual avatara (divine incarnation) of Krishna and his consort Radha. As with all the Vaisnava sects, Caitanya emphasized the chanting of the Lord's holy names as essential in the process of working the soul into a state of divine awareness. Since the 1965 westward missionary pilgrimage to New York of Swami Prabhupada, the chanting and cymbal-playing devotees of Krishna have become a world-wide phenomenon, known by their mantra, 'Hare Krishna'. On the whole the West tends to view the International Society for Krishna Consciousness (ISKON), which Swami Prabhupada established, as a bizarre new cult, not realizing the ancient roots of the tradition or the contribution of Christianity and Islam in creating and shaping this missionary face of devotional Hinduism.

Tat Tvam Asi – That Thou Art
Statement of Advice

1.

Aum

The chant Aum (commonly known as Om) has an extraordinary effect on human beings. Only by chanting it ourselves can we understand why millions upon millions of people over the ages have found harmony, peace and bliss in this simple, but deeply philosophical, sound. Aum belongs to no language or culture (although it appears in the religious vocabulary of many, e.g. Amen, Amin, ominiscient, omnipresent, etc.). Aum is not a word but rather an intonation which, like music, transcends the barriers of age, race, culture and even species. Aum is chanted in meditation and before and after all prayers and teaching.

Aum is the entire message of the Hindu scriptures. It is the sound symbol for the Absolute and Infinite Truth, known to Hindus as Brahman. It is the goal of all spiritual practices and austerities. Brahman is not knowable by any of our human faculties. It cannot be intellectually, emotionally or physically grasped. So we need a symbol – an idol – to help bring us closer to realization of the Unknowable.

When we meditate our mind should chant Aum. The momentary silence between each chant symbolizes Brahman. Mind moves between the opposites of sound and silence until, at last, it ceases the sound. In the silence, the single thought – Aum – is extinguished. There is no thought. Mind and intellect are transcended as the individual Self merges with the Infinite Self in the sacred moment of realization.[1]

1. Parth.

2.

*That word which all the Vedas declare, which all the austerities
proclaim, for which people live the life of a religious student, that
word, I will tell you, in brief. That is Aum.*

Kathopanishad I.2.15

Why Aum?

Sound symbols are the subtlest idols, those closest to the
spiritual realm, because only one of the five senses can perceive
them – the ear. At the other extreme are stone idols which can be
perceived by all five sense organs and are therefore the grossest –
the most materially bound – idols. For this reason, verbal
teaching, chanting and music have always played a predominant
role in Vedic philosophy.

A-U-M is the most complete utterance and therefore the best
sound symbol for the complete Reality. It begins at the very base
of the throat (A), rises to be shaped by the mouth (U) and then
finally vibrates on the lips (M).

The three sound constituents of Aum represent the three
constituents of material existence – waking (A), dreaming (U)
and deep sleep (M). These three states, experienced as a single
seamless life, are manifested Brahman. They are pervaded by the
fourth state, the pure Consciousness of unmanifested Brahman,
just as the sound A-U-M is pervaded by silence. Out of silence
come these tones, within silence they exist and into silence they
merge. Similarly, waking–dreaming–deep sleep arise out of
unmanifested Brahman, exist within It and merge back into It.[1]

1. Parth.

1   Tat Tvam Asi – That Thou Art

3.

*By whom willed and directed does the mind alight on its objects?
By whom commanded does the prana [vital breath], that precedes
all, start. By whom willed do men utter speech. What intelligent
power directs the eye to see, the ear to hear?*

Kenopanishad 1.1

This first verse is a student's question to his teacher, 'What is
God?' The wording of the question reveals the student's
understanding of what he asks. He is an advanced student who
can ask about the source of life because he has studied and
grasped the nature of life. We must understand what we ask
before we can understand the answer.

The student therefore defines existence in his question. He
alludes to the material layers which constitute personality.

The layers of material existence (*pancha-kosa*) fit one inside
another. Outermost are the organs of action – hands, feet, mouth,
genitals and organs of evacuation. This is represented, in the
question, by the reference to speech, the action of the mouth.

Further in are the organs of perception – eyes, ears, nose,
tongue and skin – represented in the question by ears and eyes.
The organs of perception and action constitute the gross body.

Further in still is the prana, the vital breath which enlivens the
body. The prana is on the boundary between the gross body and
the subtle body. The subtle body is the mind and intellect,
collectively referred to here as the mind.

In essence, the student is saying, 'I see how life functions, but
what is its source? What is God?'[1]

1. Parth.

4.

It is the ear of the ear.
It is the mind of the mind.
It is the speech of the speech.
It is the breath of the breathing.
It is the eye of the eye . . .

Kenopanishad 1.2

The teacher replies to the student's question, 'What is the source of all existence?' in words which may first seem nonsensical, but which are simple, known quantities – the same ones used in the question (see above). The teacher proceeds from the known to the unknown. This a fundamental principle of education. It is how the great Vedic teachings have always been taught. So the teacher begins, 'It is the ear of the ear.'

We understand the concept of the ear. If I asked you, 'What do you hear with?' you would no doubt answer, 'With my ears.' If you thought a little longer you would realize that a set of ears on their own are as deaf as a post. Follow the sound vibrations through the eardrums along the nerves. It is the brain which is actually 'hearing' those vibrations. But that's not the end of it. If the Consciousness leaves the brain you won't hear. Even if that Consciousness simply shifts the focus of your brain for a moment, the ears are still transmitting sounds to it as it ticks away, but you are deafened. Someone might ask three times if you want sugar in your tea, but all you know is that you forgot to lock the door when you left the office. Therefore, it is Consciousness which enables you to hear. It is the 'ear of the ear' because it is that which makes you conscious of sound.

By the same token, Consciousness is the see-er in the eye, the mind in the mind, the speaker in speech. That, says the teacher, is the source of existence, is God (Brahman). So God is the *subject* of *all* you see, hear, smell, touch, taste, feel or understand. Therefore, God can never be an *object* of perception or comprehension.[1]

1. Parth.

5.

It is different from what is known. It is beyond the unknown. This have we heard from the ancients who explained it to us.

Kenopanishad 1.4

That which you are seeking is beyond the known and unknown because both are intellectual concepts. In Hinduism, the known and unknown, the perishable and imperishable, are symbolically placed at the right and left. To the right are the five material layers: food (the organs of action, organs of perception), vital breath (prana), mind, intellect and unmanifested desires (vasanas – see pp. 47–8). On the left is the imperishable, unknown Consciousness. But God is more than this.

An analogy may help to explain:

I ask you, 'Do you know my name?'

You reply, 'Yes, I know your name.'

'Do you know my grandfather's name?'

'No, I do not know your grandfather's name?'

'Are you sure?'

'Yes, I know that I know your name. I know that I do not know your grandfather's name.'

In other words, you are saying: I know this knowledge. I know this ignorance.

So there is a Pure Knowledge that illumines your knowledge and your ignorance, but is beyond both. That Pure Knowledge is Pure Consciousness is God. It is beyond the known and the unknown.

Note also that even the Upanishadic sages who were totally in God-Consciousness do not take credit for the wisdom of their words but refer to their gurus. That humility is the key to fine teaching.[1]

6.

That which speech cannot express but that by which speech is expressed is Brahman. Know that alone as Brahman, not that which people worship here.

1. Parth.

*That which cannot be felt by the mind but that which enables
the mind to feel, that is Brahman.*

Kenopanishad 1.5-6

The Truth which is God cannot be expressed in words, but it is
that Truth which enables us to speak – whatever we say. Whether
our words are full of spiritual wisdom or a denial of God, it is
God that is the ultimate speaker of our speech. It is God that
enables our mind to feel and comprehend (mind is used here in
the collective sense of mind/intellect) whatever the feeling or
thought – good, bad or indifferent.

When we go to the temple, mosque or church to pray or chant,
and we feel full of joy and purity, it is God that enables us to feel
this – but God is not that feeling. God cannot be felt. What you
feel is terrestrial. What enables you to feel is transcendental.

But we are lost in the idols. So many people come to worship
idols which represent the ideal of God, as God Itself. God is not
the temple, the church, the mosque. God is not the statue of
Krishna or the crucifix or the Kabah. They are all only symbols.
Even the sound 'Aum' is just a symbol.[1]

7.

*That which cannot be seen with the eye but which enables your eye
to see, understand that alone to be God, not what the people
worship here.*

Kenopanishad 1.7

A light can be focused on anything in a room. Focus on a table –
see the table. Focus on a chair – see the chair. A flashlight will
expose anything in a dark room, except one thing – the battery
cell. If we have a flashlight as the sole source of light and want to
see the flashlight battery, we can't. It is impossible.

Similarly, we can see and understand everything except the
source of sight and understanding – the Atman, the Divinity in
us. But just because we cannot sense, feel or comprehend It, it
does not mean we should worship what is illuminated by God as

1. Parth.

God, any more than we should declare a chair 'a light' because it is illuminated by a light.

Thousands of people go thousands of miles on pilgrimage to experience God. This is the first stage of spiritual development, but we must grow. That which enables us to see is God so, by looking at anything, we can realize God.[1]

8.

He who dwells in the light but is within it, whom light does not know, whose body is light, and who controls light from within, is your Self, the inner controller, the immortal. That as regards the divinities, now as regards beings . . .

. . . He who dwells in the intellect, yet is within the intellect, whom the intellect does not know, whose body the intellect is, who controls the intellect from within, he is your Self, the inner controller, the immortal.

Brhadaranyaka Upanishad III.7.14,22

Pure light cannot be seen. It is black. All we can ever see is light reflected off an object. We see the sun with its billions upon billions of tons of matter reflecting its own light. Down here on earth the birds and trees, the blue atmosphere and white clouds are seen because they reflect that same light. So why is it eternally dark between the outer edge of the earth's atmosphere and that blazing ball of matter? Logically, the great vacuum of black space between us and the sun must be bathed in sunlight. And indeed it is, only we can't see it as there's nothing off which it can reflect except the moon.

Similarly, pure knowledge is darkness to us until it contacts something and we experience it in the shape of that thing. All the knowledges of the world are pure knowledge conditioned in this way by the material world. They are knowledge *of* something. We have knowledge of politics, knowledge of London, knowledge of Hinduism. Even though we know the

1. Parth.

knowledge is not the same as the object upon which it reflects. If I asked you to tell me about the knowledge (excluding the object) you would have nothing to say. Your intellect does not know that knowledge. That knowledge is ignorance to you as light is darkness to light.[1]

9.

The Atman appears to be limited because of ignorance. When that is destroyed, truly the Atman shines alone as does the sun when the cloud passes away.

Atmabodha 3

A passing cloud hides the sun which is billions of times larger than it. Standing beneath the cloud we say the cloud has covered the sun as a child, puttings its finger over its eye, says the finger has covered the world. Similarly, you say that you are ignorant of the Atman but your ignorance is far too insignificant and transitory to cover the infinite, eternal Atman.

The Atman is ever present whether we say it is there or not, just as sun is always shining despite our observation that 'the sun has gone out'. In fact, it is because the sun is shining that we are able to see the cloud covering it. Similarly, when an atheist denies the existence of God, it is God in him that enables him to do so. God (the Atman) illumines all thoughts, perceptions and actions. When the veil of ignorance at last passes away, it is revealed as the One and only illuminator of all.[2]

10.

That is unmoving. One. Faster than the mind . . .

Isavasyopanishad 4

What is movement? Movement of any object is from a place where it is to a place where it is not. Therefore, to move, It

1. Parth.
2. Parth.

(Brahman) must have a place where it is not. You are everywhere in your body so there is no place within it to which you can move. Similarly, since Brahman (God) is all-pervading, there is no place where It is not. Therefore It cannot move. It is One because there is nothing but Brahman, just as the mind is one even when we experience a pluralistic world of dreams.

Atman is faster than the mind, even though the mind can travel 93 million miles to the sun within a split second of hearing the word 'sun'. The Atman must be faster because it is everywhere and so already there.[1]

11.

... *The gods could not overtake it. It ran ahead. Remaining stationary, it outruns all runners. It being present, the cosmic wind sustains all life.*

                                        Isavasyopanishad 4

The gods (*devas*) represent the senses. Before the eye can see or the ear can hear, the Atman is there enabling the eye to see and the ear to hear. Similarly, before the organs of action can perform they must be powered by the Atman. Therefore, 'it outruns all runners.'

Imagine a race of fishes. The fastest fish in the world swims to the finishing post, but what beats it there? Water. No fish can beat water because water enables it to swim and it is everywhere.

The final explanation of the Brahman, in terms of material layers, is the prana, the vital breath in the cosmos and in each individual. There is a popular misconception that breathing keeps us alive, but it is the Atman (Brahman) which sustains the prana to give us life.[2]

1. Parth.
2. Parth.

12.

That moves. That does not move...

Isavasyopanishad 5

This verse continues the string of knowable paradoxes as indicators to the unknown Self. The teacher now moves from the familiar constituents of the microcosm (see above) to the familiar constituents of the macrocosm – time, expressed as movement, and space, expressed as distance (see below).

When does something move and not move?

You, yourself, have managed this feat. For example, you travel hundreds of miles in a train. I meet you at the station and ask you how your trip was and you reply, 'Wonderful, I slept all the way.' So you have moved hundreds of miles and yet, at the same time, remained slumped in your seat, unmoving. You go unmoving with the train, just as the Atman is unmoving in every aspect of the ever-moving world.[1]

13.

... That is far. That is near. That is inside all this and is also outside.

Isavasyopanishad 5

The Atman (Eternal Self) is both far and near because it is everywhere. For the wise, it can therefore be found very near – in your own self, in a lizard on a rock, in the rock under the lizard, anywhere you care to look. The ignorant have a long spiritual journey ahead of them which they turn into physical miles. They go on pilgrimage to Mecca, Jerusalem, Canterbury, the Himalayas, etc.

The Atman is inside all this universe because It is the very substratum of it. The universe is the conditioned state of the Atman. But the Atman is also outside all this, just as your mind is everything in your dreams, but it is also beyond those dreams.[2]

1. Parth.
2. Parth.

14.

[Krishna said:] O Lord of Sleep, I am the Atman seated in the heart of all beings. I am the beginning, I am the middle, I am the end of all beings.

Bhagavad Gita 10.20

Whenever Krishna says 'I' in the Bhagavad Gita he doesn't mean me, Mr Krishna, he means 'I', the Eternal Self, the Atman.

The very core of our personality is that same Atman. There are two things Krishna is talking about here: the Transcendence and the Immanence. The Transcendence is the Atman (Brahman) which is everywhere. We all come out of, live in, and merge with the Atman, but he is telling us how to locate it while we are living – in the heart of all beings. Once we have spotted it in ourselves we will understand it is all-pervading.

The government is throughout the nation. Anywhere in the nation, if we violate the law, we will experience that government. But if we want to locate the government of India, we go to the capital city. So the government is all-pervading and, at the same time, it has a location. Similarly, the Atman is everywhere, but we locate it within. Then we can merge with the whole.

Arjuna is addressed as Lord of Sleep because he is awakening, he has conquered spiritual sleep.[1]

15.

It is like a flash of lightning.
It is like the eye blinking.
This is the illustration of Braham taken from the cosmic powers.

Kenopanishad 4.4

In three lines this superbly constructed verse reaches from our furthermost point of contact with the objective world to the closest point of contact. Where does our objective world end? The sky. Where does it start? The eyelid. Everything this side of the eyelid is identified as 'me', the subject. Everything that side

1. Parth.

of the eyelid is the world, the object. Thus, 'It' (Brahman) is described in terms that span the limits of our objective experience.

Brahman is the pure white Consciousness covered by thought. From birth to death we entertain a constant stream of thoughts so we never see God, or It comes as a flash between two thoughts so quickly that we barely recognize It and are left disoriented in the darkness of thoughts and desires.

Thus, It is like lightning on a dark night, illuminating the landscape with a flash that blinds us for a moment so we are plunged back into even greater darkness and risk missing our step.

But, for the Self-realized person, living in a state of realization is like blinking. Every few seconds, we blink. Nevertheless, we have a constant vision of the world, though the eye is regularly shutting it out. Similarly, a God-realized person has a constant vision of Brahman, the Absolute Self, in spite of the constant flicker of routine material existence.[1]

16.

Now as regards the illustration of the Brahman from within the Self – the mind goes to Brahman as speedily as the mind entertains thoughts.

Kenopanishad 4.5

This subjective illustration of Brahman follows the previous illustrations in terms of the objective world (see above). Just as Brahman can be seen in the external world of nature so can It be seen in the internal world of the human psyche.

You know from experience that your mind goes in a flash to wherever it wills in the objective world. You simply have to read the words, 'London', 'New York', 'the sun', and your mind is there. In a split second it can travel millions of miles or millions of years in time.

Similarly, the Atman (the Brahman in each of us) appears and

1. Parth.

disappears in a flash. The moment a thought stops, the Atman appears; when the thought starts the Atman disappears. It flickers in concert with the thoughts of the mind.

A disciple asked the great saint, Sri Ramakrishna (see p. xxxvi), 'Where do I find God?' Sri Ramakrishna answered, 'Look between two thoughts.'[1]

17.

That which is Supreme Brahman, the Self, the great support of the Universe, subtler than the subtle, eternal. That alone Thou art. Thou art that Alone.

Kaivalyopanishad 16

You are the Supreme Self which upholds the Universe, and which is so subtle it is beyond comprehension: 'That thou art'. In the superbly laconic Upanishads in which one word has a book's worth of meaning, the guru says this twice because this is the aphorism of all religion, all scriptures. You are God. The Kingdom of Heaven is within you. Don't ever forget it.[2]

18.

Two birds of beautiful plumage inseparably bound in friendship sit side by side on the very same tree. One of the two eats the fruit of this sacred tree with pleasure whilst the other looks on but does not eat.

Mundakopanishad II.3.1

The tree is taken to be the physical body. The two birds are souls or parts of the soul within the body. One explanation holds that the bird which eats is that part of the individual soul which is associated with the sense organs, mind and emotions and which is attached to sensations and results of actions.

1. Parth.
2. Parth.

The other bird is the other part of the individual soul which retains the characteristics of God, the Supreme Soul. Aware of true Reality, this part of the individual soul remains detached and aloof from entanglements with the partial reality of the temporal, finite world.

The two aspects of the single soul are inseparably bonded and in harmony. There is no acrimony or conflict between them, but merely watchful expectation from the aspect which is God-within-man. It waits for the time when the world-orientated aspect will realize its oneness with the Supreme Soul so that the pain and pleasure from good and bad actions, as well as bewilderment at its impotence, will pass away.[1]

19.

Purusha [the primal being] that is in the sun, that spirit am I. Aum, the eternal Brahman.

Yajurveda 40.17

A thousand candles lit from a single flame carry the same flame. The spark of life in individuals comes from the one and only flame, Brahman. That makes us all as pure and bright as Brahman.[2]

20.

In Him all things exist, from him all things originate. He has become all. He exists on every side. He is truly the all. Salutations to Him who is the soul of every being.

Mahabharata Shanti Parva 47.56

God is the source of all things. He is the source of light and that light is wonderful. When the sunlight is there, we are happy and full of life. When it is dull we feel depressed. That happens because we see only the externals. We miss the divine glow that

1. Chand.
2. Choud.

radiates from our true self. Popular Sanskrit literature says,
'That day is not a bad day when the sun is not seen, but that day is
a bad day when we don't think of God.' If the internal perception
of God does not come to us, then life is dry.[1]

21.

*This Atman [Supreme Self within] is honey for all beings and all
beings are like honey for this self. This shining immortal being who
is this self and the shining, immortal person who is in this
individual self, he is just this self, this is immortal, this is Brahman
[Supreme Self without], this is all.*

*This Atman is truly the ruler of all beings, the king of all beings.
As all spokes are held together in the hub of a chariot wheel, just
so, in this Self, all beings, all gods, all worlds, all bodily organs,
all these selves are held together.*

Brhadaranyaka Upanishad II.5.15

Reality is both immanent and transcendent. 'Brahman', meaning
'bigness', only indicates that the nameless and formless Reality is
vast and all-pervading. It is beyond the caused world, yet it is the
very basis of it and of every individual in it. It is one and the same
as the Divinity – the Atman – within us.

For want of understanding, limited by our own human
situation, we couch this Reality in terms of a personal God. But
the moment we start realizing it is here within our self, we start
realizing it out there also. Knowledge of this Reality is the goal of
life. There can be no peace and happiness in our soul until we
know it.[2]

22.

*O Lord, who blesses all creatures by revealing the highest
Knowledge. You who make us happy by your calm and blissful*

1. Bhav.
2. Bhav.

Self that roots out terror as well as sin.

Samaveda 16.2

Although acknowledging Brahman as our unknowable Self, Hinduism also acknowledges the human need for a personal God. We live in a dualistic world of subject and object so we need to see God 'out there'.

In religious terminology, Brahman is kind and responsive because it is by His Grace that we perceive all this world and, ultimately, the Truth that is Brahman. The root of all sin is ignorance. It blinds us with fear, preventing this perception.[1]

23.

Write number one and put a zero by its side, it becomes ten, another and it becomes a hundred, another and it becomes a thousand. Remove that one and there is nothing.

Sri Ramakrishna

We must have that one. It is there but we do not recognize It. Those who have recognized It we recognize as great men and women. They have become the Truth and that power of Truth makes an impact on us because we also have It buried within ourselves. Be true to yourself all hours of the day and you will multiply a thousandfold.[2]

24.

O Brahman, lead us from the unreal to the real.
Lead us from darkness to light.
Lead us from death to immortality.

Brhadaranyaka Upanishad I.3.28

When Hindus offer prayer they offer their limitation as beings in the created world. They understand that they are not yet estab-

1. Bhav.
2. Bhav.

lished in Reality, although part and parcel of it, so they pray to God (Brahman) to lead them from this unreal, limited existence to Reality which is infinite and eternal.

They pray for God to give them insight into the ultimate Truth hidden by the darkness of ignorance. Seeing that everything in the world meets death, and yet feeling the echo of their own immortality within, they pray to the Immortal to lead them there.[1]

25.

Just as when a drum is beaten, one cannot grasp the sound but by grasping the drum or the beater of the drum, the sound is grasped.
Brhadaranyaka Upanishad IV.5.8

Due to our material make-up we experience a dual reality – this or that, to be or not to be, me and you, in and out and so on. Therefore, the notion of an all-encompassing God who is all that is and that isn't is a notion that slips through our mind like sound through our fingers. If we put God into our own dual terms of the visible and the invisible, however, we can grasp that invisible by grasping the visible. We can see God in the movement of the wind in the trees, the animals grazing in the fields and the toil of our fellow human beings. He has concealed himself in all these forms. He is functioning in and through them. God is not out of our reach. He is this created world.[2]

26.

The Vedanta [philosophy of the Upanishads] recognizes no sin, it only recognizes error and the greatest error, says the Vedanta, is to say that you are weak, that you are a sinner, a miserable creature and that you have no power and you cannot do this and that. In you is all power. Summon up your all-powerful nature

1. Bhav.
2. Bhav.

*and this whole Universe will lie at your feet. It is the Self alone
that predominates and not matter.*

Swami Vivekananda

Each one of us is the universal Reality. If we learn how to see the
inner Reality in all the names and forms of the world, we purify
and strengthen ourselves.

Even in the happiest of moments there is a corner of ourselves
which says, 'This is not really It, this is not really It.' We must
tune our innermost being to that knowledge so that, whatever the
activities in which we are engaged, whether spiritual or sensual,
we know there is something beyond.[1]

27.

*Assuming the self as Brahman, separate from the three bodies, one
should always offer devotion to the Lord.*

Shikshapatri 116

Our miseries persist because we believe ourself to be the physical
body. But our body is more like a garment covering the Atman.
Just as it would be foolish to consider our tailor and his wife as
our father and mother because they provided us with a new set of
clothes, similarly it is foolish to consider our parents as our
creators because they have given us a physical birth.

When we transcend the three bodies, namely, the gross body
(physical body), the subtle body (mind and intellect) and the
causal body (desires), and become aware of our own Atman
(soul), we experience a pure soul, the self as Brahman. Divine
bliss par excellence is experienced only when one is in this
brahmic state. In this state there is no hindrance whatsoever in
the sublime devotion to God.[2]

1. Bhav.
2. Panch.

28.

*... I am of One form. No one knows Me. I am always pure
Consciousness.*

Kaivalyopanishad 21

A prince approached a guru in the Himalayas and said to him,
'Swami, you must be in contact with God?'

'Yes.'

'Now I want to reach God, can you help me?'

'Sure, that's my business.'

'How do I go about it?' asked the prince.

'Well, how do your subjects go about seeing you?'

'Oh, I'm accessible to anybody, all they have to do is let my
secretary know.'

'Oh, that's easy then,' said the Swami. 'God follows the same
principle. Just give me your card and I'll pass it on. No problem.'

So the prince gave him his card. The Swami looked at it and
said, 'Isn't this your name?'

'Yes.'

'God wants to know who is coming. He doesn't want to know
your name. The name belongs to you. It is your possession, but
God wants to know who the possessor is.'

So then the prince wrote on the card that he was the prince of
the country and then the Swami said, 'Son, isn't this your
position?'

'Yes.'

'He doesn't want to know the position. This is your possession.
Who are you?'

This went on with the prince scribbling all over the card until,
finally, he wrote, 'Human being' to which the Mahatma said,
'Yes, I know you are not a bird or fox. You are a human being.
That is your species. You belong to it. But who are you?'

The prince took the card back and went away because he
understood he did not know who he was. He thought and
thought until he understood. And then he never went back. He
had met the person he wanted to meet.[1]

1. Parth.

29.

He is an atheist who does not believe in himself.
                                    Swami Vivekananda

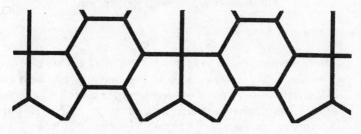

2   Srishti – Creation

30.

Aum.
That is infinite.
This is infinite.
From the infinite, the infinite has come out.
When this infinite is taken from that infinite, what remains is
infinite.
Aum. Peace, peace, peace.

Isavasyopanishad: Invocation

'That' refers to Brahman, the all-pervading Consciousness. 'This' refers to this Universe. So when the infinite Universe comes out of the infinite Brahman, Brahman is no less. It is still complete and infinite. Infinite minus infinite equals infinite. It is a mathematical fact. The concept is beyond our intellect but can be partially grasped through what we already know.

Consider your dreams. When you dream, where does the dream come from? Your mind. You might have a marvellous dream, full of kings, queens, moons, stars and great events in a world that has no apparent limits. When you wake in the morning, is your mind any less for having produced this boundless world?

Peace is chanted three times in this invocation as it is at the beginning of all Upanishads. The first and loudest time is addressed to the greater cosmic forces, the second time is to our immediate environment and the third and softest time is to our own mind and body. To be at peace is to know Reality.[1]

1. Parth.

31.

*In the beginning, this [world] was only the Self in the shape of a
person. Looking around he saw nothing, nothing else than the
Self. He first said, 'I am.' Therefore arose the name I. Therefore,
even to this day when one is addressed, he says first, 'This is I' and
then speaks whatever other name he may have...*

Brhadaranyaka Upanishad I.4.1

'Who are you?' 'I am...' 'What are you doing?' 'I am...' Every
approach we make to the world we begin with the 'I'. But we
compulsively qualify that 'I am' with material existence because
we identify with that existence. 'I am Mary'; 'I am tall'; 'I am
going to the market'. 'I' affirms itself and then it affirms the
world. Our starting point, 'I am' unwittingly acknowledges the
pure Consciousness that is God inside us.[1]

32.

*Who truly knows? Who can here declare it?
Whence it was born, whence is this manifestation?
On this side of the manifestation are the gods.
Who then knows where it has arisen?*

*Whence has this manifestation arisen
Whether created or not?
Only He who is its overseer in the highest abode
Knows or Knows not.*

Rig Veda X.129.6–7

Time, space and causation are the very definition of the world.
They do not exist beyond it. So that which is beyond the world
cannot be given a time, place or reason. To ask 'when' or 'why' or
'where' is the source of the Universe is a non-question. The
verses above make this point. We might as well ask: when is a tree
not a tree? Where is a tree not a tree? Why is a tree a tree?

You cannot get to the end of the world's time, space or

1. Bhav.

causation, you can only awaken from it. The dreamer can walk or even fly for ever and never find the end of his world as long as the waker sleeps. Only when the waker awakens does the dreamer find the end of his world – and its cause. Then only does the waker know he was dreaming. Before he knew not.

33.

He truly had no delight. Therefore He who is alone has no delight. He desired a second. He expanded to a man and a woman in close embrace. He caused that Self to fall into two parts. From that arose husband and wife. Therefore, as Yajnavalkya used to say, this [body] is one half of yourself, like one half of the two halves of a split pea. Therefore this space is filled by a wife. He joined with her. From that human beings were produced.

She thought, 'How can he unite with me after having produced me from himself? Well, let me hide myself.' She became a cow, the other became a bull and was united with her and from that cows were born. The one became a mare, the other a stallion ... thus, indeed, he produced all that exists in pairs down to the ants.

He knew, I indeed am this Creation for I produced all this. Therefore, he became the creation. He who knows this as such comes to be in that creation of his.

Brhadaranyaka Upanishad I.4.3–5

Who is the first cause?

The answer is that 'nothing started'. There is no 'first' because there is no 'second'. It is all a misconception exactly as in a dream. In a dream, thoughts and desires manifest themselves as an entire dualistic world of men and women, night and day, hot and cold, beginnings and endings and so on. This dream world has its own history and future stretching endlessly back and forward and yet, in the waker's life, it is thirty seconds long. All that was, is, and will be, is the waker's mind. That is the One which contains all multiple dualities of the dreaming world. That mind is not part of the chain of cause and effect in the dream. It is the substratum of it.

Similarly, this world is full of cause and effect but the cause of this, the substratum of this, is Brahman, our own Supreme Self, manifesting first as thought.

34.

*God the Creator, desiring offspring, did penance in the form of
meditation, and from this sacrifice created the pair Matter and
Energy which, by interaction, were to produce life forms of the
many different types.*

Pranopanishad V.4

In Hindu scriptures there are many stories about the Creation,
but this approach is the one most closely echoed by modern
scientific ideas. God is depicted as a diffuse form of energy which
becomes condensed into active forms of energy, including the
creative force Brahma. Other parts of this energy become
thickened into matter. Some matter, when infused with soul,
becomes life forms; and some life forms, when imbued with
Consciousness, become higher living creatures, including man.

Other forms of active energy become forces which are
personified as the gods, the renewing and preserving principles
of the world as well as its many other natural laws.[1]

35.

*From this are born life, mind, and all the senses, space, air, light,
water and earth which is the support of the Universe.*

Kaivalopanishad 15

The above verse gives a chronology of 'this', the manifested
Brahman, the substratum of the Universe.

The creative urge is inherent in Brahman – everything is
inherent in infinity. This urge becomes Lord Brahma, the
Creator, the first thought. As Lord Brahma the urge combines
with Consciousness (Brahman) to create life. Life develops
thoughts which, in turn, solidify into the senses. These perceive
objects, thereby creating the five elements. This is the theory of
the world 'creation'. From the ultimate point of the world there

1. Chand.

is no such world. It is an urge, a thought of the Brahman. It is the
chronology of every individual.[1]

36.

*Earth, water, fire, air, space, mind, intellect and ego – altogether
these are the eightfold divisions of my lower nature...*

Bhagavad Gita 7.4

The eight divisions of Brahman's material nature are the five
elements, mind, intellect and ego. The first five elements
together constitute gross matter. Mind, intellect and ego are
subtle matter. All eight divisions which constitute the pluralistic
world are nothing but rays of the higher Brahman just as all the
dream world is nothing but rays of the waker's mind.[2]

37.

*... O mighty-armed [Arjuna], different from this lower nature,
know my higher nature as the life element by which the universe is
upheld.*

Bhagavad Gita 7.4

This higher, transcendental, nature of Brahman is the life spark
in us and all things. It is that which enlivens the eightfold
insentient matter (see above).

To understand how this higher, indivisible nature exists as
each individual, imagine the sun splashing a wall with sunlight.
There is light all over the wall but, if we use a mirror to reflect the
sunlight onto the wall, an individual spot of light is created. That
bright spot appears separate but there is no division between it
and all the sunlight, just as there is no division between the
Brahman in us and all infinity.[3]

1. Parth.
2. Parth.
3. Parth.

38.

The world appears to be real as long as the non-dual Brahman, the substratum of all, is not realized like silver in an oystershell.

Atmabodha (Sankara) 7

On a moonlit night, a beach strewn with oystershells can appear as if strewn with silver. The illusion lasts so long as we do not recognize the oystershells. The minute we recognize them, the silver vanishes. The silver is evidence of the shell's existence which is, conversely, the prerequisite for the existence of the illusion. Similarly, the world is evidence of the supreme Brahman, the prerequisite for the existence of this illusory world.

As long as you have not awakened to God-Consciousness the pluralistic world appears as real as silver on the beach before you have recognized the oystershells. That world will disappear as soon as you are God-realized.[1]

39.

Thousand-headed was Purusha, thousand-eyed, thousand-footed. He embraced the world on all sides and stood beyond by the breadth of ten fingers.

Rig Veda X.90.1

The 'Creation' is the creation of the world by every individual. This world is nothing but names, forms and activities, represented by the heads, eyes and feet of Purusha (Brahman). Speech emanating from the head is the source and all-pervading feature of names. The eye is the source and all-pervading feature of forms. The feet represent the body as the source and all-pervading feature of activity. In other words, the speech (head) is the Brahman of names. The eye is the Brahman of forms. The body (feet) is the Brahman of activities. A 'thousand' is used poetically in the Vedas to denote infinity. Purusha is the infinite names, forms and activities which constitute this world.

'It is this infinite Universe and stands beyond it by the

1. Parth.

breadth of ten fingers' – the traditional measurement for the
space of the human heart which, in poetic terms, is known as the
abode of the Atman (Eternal Self).

It is like poetic calculus, but the point is that each one of us has,
within our very core, that infinite Reality which is all this and
beyond all this, just as the waker's mind is all the dream world
and beyond it.

40.

*That Purusha is this all, what was and what shall be. He is Lord
of Immortality which he grows beyond through [sacrificial] food.*
                                         Rig Veda X.90.2

The Purusha is 'this all, what was and shall be' – in other words,
time, space and causation. He is the 'Lord of Immortality', the
eternal spirit sustaining the universe. In truth, you are the
Purusha, but to grow beyond this world to your full, infinite
stature you must follow the universal law (dharma) of sacrifice
(see below). By living our life as an act of sacrifice (see pp.
212–27) you will realize yourself as Purusha.

41.

*... When the gods spread out the sacrifice they bound the Purusha
as a victim.*

*With the sacrifice the gods sacrificed the sacrifice. These were
the first ordinances...*
                                         Rig Veda X.90.15–16

The act of sacrifice is the Purusha (Brahman) giving itself in
bondage as the material world. Thus the world is maintained
through a permanent state of sacrifice on the part of the spirit to
the bondage of material existence. There is no beginning or end
to this state, only release from it.

Having given rise to the world through thought (see pp. 25–7),
the Purusha is bound by the internal forces of the world – the

gods. This is our own eternal Self being bound by our material nature.

But, having been given the sacrifice, the gods sacrifice the sacrifice. Having been given the world they sacrifice it, they overrule their desire for it. We become gods when we cease to covet this existence and give all our thoughts and actions back to that Supreme Self (Brahman).

Sacrifice is the dharma of material existence. As long as we are bound by material existence we must live in the spirit of sacrifice, becoming first a god (the sacrificer) and then the Purusha (the sacrifice).

42.

At the beginning of Brahma's day, all living entities become manifest from the unmanifest state, and thereafter, when the night falls, they are merged into the unmanifest again.

Bhagavad Gita 8.18

The Vedic (Hindu) culture sees time and the universe in a cyclical, rather than a linear, way as something which began and will end. The days and nights come and go, the seasons come and go, the lives of an individual come and go, civilizations come and go, so it is natural to suppose the whole Universe comes and goes. Nowadays, of course, physics also considers that the Universe comes and goes, expanding and contracting in and out of existence.

One universe's life is one breath of Mahavishnu (the Supreme Soul). His breathing causes bubbles and each universe is a bubble.

Material creation is engineered by Lord Brahma. Before Brahma begins the creation, material universes are un-manifested. They are there but they are not manifested. Each of the innumerable universes is designed by the Supreme Soul so, for each universe, there is a Brahma. When Brahma comes the Universe becomes manifest and when Brahma dies the Universe dissolves.[1]

1. Char./Das.

43.

Again and again, when Brahma's day arrives, all living entities
come into being and, with the arrival of Brahma's night, they are
helplessly annihilated.

Bhagavad Gita 8.19

One day of Brahma consists of a thousand cycles of four yugas or
ages. The four yugas are known as Satya, Treta, Dvapara and
Kali. Satya is an age of wisdom, virtue and religion, lasting for
1,728,000 years. Treta, in which the seeds of vice begin, is
1,296,000 years. Dvapara, in which trouble and irreligion
increases, lasts for 864,000 years. Finally, there is Kali in which
the Universe is overrun with strife, ignorance and irreligion; this
lasts for 432,000 years.

Altogether, these ages make up 4.32 million years. This cycle
of ages occurs 1000 times to make a day of Brahma, and then the
same again for a night of Brahma. He lives for 100 years, totalling
311,400 billion earth years. At this point there is total devastation
before the Universe is born again.

The cyclic nature of creation and destruction permeates all
Creation right down to the cycle of seasons, the life and death of
an individual and the passage of day and night.[1]

44.

[Krishna said:] It is said that there is an imperishable banyan tree
that has its roots upward and its branches down and whose leaves
are the Vedic hymns. One who knows this tree is the knower of the
Vedas.

The branches of this tree extend downward and upward,
nourished by the three modes of material nature. The twigs are the
objects of the senses. This tree also has roots going down, and these
are bound to the fruits of action of human society.

Bhagavad Gita 15.1–2

1. Char./Das.

What is the tree that we see with its roots upwards and branches downwards? It is the reflection of a tree in water. The material world is a reflection of the spiritual world.[1]

45.

Like bubbles in water, the worlds arise from, exist in, and dissolve into the supreme Lord, who is the material cause and supporter of everything.

Atmabodha (Sankara) 8

Every creation has three causes – material, efficient and instrumental. For example, the making of a pot requires the mud, the potter and the potting wheel respectively. In the case of the Creation of the manifest world, the three causes are one – Brahman. Brahman uses Itself to create the world out of Itself. Thus, It supports everything in the sense that It is Self-supporting.

The pluralistic world arises out of the ocean like bubbles. The bubbles are, at once, separate and a part of the ocean. They are made by the ocean out of itself. If we understand the water that is the bubble, we understand the water that is the ocean. If we understand the Divine Spirit (Atman) that is us, we understand the Divine Spirit (Brahman) that is the Universe.

Within every bubble is air which expands with heat. This is like our unmanifested desires accumulated though karma (see p. 52) which expand with the heat of passion until the body succumbs to the stress and dies. The water merges again with the ocean which it has never left.[2]

1. Char./Das.
2. Parth.

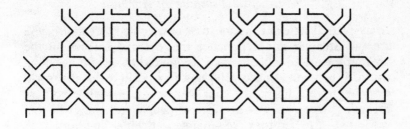

3 Maya – The World Illusion

46.

*That same Self, completely deluded by maya [illusion], abides in
the body and does everything. In the waking state he derives much
satisfaction through the varied pleasures of women, food and
drink.*

Kaivalyopanishad 12

The all-pervading, immortal self is the very same self that lives
as 'you' in this world, believing it to be pluralistic and ever
changing with yourself as just one of the many ever-changing
forms.

In the first of the three states of consciousness you currently
know, you are the waker and enjoy the external and internal
pleasures of the waking world. Because you accept the illusion
which is manifested out of eternal Brahman like a rope out of a
snake, you are able to experience its pleasures and its sorrows,
just as you experience fright when you accept the illusion that
the rope is a snake.[1]

47.

*In the dream state that jiva [individual self] experiences joy or
sorrow in the worlds created by his own maya . . .*

Kaivalyopanishad 13

1. Parth.

In the second state of consciousness of which you are aware, you are the dreamer and experience the joys and sorrows of the dreaming world as convincingly as you did those of the waking world. When you awaken you know immediately that the world was the maya (illusion) of your own mind, but while you are dreaming, there are any number of people and things in that world to assure you they are separate individuals in a very 'real' world. That world is totally self-validating, just as the waking world is totally self-validating.

Whichever illusion you are caught up in, waking or dreaming, you have to play the game. If you don't flee the tiger in the dream, you will be mauled and suffer pain. It's all illusion but, until you wake up, that pain is very real to you, the dreamer. Similarly, when you are immersed in the maya of the waking world, you have to play the game. Until you awaken and realize the Eternal Self, the joys and sufferings of the waking world are very real to you, the waker.[1]

48.

... In the state of deep [dreamless] sleep in which everything vanishes, overcome by ignorance, he attains the state of bliss.

Kaivalyopanishad 13

The third state of consciousness is deep sleep when the mind is temporarily at rest. In this state the individual self (jiva) experiences relative bliss because the desires which create his waking and dreaming world do not express themselves. The deep sleeper is nothing, but he is also something because he will awaken as he was when he went to sleep, so he has been maintained in an unmanifest state. He is the seed of the dreamer and the waker. He is at peace in the sense that he is oblivious of the desires which constitute his personality, but it is not ultimate bliss because he is also oblivious of his Supreme Self (Atman).[2]

1. Parth.
2. Parth.

49.

... From him the entire pluralistic world is born. He is the substratum. He is the bliss. He is the indivisible consciousness and in him the three cities are resolved.

Kaivalyopanishad 14

In the dreaming and waking worlds your personality becomes aware of itself through the constant flow of experiences: perceptions, actions, thoughts.

In the 'nothingness' of deep sleep your desires exist unmanifested like mud yet to be made into pots. As such you do not experience anything. It is a state of no-sorrow, no-joy – relative bliss. As long as you have those unmanifested desires (vasanas) you will have a personality of a particular shape. The personality's experience of the Atman (Supreme Self), which it mistakes for the world, will always be in its own shape.

At any time, your individual self (jiva) only recognizes one state. When it is waking, that is the total reality, when it is dreaming, that is the total reality, when it is in deep sleep, that is the total reality. And yet Reality is that which persists through all time, so it is none of these states. It is pure Consciousness, the Atman, the fourth plane of Consciousness which is the substratum of all three states. It is the state of pure 'colourless' bliss (ananda) which is experienced as the 'coloured' waking, dreaming or deep-sleep worlds, like water seen through different-coloured glass.[1]

50.

In these three states of consciousness is the object of enjoyment, the enjoyer and enjoyment. I am different from these, the witness, pure Consciousness. Ever auspicious.

Kaivalyopanishad 18

Life is nothing but a flow of experience. In any experience there are three components: the subject, i.e., the experiencer; the

1. Parth.

object of the experience, i.e., the experienced; and the relationship between the two, i.e., the act of experiencing. The true Self (Atman) is all of these while being different from them.

This is best understood by thinking in terms of what you know. In the dream experience, there is the dreamer, the dream objects and the relationship between them, the experience itself. When the individual wakes from the dream these three components merge into the waker's mind which is their source while at the same time being totally different from them.

Atman is the witness (*sakshi*) because It is pure Consciousness unswayed by perceptions, activities and thought. It is 'ever-auspicious' – undisturbed – by them, as the waker is undisturbed by the dream world.[1]

51.

> *Truly, this world is a triad of name, form and action. Of those names, speech is the source. It is their common feature for it is common to all names. It is their Brahman [Supreme Self], for it sustains all names.*
>
> *Now of the forms, the eye is the source, for all forms arise from it. It is their common feature for it is common to all forms. It is their Brahman for it sustains all forms.*
>
> *And of actions, the body is the source, for all actions arise from it. It is their common feature for it is common to all actions. It is their Brahman for it sustains all actions. These three together are one, this Self. The Self, though one, is this triad. Prana truly is the immortal; name and form are the real. This is the immortal veiled by the real.*
>
> Brhadaranyaka Upanishad I.6.3

The names, forms and activities which constitute the world are nothing but the all-pervading Brahman which is our self. But the Brahman has no name because there is nothing that It is not. It has no form because there is nothing outside It to define It. It has no activity because there is nowhere It is not.

How can something give rise to qualities it does not possess? The square does not have unequal sides, nor acute angles, nor

1. Parth.

The square does not have unequal sides, nor acute angles, nor three sides, but divide it diagonally and two triangles are created with just these properties. It is only a matter of new sets of relations.

Hydrogen atoms are highly combustible and oxygen aids combustion. Both are gases and light, in the case of hydrogen extremely light. Together they create water, which extinguishes combustion, is heavy and is liquid. A new configuration creates properties which bear no relation to those of its constituents.

Diamond and carbon are both carbon atoms. One is soft, black, cheap. The other is harder than iron, beautiful, glittering and enough to drive men to murder. All this arises out of a minor rearrangement within their atoms. It is not the content but the form which makes this world.

At the Absolute level, the Infinite has no properties because it has nothing which is not Itself with which to establish relations. Names, forms and activities are within the Infinite and are based on the illusion of the One as plural. But it does not possess the qualities of these names and forms, any more than the square has acute angles or the waker has the qualities of the trees, mountains and houses in his dream world.[1]

52.

Then Gargi Vachaknu asked him, 'Yajnavalkya, since all this here [the earth] is woven like warp and woof in water, on what, pray, is water woven like warp and woof?'

'On air, O Gargi.'

'On what, then, is air woven like warp and woof?'

'On the worlds of the sky, O Gargi.'

'On what, pray, are the worlds of the sky woven like warp and woof?'

'On the worlds of the gandharvas [celestial singers], O Gargi.'

'On what, then, are the worlds of the gandharvas woven like warp and woof?'

'On the worlds of the sun, O Gargi.'

'On what, pray, are the worlds of the sun woven like warp and woof?'

1. Parth.

'On the worlds of the moon, O Gargi.'

'On what are the worlds of the moon woven like warp and woof?'

'On the worlds of the stars, O Gargi.'

'On what are the worlds of the stars woven like warp and woof?'

'On the worlds of the gods, O Gargi.'

'On what, pray, are the worlds of the gods woven like warp and woof?'

'On the worlds of Indra [king of the gods], O Gargi.'

'On what, pray, are the worlds of Indra woven like warp and woof?'

'On the worlds of Prajapati [Lord of Creatures], O Gargi.'

'On what are the worlds of Prajapati woven like warp and woof?'

'On the worlds of Brahma [Creator], O Gargi.'

'On what are the worlds of Brahma woven like warp and woof?'

Yajnavalkya said, 'Gargi, do not question too much lest your head fall off. Truly, you are questioning too much about a Divinity about whom we should not ask too much. Do not ask too much, O Gargi.'

Thereupon Gargi, daughter of Vachaknu, held her peace.

Brhadaranyaka Upanishad III.6.1

In the debate at the court of King Janaka in which the nature of Reality was to be explained to the best of the participants' capacity, Gargi, a brilliant and highly educated thinker in her own right, questioned them closely.

In this interchange, she asks the question that all religion and science ask – what is the fundamental source and law of the Universe? 'What is the warp and woof?' conveys the idea of something that is all-pervading because it is within and without.

The answers given by the leading contestant, the great sage Yajnavalkya, begin with the perceived external world of the five elements. They progress through subtler and subtler names and forms, each pervading the one that preceded it. The internal world of the senses, mind and desires, represented by the gods, are crossed to arrive finally at thought, represented by the Creator, Lord Brahma (see pp. 25–6). This debate follows the standard Vedanta practice of 'not this, not this'. By eliminating all that is not the ultimate Reality we come as close as we can to knowledge of the unknowable.

Through the exchange of questions and answers, the nature of the Self-existent Reality becomes apparent as an indissoluble whole which can be approached by the intellect but never reached. Thought is the fundamental principle which creates names – ideas of individual things which are 'this but not that' – and so creates forms which are 'this but not that'. Therefore, our intellect can take us to the depths and heights of the infinite configurations it has created as this world, but to see beyond we must abandon it to focus on the Infinite One, which is its warp and woof. Gargi understood immediately what Yajnavalkya was telling her and held her peace.

53.

. . . When he goes to sleep he takes along the material of this all-embracing world, tears it apart himself, builds it up himself, he dreams by his own radiance, by his own light. In that state the person becomes Self-illuminated.

                                        Brhadaranyaka Upanishad IV.3.9

Dreams are pervaded by your mind. When waking each morning you realize that the dreams of the previous night were nothing but a projection of your mind. Nevertheless, while you were dreaming, everything seemed as real as this world seems now. There was you, the subject, and there was the outside objective world – a wife or husband, family, friends, enemies, houses and so on. If I came to you, if the gods themselves came to you in that dream and said all this world, themselves included, was a projection of you, you would laugh it off. But once you cross the barrier of the dream world into the waking world, you understand that the moon, the sun, the stars, the trees and people were all only rays of your mind.

Now in the waking state as you read, you are being told this world is pervaded by the Lord. Brahman is the very substratum of the world, just as your mind is the substratum of your dream world. You are the Brahman just as everyone in your dream is your mind, every mud pot is mud and every gold ornament is gold. But until you cross that barrier out of this waking world into the fourth plane of Consciousness, you can no more conceive of It than the dreamer can believe that the dream world is his invention and no more.[1]

54.

Like all-pervading space, the infinite Reality appears to be diverse on account of its association with various types of equipment and becomes one on their destruction.

Atmabodha 10

Space is one, all-pervading and indivisible. Nevertheless, we have a concept of living-room space, bedroom space, pot space, etc. The walls of a house are the 'equipment' which appear to separate the space; in fact, the walls have no impact on the indivisible, limitless nature of space. The air in space may be separated from that which is outside the walls, but the space itself is neither contained nor divided by the walls.

Just as walls create the sense of individual room space so the physical body, mind and intellect create the impression of an individual self. Thus, the pluralistic world emerges through identification with the 'walls' within the Self.[2]

55.

To the non-discriminating, the Atman appears to be active when the sense organs are functioning, just as the moon appears to be moving when the clouds are moving.

Atmabodha 19

1. Parth.
2. Parth.

The movement of clouds on moonlit nights creates the impression that the moon is moving because your attention is on the clouds and moves with them. But if you shift your focus to the (relatively) stationary moon you realize that it is, in fact, the clouds which are moving.

Similarly, the Self (Atman) appears to be active because your attention is focused on the body, mind and intellect and you go with them.

If we consider this metaphor further we see also that it highlights the point that motion can only be recognized if there is a stationary reference point. You recognize movements, i.e., changes, that occur at all levels of your personality because of an unchanging substratum which is the Supreme Self.[1]

56.

Mistaking oneself for the living being as the rope is mistaken for the serpent, one is overcome with fear. If one is known not as the living being but as the Supreme Self one becomes free from fear.
Atmabodha 27

The snake–rope analogy is one of the great contributions to the science of Vedanta, explaining its highest philosophy in the simplest terms. When you see but do not recognize a rope, you misapprehend it, for instance, as a snake. The cause for misapprehension is not the rope itself, but your non-recognition. As soon as you recognize the rope the snake vanishes along with all the fear and agitation of mind and body.

Similarly, when you recognize the world and yourself as the one, all-pervading Reality, the pluralistic world dissolves along with all your fears and agitations. Indeed, there is nothing and no one to fear because there is only the Supreme Self.[2]

1. Parth.
2. Parth.

57.

'Why did God forget himself into a man, into a little egotistical self?' ... In this question of yours there is a fallacy of the circle in the proof.

To whom are you putting the question? Are you putting this question to the dreaming subject or to the wakeful subject? To the dreaming subject you should not put the question because the dreaming subject has not forgotten anything, being a creation like the other objects it sees, and to the real subject in the wakeful state you cannot put the question. Who will put the question? The questioner must be in the dream itself, and when the dreaming subject is removed then who will put the question? ... Let the dreaming subject be removed and the whole panorama, the whole dream vanishes, and nobody is left to put the question.

Swami Rama Tirtha, 'Maya' lecture, 15 January 1903

Pragnanam Brahma –
Consciousness Is Brahma

Statement of Definition

4 Samsara – The Endless Cycle of Birth and Death

58.

The Supreme Personality of Godhead [Krishna] said: While speaking learned words, you are mourning for what is not worthy of grief. Those who are wise lament neither for the living nor for the dead.

Never was there a time when I did not exist, nor you, nor all these kings; nor in the future shall any of us cease to be.

Bhagavad Gita 2.11

When the warrior-prince, Arjuna, baulks at a battle in which the enemy army is peopled with his own relatives and friends, Krishna explains to him why his grief is misguided. True wisdom involves understanding that the body is born to die. Death is an inevitable fact not worth lamenting as the soul is destined to live for ever.

This introduces the fundamental principle behind the Bhagavad Gita that every single living being is eternal, beyond both past and future. Generally, in the West, immortality of the soul is taken to mean that the soul, having come into existence, will live for ever. But in the Vedic (Hindu) view of the world not only does the soul never die, the soul was never born.

The spiritual life begins with the understanding that the Self is that eternal 'I' which is beyond the body.[1]

---

1. Char./Das.

59.

As the embodied soul continuously passes, in this body, from boyhood to youth to old age, the soul similarly passes into another body at death. A sober person is not bewildered by such a change.

O son of Kunti, the non-permanent appearance of happiness and distress and their disappearance in due course are like the appearance and disappearance of winter and summer seasons. They arise from sense perception, and one must learn to tolerate them without being disturbed.

Bhagavad Gita 2.13–14

In Hindu society the idea of transmigration of the soul is as much a fact of life as birth, old age and death. Many can remember having a tiny child's body and looking out through those eyes. Now we have a completely different body and one day we will look out through the eyes of an old body, yet it will be the same person who once had the child's body. So the body is changing but there is an inner core that doesn't change. If we can identify with our inner core then we will not be bewildered by life or death because we will understand that the body is simply changing as the cycle continues.

Once we have each realized that we are eternal, while everything around us is temporary, then we can become aloof to this changing world.

It is important to understand the Vedic meaning of happiness and distress, based on the understanding that life is the struggle of the spirit. When the struggle is heightened we call it distress. When the struggle is lessened we call it happiness. But, in fact, we are in a distressed condition as long as we are in this material world because it conflicts with our spiritual nature. Happiness is simply the minimizing of that distress. The two are not diametrically opposed. Bliss is the true opposite of distress and this is found beyond the material world.[1]

---

1. Char./Das.

60.

The man of Self-realization knows the radiant supreme Brahman to be He on whom the world is based. And those men of discrimination who, without any wordly desire, are devoted to such go beyond the cycle of birth and death.

Mundakopanishad III.2.1

The soul is unborn and does not die. It is in a state of material bondage from beginningless time. When our body gets old and worn, the soul transmigrates to another body.

Out of ignorance it is drawn to pleasurable objects of the senses. Thoughtlessly it enjoys. Enjoyment, far from extinguishing the flame of desire, adds fuel to it. The soul craves for more and more; it enjoys more and more. The desires harden. One life is too short a time to satisfy these desires. Consequently this hardened, unsatiated core of desires, called vasanas, is the cause of births and rebirths.

To break this almost unbreakable cycle we have to divest ourselves of desire and develop the qualities of Brahman.[1]

61.

This then is the truth: As from a blazing fire there spring forth thousands of sparks like little fires, so, my fellow seeker, from God the Imperishable diverse life forms are produced and indeed go back again to Him.

Mundakopanishad II.1.1

One aspect of God is the Universal Soul. This fragments into myriads of individual souls each of which becomes trapped inside the five sheaths of earthly existence, which are the anatomical, the physiological/metabolic, the logical, the intuitive and the blissful. These sheaths become fixed around each individual soul by the load of sin which accumulates during lifetimes.

Obsession with pleasures and emotional attachments to the

1. Panch.

world, as experienced through the senses, incurs demerit, which can only be removed by the merit from good deeds assiduously undertaken and performed during a succession of lifetimes and rebirths. When, finally, according to the laws of karma, the soul is freed from its load of sin, the sheaths can fall away and the individual soul can return to God the Universal Soul and experience perpetual Bliss.[1]

62.

. . . I have already slain these men, you are only an instrument.
Bhagavad Gita 11.33

Krishna is talking as a God-realized man. He is the Supreme Self which embraces within it the entire Universe, including the men who are to die in the battle. He is their own Self which is in search of Itself. Each individual soul (jiva) makes its own way back to the Self as a river to the sea. The hill might apologize for forcing the river down but, whether the hill was there or not, the river would have found a way down.

All of us are born to die. It is the nature of birth. The seeds of desire left from previous lives have pushed us into this world and they will affect the manner in which we go out. These unmanifest desires (vasanas) are the blueprint of our destiny. How we use it is up to us. If you have a difficult destiny on account of past actions you will need much self-effort to achieve, but it is not impossible. It is the difference between a smooth, fast-flowing river and one that is stagnant and full of obstructions which will take you a shorter distance for the same degree of effort.

Arjuna's opponents had mapped out their own destiny by their actions, which included usurping the kingdom of the Pandavas. So their death in the battle is a *fait accompli* by the Atman (Self). As their ultimate destination It is the fundamental force of their existences for which they will continue to die and be reborn as many times as necessary. Arjuna is merely an

1. Chand.

instrument for their inevitable evolution just as the world is an instrument for his evolution.[1]

63.

As a person puts on new garments, giving up old ones, the soul similarly accepts new material bodies, giving up the old and useless ones.

Bhagavad Gita 2.22

The body is made up of subtle and gross bodies. The subtle body refers to mind, intellect and ego while the gross body refers to our purely physical makeup.

With our many bodies for our many lives, we are all like the actor who puts on different costumes for his different roles. And, like that actor, we may also become deluded by our part and begin thinking 'I am this part.'

Nevertheless, the body awarded to the individual soul is perfectly cast for the soul at that time. It reflects the development of the soul's consciousness. So we should not reject this identity. We should learn to carry it with dignity but understand that this is not the real Self. The real Self is the eternal being within.[2]

64.

One who has taken his birth is sure to die and, after death, one is sure to take birth again. Therefore, in the unavoidable discharge of your duty, you should not lament.

Bhagavad Gita 2.27

There is a riddle asked in the Mahabharata: 'What is the most amazing thing in this world?' The most amazing thing in the world is that every person in the world sees that his or her forefathers have died and yet each of us thinks 'I will never die.'

1. Parth.
2. Char./Das.

Arjuna is of the kshatriya caste, the warrior class, so it is his duty to fight other warriors – never civilians – when the circumstances decree. The universal law, dharma, does not support unnecessary slaughter, but the battle was an unavoidable reaction in the cycle of action-reaction. It is dharma that, for every act (karma), there is an inescapable reaction. The cause of the battle had already happened, now the effect could not be avoided. Krishna reminds Arjuna that, in this karmic cycle, he must follow his personal duty, svadharma, arising from his own past actions. Arjuna's caste as a warrior is part of his svadharma. Therefore he must perform his duty or suffer the harmful consequences that will inevitably rebound.[1]

65.

In this endeavour there is no loss or diminution and a little advancement on this path can protect one from the most dangerous type of fear.

Bhagavad Gita 2.49

The endeavour is to work, not for material gain but for the Lord. The more submissive we become to the Lord, the closer we come to Him. Even if we cannot complete this yoga (spiritual practice), this will not mean failure as it does when we do not complete an endeavour on the material plane. If a person can make just a little progress toward the Lord he will save himself from having to fall down into a lower species in the next rebirth. Whatever is attained in this life is never lost, it is carried over to the next so the soul can begin from that point to make further advancement. In this way, through many lifetimes, we can gradually progress to moksha, the final release from the material world.[2]

1. Char./Das.
2. Char./Das.

66.

After many births and deaths, he who is actually in knowledge surrenders unto Me, knowing Me to be the cause of all causes and all that is. Such a great soul is very rare.

Bhagavad Gita 7.19

When a person takes up the spiritual life he gradually advances. The first stage of spiritual life is the endeavour for knowledge. After many, many births one reaches the stage of spiritual knowledge and then the person realizes that the Lord is the cause of all causes. But few reach that stage at any one time. When a person does reach that stage he is qualified to go back to the Lord.

It is a process that goes on over many, many lifetimes. If a person is spontaneously attracted to the service of God it is because he has been following that path over many lifetimes. Sometimes we may see a person suddenly awaken and become absorbed in the spiritual life; this is a sure sign that, previously, he was already advanced on the path and is resuming from where he left off.[1]

67.

Whatever state of being one remembers when he quits his body, O son of Kunti, that state he will attain without fail.

Bhagavad Gita 8.6

This summarizes the principle under which the soul transmigrates into another body. The focus of consciousness at the time of death will naturally attract the soul as the focus of its future existence. So if the consciousness has become degraded, has become animal-like even whilst in the human body, then the soul will slide downward to an animal birth; whereas if the consciousness has become elevated to finer and finer levels of awareness, then the soul will naturally gravitate upward. These

1. Char./Das.

are all within the sphere of material existence, lower and higher
levels of existence. But, of course, the ultimate stage is when the
soul is focused completely on Krishna; then one will not take
birth again in this world but will return to the spiritual world to
associate directly with Krishna.[1]

68.

*On account of his connnection with the deeds of previous
incarnations, the individual self [jiva] dreams and awakens. He
plays in the three cities...*

Kaivalyopanishad 14

The law of karma says that for every action there is a reaction.
This operates at the level of personality through an endless chain
of action and desire reacting to one another. Driven by the
stream of thoughts in one direction, which constitutes desire, an
action is performed. From the action performed with desire,
desire for more of the same or something different arises. We are
born because we have ended our last life still caught in this chain
of action and desire. In other words, your personality is simply
the conglomeration of desires accumulated through all your
deeds from this moment backwards beyond birth to your
previous life and even further.

As long as we have even one desire we are still caught in the
wheel of karma and will take rebirth in this world to try to satisfy
that desire. We will play again in the 'three cities' of waking,
dreaming and deep sleep. The three cities are also known as the
gross, subtle and causal bodies, which refer to the physical
(waking), the mental (dreaming) and the unmanifested desires
(deep sleep).[2]

1. Char./Das.
2. Parth.

69.

But if he were born again and again, and again and again he were to die, even then, victorious man, do not grieve.

Bhagavad Gita 2.26

No one wishes to die, yet everyone dies. It is the greatest change which happens to us on the material level. As long as we identify with material existence we identify with its definition – change. We have a great desire for change and more change. It is the process of our evolution. One way or another, consciously or not, we get that change for ourselves. The greatest material change available to us is death. When the desire for change is great enough we will die and take another birth. It may even be the fear of change, i.e., death and rebirth, that kills us. Unable to undertake it at a conscious level in our daily life, our causal body (unmanifested desires) will orchestrate it against our apparent wishes.

70.

They are brave warriors, Drona, Bhisma, Jayadratha, Karna, and have already been slain by Me. Therefore kill them and do not be disturbed. Simply fight and you will vanquish your enemies.

Bhagavad Gita 11.34

These people who have been living in total unrighteousness have come to the state where they will eliminate themselves. We are all in mortal bodies although we never believe we will die because our immortal Atman echoes within us, whether or not we know it.

The law of karma (action-reaction) is the law set by the Self, the Brahman. That law will function. As the law of gravity takes the river to the sea so the law of karma takes us ultimately to the Self. The vasanas are merely the permutations arising from this law. The Kaurava warriors have shaped their own vasanas such that they must die in the battle as their process back to the Self.

Arjuna should not make the mistake of egotism and believe he is the doer. In Shakespeare's language, there is a Divinity that shapes our ends. We are a spoke in the wheel of life. If we understand that, we are humble. Otherwise we are arrogant and think, 'I am the doer.' Arjuna has made that mistake of thinking 'I am killing.' He is only functioning on behalf of the Totality from which he has received the gift of military leadership. Therefore, whenever it is his duty to fight he must do so for that is his part in the wheel of life.[1]

71.

One who is able to withdraw all his senses from the attractions of sense objects, even as a tortoise withdraws all its limbs, he is a man of steady wisdom.

Bhagavad Gita 2.56

A recurrent theme in Hindu scriptures is the unreality of the world we perceive through the senses. The internal maps of the world which we build up, using data from the senses, are bound to be imperfect and relative, varying with the individual genetic makeup and the play of circumstances in time and place. Yet we attribute to these perceptions a constancy and reality which they do not possess.

Convinced of the reality of the world, we seek pleasures by the use and (often) abuse of the senses and body functions, thereby becoming attached and even addicted to certain types of stimulation. Attachment keeps the soul earth-bound for many cycles of life and death and prevents liberation from the bondage of illusion (maya). Liberation is necessary for us to achieve closeness to God and immortality through final union with Him.

Detachment from addictions and earthly attachments can start with the realization that body functions and senses are imperfect and are activated by the Divine force in us. The ultimate Reality and everlasting Bliss come from developing awareness of the activating Spirit rather than developing awareness of the false and imperfect ability of the senses.[2]

1. Parth.
2. Chand.

72.

Existing in the midst of ignorance, thinking themselves wise with a surfeit of worldly knowledge, deluded beings wander about suffering again and again, like the blind led by the blind. Preoccupied with the manifold deceits of ignorance, such people believe they have achieved the goal of life. They are, however, subject to emotional attachments and therefore never find the Truth but are cast down in dejection when the rewards for any good actions are exhausted.

Mundakopanishad I.2.8–9

Secular learning does not bring liberation from the cycle of rebirths. Only spiritual enlightenment can bring true realization of God and freedom from attachments and emotional storms which arise from desires. Good works alone may bring the reward of a brief period of happiness in heaven after death; but this period is finite and, when it is over, rebirth occurs into the hardships, suffering and enslavement to desires which are so commonly found in lives on earth.

The sad fact is that many intellectually gifted men and women become totally engrossed with the pursuit of secular knowledge and do not realize the need for spiritual development to free them from the endless cycle of rebirths.

Psychologists and medical researchers have shown that one part of the brain deals specifically with the logical chains of thought which impose some sort of order and constancy on the deluge of data transmitted by our senses from the world around us.

Another part of the brain, however, deals specifically with the intuitive processes of the mind and might well be the physical basis by which we communicate with God-within-us and, through this channel, with God-in-the-Universe-at-large. Meditation is one way by which this intuitive part of the brain and its spiritual and transcendental connection might be strengthened, amplified and extended.[1]

1. Chand.

73.

*From constant thinking about objects of the senses attachment
arises. From that attachment, desire develops, and from desire,
anger arises.*

*From anger, delusion arises. From delusion comes confusion of
memory. From confusion of memory comes loss of discrimination.
When discrimination is lost, you fall down into the material pool
again.*

Bhagavad Gita 2.62–63

These two verses describe the spiritual fall precipitated by desire.
It begins with a thought – an expensive car, a handsome man, a
beautiful woman. A thought goes out, followed by another along
the same lines, making a groove so the stream of thoughts
becomes attachment. It is like the mighty Ganges in India which
starts as a few drops here and there, collecting into a trickle high
up in the Himalayas. The trickle becomes a tremendous flow of
water plunging down the mountainside. This happens when
thoughts begin flowing in one direction. More and more
thoughts are drawn into the groove, establishing a river of desire.
Attachment turns into a desire.

When a desire is blocked it is deflected onto another object or
being. This is anger. In a state of anger we become disorientated.
We forget who is boss and who is the subordinate, who is the
loving spouse and who is the beloved child. Once we forget this
our judgement goes awry. We perceive others as objects of
hatred. The ability to discriminate is the glory of humanity. It is
what makes us the most highly developed created being. If we do
not use it to analyse and control our thoughts we slip down the
ladder into the uncontrolled desires of animal existence. We let
slip our chance for godhood.[1]

74.

Truly, these worlds are demonic which are covered by blinding

1. Parth.

darkness. Those people who slay their own Self [Atman] go to such worlds after death.

Isavasyopanishad 3

This is the spiritual death of people who totally immerse themselves in this world as an end in itself. The world cannot harm us if we use it to reach a higher level, but once we commit ourselves to it alone, we condemn ourselves to run in circles in a sunless, demonic world. There is no time for enjoyment. We are too busy attaching ourselves to material happiness which keeps slipping away from us.

If we use earthly pleasures to satisfy our spiritual needs (whether or not we recognize them as such) we become addicts of the material world, like the drinker who gets a kick from his first alcoholic drink and drinks more. Then he drinks more and more to get that same kick. Finally, it is no longer a kick but only hell – hell if he drinks, greater hell if he doesn't. For he has nothing else, he has shrouded all the higher aspects of life.

People who slay their own Atman with addiction to the material world return to it constantly. 'After death' does not refer only to the death of the body, having been reborn into another hellish lifetime. It means also the daily deaths – ends – of activities. After each action in pursuit of kicks people find themselves still trapped in the same overstimulated, boring, sunless life.[1]

75.

There are three pathways to hell which destroy a human being: lust, anger and greed. Therefore give up these things.

Bhagavad Gita 16.21

There is a Ramakrishna swami who always tells the novices, 'I'm not afraid of hell or heaven. You know I have beautiful handwriting. If I go to heaven, God will say, come here and do my correspondence. If I go to hell, the day the god of hell

1. Parth.

discovers my handwriting he will put me to the same job. So it doesn't make any difference where I go.'

We make our heaven or hell depending on how we use our opportunities. Heaven is a calm and healthy mind.[1]

76.

Those who know the three Vedas [scriptures] and drink soma juice [alcoholic oblation], purified of their sin through worshipping Me, reach the heavenly world of the god Indra where they enjoy the divine pleasures.

Bhagavad Gita 9.20

If you are after the world, you get the world. If you are after Reality, you get Reality. These verses are talking about people – good people – who perform the rituals as laid down in the Vedas (scriptures), but hang on to their desires. They do not have single-pointed dedication to the Atman (Eternal Self). It is a case of obeying the letter of the law rather than the spirit. Their spiritual activities are an end in themselves, with the added benefit that business seems to have been doing better since they started worshipping regularly.

This type of person includes the majority of religious people. They go on pilgrimages and to the temple or church regularly, and there's nothing wrong with it. The letter of the law is better than no law. Such people achieve a lot of punya (good results) and enter a realm in which they enjoy those good results. That realm is called heaven. The heavenly pleasures are in accordance with their desires. They achieve limited goals because that is what they have set for themselves.

Heaven is not a geographical place. It is a state of mind. In these verses it is referred to as the heaven of Indra, because he is God of the mind, Lord of the senses. In John Milton's famous words: 'The mind is its own place. It can make a heaven out of hell and hell out of heaven.'[2]

1. Bhav.
2. Parth.

77.

Such people, having enjoyed the vast heaven, enter the mortal world on the exhaustion of the punya. Abiding by the principles of the three Vedas, desiring the objects of desire, they achieve the world of birth and death.

Bhagavad Gita 9.21

People who study the scriptures and do good actions in the world, but nevertheless get involved in their activities, desiring the fruits (see above), reap benefits on the material plane. For a while they exist free of anxiety and fear. They are not plagued by the myriad forms of death – death of their self-esteem, death of their business, death in their family, death of a friendship, etc. They experience relative immortality, but when their punya, the good results of their good actions, has exhausted itself, they return to the mortal life of birth and death, change, worries and agitations.

The relative heaven achieved by mechanically observing religious principles is akin to the painkiller the doctor gives you for a brain tumour. For a while you feel fine again, but once the drug wears off, you will be back where you started. The painkiller is a temporary measure. But to cure yourself, you have to rid yourself of the tumour. Similarly, to cure yourself of desire, you have to rid yourself of the desires that bind you to this world.[1]

78.

Out of many thousands of men scarcely one strives to know me. Of those who strive, scarcely one knows me in Truth.

Bhagavad Gita 7.3

There is a story of a mahatma (great soul) who, for many years, got up each morning and began pushing a huge boulder to the top of a hill. For six hours he would struggle with this boulder until he reached the top. As soon as he did so he kicked the

1. Parth.

boulder and it came tumbling down. Within minutes it lay at the
bottom of the hill again. The mahatma laughed out loud and then
he came down for the day. As you can imagine, he became a
tourist attraction. Everybody came to see the potty old fellow
until, one day, two of his disciples turned up. They had been
searching for him to ask him to return to the Himalayas and teach
them.

'He's crackers,' said the local people.

'But you see,' said his disciples, who were themselves very
developed souls, 'all his tremendous effort has been to bring you
and me to understand what we have never understood. Each one
of us has spent millions upon millions of lifetimes struggling to
the top of material evolution. We are within reach of godhood
and then, for the sheer thrill of worldly pleasures which will be
gone in a flash, we kick ourselves down again.' [1]

1. Parth.

5 Kama – Desire

The Three Bodies: Gross, Subtle and Causal

79.

*Desire first stirred in It, desire that was the first seed of the spirit.
The connection of the existent in the nonexistent the sages found,
seeking in their hearts with wisdom.*

Rig Veda X.129.4

All this world arises from pure Consciousness. That state is
absolute peace and fulfilment. But within the Infinite is the
infinity of possibilities, including disturbance. The first
disturbance of peace is thought – the desire for another. That is
the seed which grows into this world of names, forms and
activities and from their fruit are sown more seeds of desire to
perpetuate this world.

80.

*[Arjuna said:] O Krishna, by what impulse does man commit sin,
though against his wishes, constrained as it were by force?*

Bhagavad Gita 3.36

Sin means agitation. It is not the action, but the reaction which
determines sin. For instance, killing a man is not in itself a sin.
Suppose a man outside your house took out a machine-gun and
began shooting down passersby in the street. You had a loaded

gun at your disposal and could choose to shoot him and save the
lives of the dozen still in range or make a cup of tea while he
continued his killing spree. It is the making of a cup of tea, not
the killing of a man, that is likely to rebound in such a way as to
agitate your mind. When an action rebounds and agitates your
mind, you have committed a sin. Sin is a state of mind.

So the problem is not knowledge. We know what is right and
wrong. We know what agitates us. The problem is how to keep
ourselves on the path which we think is right and to avoid what
we think is wrong. Arjuna is asking what is it that makes him act
against his better judgement for peace of mind. This is the sinful
life which plagues us all. We want to get up early in the morning
and do exercises but we can't; we want to read the great
philosophers but we can't; we want to control our anger but we
can't. What prevents us from doing the good we want to do in
life?[1]

81.

> [*The Blessed Lord said:*] *It is desire. It is anger, Arjuna, and it is
> begotten by the quality of rajas* [*passion*]. *It is a great devourer. It
> is all-sinful. Know this as the enemy.*

Bhagavad Gita 3.37

Desire, the characteristic of a rajasic nature, is the enemy that
prevents us following our better judgement.

How do we get this rajasic nature? When we see an object, we
start thinking of it indiscriminately. When the thoughts are going
constantly between us and the object, creating a stream of
thoughts, it is called desire. Whenever these desires are
obstructed by an object or being, the thoughts are refracted. This
is anger. Therefore, anger can never come without desire. It is
the other side of the coin. It is a desire which takes us away from
the chosen path.

Some of you may have a long list of desires but most of you will
have a very modest list – one or two things, perhaps, that you

1. Parth.

desire. And you genuinely believe that when you fulfil these few
desires you will be fulfilled. But desire is insatiable. One desire is
enough. A desire for gambling, drink, another person, money,
fame, can take you and take you until it has devoured your life.
And because it is never satisfied you are constantly agitated by it.
You are permanently in a state of stress. This is sin.[1]

82.

*O son of Kunti, knowledge is enveloped by this constant enemy of
the wise in the form of desires, insatiable as the fire.*

Bhagavad Gita 3.39

The desires of the mind are insatiable and are compared to the
fire. Any amount of fuel we give to the fire will not satisfy it. We
can throw the whole house, the whole country, the whole world
into the fire and at no point will it say, 'No thank you, I've had
enough.' This is the nature of fire. This is the nature of desire.
The more we feed it the more its appetite increases, the higher
and wider is its sweep.[2]

83.

*Desire has three headquarters: the senses, the mind and the
intellect. Through them desire covers true knowledge of the living
being and bewilders him.*

Bhagavad Gita 3.40

There is a story of a young man who went into the Himalayas to
find peace in which he could realize the Self. When he got there
he found there were more distractions than in the city. The
monkeys would come to the cave where he meditated to scream
and chatter until he gave up meditating and chased them off.

1. Parth.
2. Parth.

Everyone else seemed to be able to meditate in peace, so finally, he sought advice on the matter.

He was told to put a little channa (nuts) in a kuja (narrow-necked prayer jug), which he did, and then he sat and waited. Sure enough a monkey appeared and followed its nose to the channa. In went the paw. The young man got up but the monkey didn't scamper off. Its hand was caught because it could only come out of the kuja if the monkey let go of the channa. The man struck it with the stick but the monkey was trapped because it wouldn't let go of the channa. The man was able to strike it again and again and still the monkey kept clutching the channa. Only when it was more dead than alive did it let go of the channa and flee.

We are like that monkey. We cling to our objects of desire, physically, emotionally and intellectually, even when we are being pummelled to death because of them. Our wealth, our family, our ambitions are the channa of our desire in which we invest our being, blind to the damage we inflict on ourselves. Our intellect, the greatest weapon we have for our own salvation, our judgement becomes party to our damnation.[1]

84.

> ... *The person is identified with desire. As is his desire so is his will. As is his will, so is the deed he does, whatever deed he does, that he attains.*

Brhadaranyaka Upanishad IV.4.5

Our desires shape our personality and we act accordingly. As we act, so are we rewarded. But what we sow, reap and eat has a seed which remains dormant within us. This is the long-term reaction of karma – unmanifest desires known as vasanas which constitute the causal body. As long as we have vasanas we will have to act them out. We attain material existence again in a suitable situation to do so.

The subtle body (mind and intellect) ferries the Self from gross (physical) body to gross body. The world is like a magnet.

1. Parth.

But it is our gross and subtle bodies which are attracted. They are the iron that goes to the magnet. That is their nature. We needlessly attach our Self to them. We are like a piece of wood bound by desire to the piece of iron. The iron attaches itself to the magnet taking the wood with it. The wood appears also to be affected by the magnet but, in truth, the magnet has no effect on the wood. It will cease to be attracted by the magnet as soon as it is detached from the iron.[1]

85.

The sons of Dhiritarashtra [the Kauravas] and all the hosts of the kings of earth, Bhisma, Drona, Karna, with our warrior chiefs, come rushing into your mouth with terrible teeth, fearful to see. Some are trapped between your teeth with their heads crushed to powder.

Bhagavad Gita 11.26–27

This horrifying vision of all the great personalities of the Mahabharata, crushed by the mouth of Krishna's divine form, is simply to convey poetically the terror they all suffer because of desires which plague them. Whenever there is desire in you, you will have to struggle in the world and will be crushed by your own actions, even as you knowingly or unknowingly try to enter that Supreme Self which is your own self.[2]

86.

A person may abstain from sense objects but the sense objects remain with him. Only by experiencing the higher Reality does a person leave his desires behind.

Bhagavad Gita 2.59

Attachment means that you depend upon an object or being. If that being or object is taken away you feel as if a part of you has

1. Parth.
2. Parth.

been taken away. You are not a whole person. You can't function without that other. So the advice here is to root out dependencies on that which is *not* you. This does not mean dissociating yourself from the world. The secret is to be truly independent so that you can associate freely without becoming attached.

If you are attached to something or someone, he will find his way to you. You need only look around you to know to what and to whom you are attached. Like attracts like. He who desires drink will be surrounded by drink and drinkers. He who desires learning will be surrounded by books and thinkers and so on.

Unless you are established in the higher Reality which is your Infinite Self, you can abstain from these things but the taste for them will remain. Your thoughts will continue to run after them. You will have achieved self-denial but not self-control. Educate yourself to higher levels so the desires dissolve and you can associate with objects and beings without becoming attached.[1]

87.

The senses are so strong and impetuous, Arjuna, that they even carry away the mind of a wise man who is striving on the path of realization.

Bhagavad Gita 2.60

The senses are constantly driving us to beautiful shapes and colours, sweet sounds, nice smells, flavoursome tastes, pleasant touches. Not only are our senses pushing us to sense objects, but the sense objects pull us toward them, whether they are a flashing neon sign for 101 flavours of icecream, a gleaming car or a seductive personality.

There is a tug-of-war that begins with the senses, backed by the mind, backed by the intellect on one side and the world on the other. Once the senses cross over to the side of the world, the mind is pulled violently. If it crosses over, the intellect takes the full strain of the pull. If the intellect crosses over we are finished. The intellect is the greatest defence we have. It is what raises

1. Parth.

humanity above all other beings and provides the means for realizing our own godhood. But, as this verse warns, even the man who is far along the road to realization is not free from the threat of his senses.[1]

88.

For the objects of the senses abide in the senses – attraction and aversion are within you. Let nobody come under the dominion of these two. They are your enemies.

Bhagavad Gita 3.34

Attraction and aversion are the two sides of the coin of desire. They are our greatest enemies yet we are very friendly with them. But what we like is not necessarily what is good for us, any more than what we dislike is necessarily bad for us.

You don't like healthy food, you love junk food. You don't like exercise, you love lazing around. You hate your mother-in-law with whom you live, you love your mother, so your mind is constantly turned away from the one to the other. You like going to parties, you don't like studying for your exams. All these likes and dislikes will harm you unless they are filtered through your discriminating intellect. They will concentrate and harden into the chains that bind you to this world.[2]

89.

As a boat on the water is blown from its course by a strong wind, the wandering senses can catch the mind and blow a man's judgement far off course.

Bhagavad Gita 2.67

The mind, carried away by the senses, can then carry away the intellect. In this metaphor, the boat is the human being on the ocean of the world. The desires of the senses catch the mind as

1. Parth.
2. Parth.

the wind catches a sail. The captain in the boat is the intellect, the discriminating faculty. He can't wait for the wind to stop blowing, any more than you can wait for the desires of the senses to blow away of their own accord. They won't.

The captain understands the principle of using the wind to take his boat out of the wind. With the help of the compass – his guru – he can sail the boat into the calm harbour, protected from the wind. Here, out of the wind, the sea is calm, just as the world is calm when the desires of the mind are calm.

Desires can sink a person lifetime after lifetime into this world, but if his intellect guides him to the calm waters of meditation, he can easily cross to the shore of Reality.[1]

90.

O bull among the Bharatas, controlling first the senses, kill the sinful thing desire which destroys knowledge and wisdom.

Bhagavad Gita 3.41

Krishna calls Arjuna a bull as an accolade and reminder of his ability to work without desire. The cow and bull are worshipped in India because their lives are devoted to the benefit of others.

He urges Arjuna to get a grip on his senses as a fundamental principle for conquering desire. Unchecked, those senses will enlist the mind and then the intellect to open the way for desire. The very means we have for draining away desire become the means by which we saturate ourselves with it.

If we immerse ourselves in the world we are like a house standing in streets swilling with the filthy water of flooded sewers. In this situation the drainpipes through which the houses release their filthy waters become the means by which the water pours in, ruining the house interior. This is what has happened to us. The world, polluted by desire, has risen higher and higher around us. Our body, mind and intellect which have the capacity to drain off our desires become the means by which those desires saturate us, destroying knowledge and wisdom.[2]

1. Parth.
2. Parth.

91.

They say the senses are great, greater than the senses is the mind, greater than the mind is the intellect, greater than the intellect is He.

Bhagavad Gita 3.42

What controls the body is the mind, what controls the mind is the intellect, what controls the intellect is 'He', the Atman (Eternal Self). The more we identify with the higher layers of our personality, the greater will be our control over desires. If we identify with the body, we have physical desires, if we identify with the mind we have emotional desires, if we identify with the intellect we have intellectual desires.

As we move to the emotional level, the physical desires are overruled. The father who loves his child gives her the sweet because the emotional pleasure of seeing her happy is greater than the physical pleasure of eating the sweet himself.

Similarly, when we rise to the intellectual level the emotional desires are overruled. As Brutus said, after killing Caesar, 'Not that I loved Caesar less, but I loved Rome more.'

The final stage is when we identify with the Atman. Then the intellectual desires drop away and then there is no desire. We realize the Atman.[1]

92.

Thus knowing that which is greater than the intellect and restraining the self by your own Self, O mighty-armed Arjuna, kill the formidable enemy.

Bhagavad Gita 3.43

We are given two complementary mechanisms for overcoming the formidable enemy, desire. The first is knowledge of Brahman (Eternal Self), the second self-restraint. If we indulge in the pleasures of material existence while studying Vedanta (the

1. Parth.

culmination of knowledge) the knowledge is likely to sink from sight into the sea of sensory experience. On the other hand, if we completely give up all sense objects we will inevitably become frustrated. So Krishna gives a very practical tip. What we need is a little knowledge of the Atman (Supreme Soul) to help withdraw a little from worldly attachments. And when we have withdrawn a little, we will be able to learn a little more and so on. These are the two pedals to the wheel which will carry us towards the Truth.[1]

93.

Know that the soul is the lord of the chariot, the body is the chariot, the intellect is the charioteer, the mind is the reins.

The senses, they say, are the horses and the material objects are the fields of pasture. The wise men say that the soul, joined with the mind and senses, enjoys the material objects.

Kathopanishad I.3.3–4

Here lies the story of life's pilgrimage for which we have been given the body. Everything on earth has its specific purpose. The sages of India have revealed that the specific purpose for which we have been granted this body is to seek ultimate salvation of our soul. Just as the chariot is used for travelling, the human body should be kept active, engaged in good deeds. If the horses of the chariot run out of control, the lord of the chariot will not reach his destination. Similarly, the five sense organs – the tongue, eyes, ears, nose and skin – should be kept under control otherwise we will not reach our spiritual destination.[2]

94.

The man whose charioteer [intellect] is knowledgeable, wise, alert and discriminating, whose reins [the mind] are in full control, only that man is able to cross the path of material life, reaching the desired goal, Lord Vishnu's supreme abode.

Kathopanishad I.3.9

1. Panch.
2. Panch.

The reins are the mind, the charioteer is the intellect and the lord of the chariot is the soul. We must employ our intellect to control our mind and senses, otherwise they will drag us into the enemy ranks of egotism, jealousy, envy, spite, prejudice, lust, etc. These enemies cause the inner turmoil each individual experiences. Given the opportunity, they will destroy us. Just as an intelligent driver pleases his employer so the intellect should take hold of the mind to direct the senses towards God with spiritual vigour. If the mind meditates upon the divine form of God, the other organs will enjoy the Divine Bliss.

Just as Arjuna handed the reins of the chariot to Lord Krishna, if we hand the reins of our life to God, it is His wish that will prevail. Believing that God is the all-doer gives meaning and joy to our lives.[1]

95.

He [the man of perfection] is not agitated by the threefold sorrows nor hankers after happiness . . .

Bhagavad Gita 2.56

The miseries of the body, mind and intellect do not worry the man of perfection (God-realized). The trouble in the world is not the joy and sorrow that visit us, but our identification with joy and sorrow. Experiencing joy and sorrow without identifying with either is the art of human life. If we do not feel joy and sorrow, we are like a plant. If we identify with joy and sorrow, we are like an animal.

There are many occasions already when we feel sorrow or joy while being unaffected by them. Suppose you are reading the newspaper one morning and there is an article about twenty-five children drowning on the other side of the country. You are very sorry. You tell your wife. You both say what a terrible tragedy it is and then you eat your eggs. This is not hypocritical. The sorrow is genuine, but you are not *affected* by it.

Now suppose there is news that twenty-five children have

1. Panch.

72   *The Essential Teachings of Hinduism*

drowned in a school where your child is studying. You will be
sorry and will not finish your breakfast. You can't work, can't
cook. Everybody is paralysed by sorrow. They have identified
with it.

Joy and sorrow are the two experiences which make an
unending procession through our lives. Learn to accept them as
visitors to your house. Acknowledge them politely and cater to
their needs patiently. Let them into your house without
involving them in the routine of the house because you know that
sooner or later they will leave.[1]

96.

*. . . [He] is free from desire, free from fear, free from anger. He is
called a man of perfection.*

Bhagavad Gita 2.56

Desire, fear and anger – get rid of the first and the other two,
merely modifications of it, will go as well. Desire is the response
to an experience of emptiness. Your stomach is empty so your
thoughts run after a particular object called food. When your
stomach is full your thoughts do not run after food. You lose that
desire – temporarily – and take up another. Your true nature is
infinite, so as long as you turn to the limited world instead of that
Self, you will never be full. That sense of emptiness is expressed
as an endless chain of physical, mental or intellectual desires.
You are like a starving person who dreams of vast banquets. It
doesn't matter how much you eat in that dream, you are still
hungry, so you keep dreaming of more and more delicious foods.
But the solution is not within the dream.

Many people become 'irrationally' angry. Anger is the effect of
obstructed desire. It is only 'irrational' because the person has
not identified the desire which is being obstructed.

On the other hand, if the desire is fulfilled you develop fear.
The more the desire is fulfilled, the more you have to fear. You
have accumulated enormous wealth so your mind is plagued with

1. Parth.

fear of the Inland Revenue or your son-in-law or both. You have a reputation as the greatest boxer in the world so every young boxer is to be feared as your downfall.

When there is no desire there is nothing about which to be angry, nothing to fear.[1]

97.

... Do not covet anyone's wealth.

Isavasyopanishad I.1

Coveting anyone's wealth, including that which you already consider as 'mine', will only agitate the mind. What you have you fear to lose; what you do not have you crave. When your mind is agitated it can't think properly. When you can't think properly, you can't act properly and so, paradoxically, you are most likely to fail in pursuit of that wealth. But the second twist to this is that all this world is your wealth anyway. To covet it is like coveting your own arm.

The injunction here, 'Do not covet anyone's wealth', is the immediate rider given as the logical and practical conclusion to a declaration that the Supreme Being is all-pervading. The ultimate Reality of you and all the world is the Supreme Being, just as the ultimate reality of all the beings and objects in your dreams is your mind. So when you covet something in the world it is one aspect of the Supreme Being coveting another aspect of the Supreme Being. It is like your mouth coveting your foot. One of the images of Lord Krishna is of a baby sucking his toe. Krishna, the most human incarnation of the Supreme, is satirizing humanity. We are all sucking our own toes when we run after wealth in any form – money, power, reputation, knowledge. It is ours already if only we realized it.[2]

1. Parth.
2. Parth.

98.

> ... *When all the desires that dwell in the heart are cast away,*
> *then does the mortal become immortal, then he attains Brahman*
> *here [in his body]* ...
>
> Brhadaranyaka Upanishad IV.4.7

If there is a spot on the projector it doesn't matter what images
you project or how many times you clean the screen, there will
still be a spot on every image you project. Similarly, you can
spend a lifetime trying to satisfy your desires and agitations, but
the problem is not external. It is not the world that needs to be
cleansed, but yourself. You cannot find internal peace, you
cannot find the Eternal Self by external arrangements.[1]

99.

> *What have I to do with things that are not of immortality?*
> Brhadaranyaka Upanishad 2.4

On the eve of entering the fourth stage of life – renunciation – the
great sage Yajnavalkya offers to divide his earthly possessions
between his two wives: Maitreyi and Katyayani. Maitreyi asks
him, 'My Lord! if this whole world belonged to me with all its
wealth, should I, through its possession, attain immortality?'
When Yajnavalkya admits that it will not bring her immortality,
she asks the above question. With the simplicity of deep insight
she hits the nail on the head. There is no point in trying to
squeeze out immortality or eternal happiness by accumulating
the material world.[2]

1. Parth.
2. Panch.

6 The Ramayana – The Conquest of Desire

100.

I praise Rama who preceded Lakshmana and belonged to the lineage of Raghu, charming husband of Sita, coming from the race of Kakutstha, compassionate, abode of virtues, loved by the Brahmins, righteous, king of kings, truthful son of Dasaratha, of dark complexion, having a calm beatitude; delight of the world, the best in the family of Raghu and the killer of Ravana. To his right stands Lakshmana with bow, to his left auspicious Sita, and Hanuman stands in front. I praise Rama again and again.

Ramayana: Invocation

This invocation is chanted before the study or performance of the Ramayana, the great epic which tells how a perfect man falls from bliss to sorrow and bondage, and then struggles back to his original state. The hero, Prince Rama, is the Atman (Supreme Soul) in all of us. He is dark-skinned because, like Krishna (which means 'dark'), he is the unknown. Both are incarnations of the God Vishnu who maintains the world and comes to earth when righteousness has been usurped by its greatest enemy – desire.

Rama's wife, Sita, and his brother, Lakshmana, represent the Atman's loyal ego and mind respectively. Nevertheless, the ego is party to the Atman's downfall. Sita is deluded and enslaved by the desires of the ten organs of action and perception, embodied as the ten-headed demon, Ravana. Having made this mistake, she then performs tapas (austerities) while she waits in perfect faith for Rama – the Atman – to save her. Hanuman, the monkey-god, represents the intellect which, inspired by the Atman, leads its forces against the demon desire.[1]

101.

The gods said to Brahma, 'Lord, there is a rakshasa [demon] called Ravana who, having secured your favour, is oppressing us all. We are powerless to defeat him...

'... We are overwhelmed with terror because of this dreadful creature, Ravana. O Lord, please find some means to destroy him.'

Ramayana I.15.6 & 11

Lord Brahma is the god of Creation. All creation arises out of thought disturbance. Brahma is the total capacity for this disturbance. He is our mind and intellect. Therefore, he is known as the grandfather of the gods because, whether they heed him or not, all arise from him. The world exists only as long as we are thinking. In deep sleep there is no world, no gods.

Lord Brahma does not command as many devotees as his counterparts, Shiva, lord of destruction, and Vishnu, lord of maintenance. Human beings have no shortage of thoughts, albeit without understanding, and, indeed, thought is seen as the forerunner of the great enemy, desire, which blinds our understanding. The Ramayana deals with this very problem in Ravana, the demon of desire, who has grasped power through the good auspices of Brahma. Thought feeds desire, fuelling its ravenous appetite, yet when the personality and its world, represented by the gods, is oppressed by desire it must turn to the intellect for help. Only the discriminating and reflective powers of the intellect can shake off this demon.[2]

1. Parth.
2. Parth.

102.

[Brahma replied:] While he [Ravana] was asking for his boon, he said, 'May I be unconquerable by the gandharvas [celestial singers], yakshas [sprites], gods, and demons.' I replied, 'Let it be so.' But since due to contempt he did not mention men, he will be destroyed by no other person but a man.

Ramayana I.15.13–14

Lord Brahma, god of Creation and thought (see above), wears an animal hide as a symbol of the austerities (tapas) people must perform to benefit from him. These austerities are dedicated study and reflection on the scriptures, control of the senses and sacrificial service to others. Brahma blesses practitioners of tapas with great intellectual power which can lead first to renunciation and then to God-realization, but can also become a corrupting force if the practitioner loses sight of the ultimate goal, the Immortal Self. Ravana had been corrupted by this power and lured into worldly domination. Once a devotee, he became the demon desire.

Desire goes out to conquer the world, whatever it perceives that world to be, and forgets to watch its back. Behind it is the intellect, the essence and glory of man. The intellect is our lifeline to the Atman (Supreme Self). It can draw on that power to destroy desire.[1]

103.

[Rama said to Lakshmana:] Here lies the rakshasa [demon] killed by me with an arrow. He took the magic form of a deer and thereby made me come away from our cottage.

As he was struck by the arrow, he imitated my voice and loudly let out a cry for help – 'Brother Lakshmana, I am dying, help me' – that could be heard from a great distance. And therefore, having

1. Parth.

heard that loud fateful cry, you have come here leaving Maithili
[Sita] behind.

Ramayana III.59.25 & 27

Rama is the Atman, slayer of desire, using the arrows given by
Lord Indra, ruler of the senses. Pierced by one of these arrows
the demon desire reveals its ugly form but, in its death throes,
calls to the mind (Lakshmana) and the ego (Sita), mimicking the
Atman (Rama). The mind and the ego fear their own dear Self is
dying. Death of desire frightens us: we fear it is our own death.
The mind is fooled by this trick of desire and races off
unnecessarily to save its immortal Self, leaving the mortal ego
wide open to another demon of desire.[1]

104.

[Vali said to Rama:] I was killed by you when you were invisible in
the battle. It would have been difficult for you to kill me otherwise.
It is like killing a man who is asleep or unconscious due to some sin
or due to drinking, almost like a sleeping serpent who cannot be
easily killed otherwise. You may give the kingdom to Sugreeva as
I ascend to heaven, but that kingdom will be tainted with sin
[adharma] since I have been killed in an unjust battle.

Ramayana IV.44.48 & 52

The great hero Rama is, in every way, the ideal man. To a Hindu
he is the perfection each man should aspire to, yet Rama shoots
the monkey, Vali, from behind a tree while Vali is locked in
combat with his brother Sugreeva. This has laid an unjust
question mark over Rama's impeccable character. Rama was
being an ideal friend to Sugreeva but, more than that, the poet
Valmiki is giving us a solution to uncontrollable desires.

Vali was lustful and immoral while his brother was virtuous
and moral. Vali had usurped Sugreeva's throne. He was able to
do so because of his invincible strength. Brahma had granted him
a boon for his tapas (dedicated effort, austerities) and he had

1. Parth.

chosen half the strength of any opponent in battle. Thus he was an infallible fighter, needing only an ounce of strength himself to defeat any adversary.

Vali and Sugreeva are the lower and higher aspects of human nature. Vali is the sensuality which enslaves us to the world. When we become entangled with objects of the senses they drain half our strength away. Our mind goes running off and, if we are not careful, the intellect follows suit. We become entangled and identified with these objects. The first time the two monkey brothers fought Rama couldn't even tell them apart to shoot Vali.

The practical solution given here is to keep out of sight of the objects of desire until we have laid them to rest.[1]

105.

O friend, behold my chariot through which I am always decidedly victorious… courage and tenacity are its wheels, immutable truth and character are its flags. Strength, discrimination, self-control and charity are its horses. Forgiveness, mercy and equanimity are the reins and devotion to the Lord is its charioteer.

O friend, whoever possess such a chariot can never be defeated. With this chariot he can not only subdue minor temptations, but transcend the trappings of this material world.

Ramayana XI.153

The chariot as symbol of the individual soul and its body is one of the recurring images of the Hindu scriptures (see pp. 70–71). These words are those of Prince Rama as he prepared to face the rakshasa (demon) king, Ravana. Rama's monkey army has just killed numerous rakshasa generals. Brimming with rage, Ravana rushes onto the battlefield to kill Rama, much to the fear of Rama's friend, Vibhishana, Ravana's saintly brother. But Rama reassures Vibhishana, using the symbol of the chariot to explain why there is no reason to fear. Any man who lives a noble life, with courage and tenacity, powered by the spirit of truth, discrimination and self-control, and blessed with a generous

1. Parth.

heart, abiding in forgiveness, charity and devotion to God, can face the demons of life without fear of defeat. Such a man will attain eternal release.[1]

1. Panch.

7 Gunas – The Three Qualities of Nature

106.

The three qualities sattwa, rajas and tamas are built into human nature. They bind and limit the divinity within the personality.

Sattwa encourages punity, virtue and clarity of thought, creating attachment to happiness and knowledge.

Rajas is of the quality of passion, giving rise to desire and attachments; it binds fast by attachment to action.

Tamas is born of ignorance, causes delusion; it binds by inadvertence, indolence and stupor.

Bhagavad Gita 14.5–8

The three qualities of nature can be equated with one of the names for the manifest Brahman, Sat-Chit-Ananda, meaning 'Existence-Consciousness-Bliss'.

An individual is constituted of all three qualities. As long as we are material beings even tamas, the lowest form, is essential. We have to sleep and dream. But tamas should not become dominant. We should not be dozing all the time. Likewise, activity is necessary for our well-being but a fear of tranquillity and a passion for action and its fruits will harm us. The contemplation and peace of sattwa make it the highest quality, but even here there is a need to translate goodness into action and to sleep. The sattwic person must act if only in taking up the life of a sannyasi (person of renunciation). There is still desire within the action but it is the noblest of desires – to do God's work and realize Brahman.

All three qualities (even sattwa) are a form of bondage. The mind has a natural tendency to become attached to whatever it contacts, whether it is the sensual pleasures of rajas or the relative bliss and knowledge of sattwa.[1]

107.

Know the three natures – goodness [sattwa], passion [rajas] and ignorance [tamas] – as emanating from Me. I am not in them. They are in Me.

Bhagavad Gita 7.12

The entire purpose of life is to rise from the lowest to the highest of the three *gunas* (natures). All human beings are a combination of the three but the varying proportion of each in an individual is what gives the specific texture of body, mind and intellect.

The lowest guna is the tamasic one. In the world as a whole, this is the nature of the plant and mineral world. It is the heaviest material coating. In the human personality it manifests as unresponsiveness, lethargy, apathy and irresponsibility.

The second guna, rajas, is the nature of the animal kingdom. It is ruled by desires. There is no discrimination and self-control so it is a nature of constant activity in response to, and creation of, constant desire. The rajasic person is full of agitations. He is always running, running, running, getting, getting, getting. He has no time to stop and enjoy.

The highest guna, sattwa, is the essential human nature. A sattwic person is serene, composed and objective in life because he is attached to nothing. He is centred in the Self so he is full of limitless energy. He is very dynamic, but not in a frenzy of agitated activity. His activity is smooth and efficient, giving the impression of perfect stillness, like the propeller of a plane turning with such power and constancy that it appears to be motionless.

These gunas are within the Atman but It is none of them, as the ocean is not the wave that is born and dies within it. The ever-changing waves are a projection of the unchanging ocean.[2]

1. Bhav.
2. Parth.

108.

Just as fire is enveloped by smoke, just as a mirror is covered by dust, just as an embryo is covered by the womb, so is this covered by it [desire].

Bhagavad Gita 3.38

'This', the Atman, is covered by three types of desire, according to personality type – tamasic, rajasic and sattwic. The sattwic is the highest and subtlest being, no more than the desire to realize the Self. When smoke is covering the fire we see the flame as well as the smoke. Even an external factor, such as a passing breeze, can take the smoke away and what remains is the pure flame. So it is with the sattwic type.

Next there is the rajasic personality, like a dust-covered mirror. The divine image is blurred. External factors are not enough to remove the dust. We have to put in an effort to rub it clear.

When we come to the tamasic desire, it is compared to the baby in the mother's womb. As long as the baby is in the womb it is completely covered. Eventually it will come out but patience is necessary. It needs time to develop.[1]

109.

The gods, nourished by sacrifice, will give the desired object. But he who enjoys what is given without having offered to them is truly a thief.

Bhagavad Gita 3.12

To whom do the fruits of this world belong? Every breathing moment we are devouring the world to fatten our physical, mental and causal (egotistic) bodies. But they are not the source of the world any more than the bulb is the source of light. They are merely conductors.

Ritual offerings to the gods in all aspects of Hindu life are a

1. Parth.

reminder that every action in life should be performed as an offering to the Absolute Self, the Brahman. The ritual is pointless if we do not then take its significance to heart. If we use the fruits of our actions to feed our ego, we have robbed the Brahman which is the true source of all action, the Consciousness which contains this world. Everything we do should be in the spirit of service and sacrifice for, in so doing, we give it back to the all-pervading Self.

This does not mean you should give away everything you earn. On the contrary, your first service to society is to earn your own living so you are then in a position to share. The darkest hour of life is when you plan to acquire unearned wealth, whether through robbery, entering a lottery or speculating on the international money market. You have sunk to the tamasic level, the lowest of the three gunas (see pp. 81–3). Tamasic people are irresponsible, idle and heedless. They are far from their own divinity.[1]

110.

Righteous people eat the remnants of sacrifice and are thereby freed from sin...

Bhagavad Gita 3.13

Sin is not an action, but a reaction. When an action rebounds and agitates us, we have sinned. If eating meat does not worry us, we have not committed a sin. If eating meat worries us, we have committed a sin. It is the state of mind which determines sin.

People who work in the world with an attitude of 'after you' are not agitated. They have more than they desire because their desires have been immolated in the fire of sacrifice. Yet the world gives to them constantly. It is their own reflection. If you give to a reflection, it gives to you; if you withhold from it, it withholds.

Such people, who have whittled away their desires to little more than the desire for the Self, are of sattwic nature, the

1. Parth.

highest of the three gunas. They are contemplative and dynamic. They understand the unity of the world.[1]

111.

... But those who cook for their own sake truly eat sin.
                                          Bhagavad Gita 3.13

In the harbourside suburb of Malabar Hill in Bombay there are many beautiful penthouses, owned by men rushing through them on their way to more acquisitions. The only people who have time to sit on the balconies and enjoy a cup of tea and the marvellous view are the frequently invited swamis.

People who are constantly preparing pleasures for themselves have no fun. They are too busy cooking up the goodies to eat them. All they eat is agitation (sin). Their nature is rajasic, the second of the three gunas. We see these people everywhere, dashing here, dashing there, accumulating wealth, power, name, fame and ulcers. Driven by desire, they are chasing their own tails.[2]

112.

[Arjuna said:] O Lord of lords, please tell me who you are. Salutations to you. Have mercy. I desire to know You who are the Original Being. I know not your purpose.
                                          Bhagavad Gita 11.31

Arjuna has asked Krishna to show his original form and, having seen It, asks, 'Who are you?' So he has not understood. If Arjuna was a sattwic (contemplative) person he would have understood. If he were a tamasic (ignorant) person he would neither have understood nor cared. But he is a rajasic (passionate) person so he

1. Parth.
2. Parth.

doesn't understand but he wants to know. He is typically rajasic
with his excitable language.[1]

113.

*Arjuna said: O Master of the Senses [Krishna], rightly the world
is delighted and rejoices in your praise. Rakshasas [demons] fly in
fear in all quarters. The hosts of siddhas [perfected ones] bow to
you.*

Bhagavad Gita 11.35

Arjuna is talking about three types of people. First, the majority
of people in the world are rajasic (active, passionate) personalities
who rejoice in and praise someone who, like Krishna, has
unfolded his own Divinity. Wherever we find a perfected
individual we always find the world flocking around him,
bringing their fearful, worried minds to be calmed, their
intellects to be delighted.

Then there are the tamasic (inactive, ignorant) personalities,
wrapped in their tiny selves, dishonest to themselves and the
world; they are the rakshasas who fly in fear from perfected
individuals.

The third category of individual, the siddhas, are perfected
individuals of sattwic (transactive, contemplative) nature. They
understand and respect perfection. There is no tamasic fear, no
rajasic overexcitement. They adore and identify with the One
Truth revealed before them as it is in them.[2]

114.

What is night for all beings is the time of awakening for the self-

1. Parth.
2. Parth.

controlled; and the time of awakening for all beings is night for the introspective sage.

Bhagavad Gita 2.69

This has a literal as well as a metaphoric dimension. Night-time is the time when tamasic (ignorant) people enjoy the sensual delights of this world and sattwic (spiritual) people sleep. In the early hours of the morning, when everyone else is asleep, those on the spiritual path are awakened. The early-morning hours are the hours of sattwa (goodness and joy); the daytime is rajasic (passionate and active) and the night is tamasic (idle and ignorant). These different times of the day draw out that particular guna (quality of nature) in each person to the degree he or she possesses it. Therefore, we should try to live in harmony with the gunas, living so as to maximize our sattwa personality and minimize our tamas.

115.

Those deluded by the gunas [qualities of nature] are attached to the functions of the gunas. Those who have perfect knowledge should not unsettle those whose knowledge is imperfect.

Bhagavad Gita 3.29

There is a great saying: 'All grumbling is tantamount to asking, "Why is a lily not like an oak?"' A lily is a lily and an oak is an oak. People who cannot see the One Reality, supporting this pluralistic material nature, attach their likes and dislikes to its different functions. They want lilies to be oaks, lions to be lambs, mother-in-laws to be mothers, hysterical bosses to be calm swamis. Once we understand that all beings have vasanas (unmanifested desires) which will be played out as they evolve, we accept the nature of everyone. We do not feel agitated because we understand that their nature will not be transformed by persuasion, threats, flattery or even experience. By the same token, having recognized the all-pervading Being in each and every one of us, we love all beings for that, not for their nature which is merely the expression of their vasanas.

Having gained this objectivity we cannot impose it upon

others by preaching at them. What we learn we practise. From our behaviour others will learn when they are ready.[1]

116.

Even a man of knowledge acts in conformity to his own nature. Beings follow their own nature. What can repression do?

Bhagavad Gita 3.33

This verse is often taken to be pessimistic but, in fact, it is optimistic. All of us have certain types of vasanas (unmanifested desires) which constitute our nature. Now, if you study the Bhagavad Gita you find yourself full of knowledge about how to live. For a few weeks you might be sweetness and light itself, but before long you will be back to the same old rakshasa (demon).

This can be very disheartening. All Krishna is saying here is that you shouldn't have high hopes of immediate results. However much you restrain yourself, if your vasanas have enslaved you to sense objects, knowledge alone will not change patterns of behaviour. You will have to reflect upon that knowledge over and over again until you have assimilated it. If you shovel food into your baby daughter's mouth and she keeps it there, it is of no use to her. Only when she swallows and digests it will it give her strength and help her grow. Similarly, only when knowledge is digested through reflection does it become wisdom.[2]

117.

Arjuna said: Having seen this gentle form, I am now composed of mind, restored to my original nature.

Bhagavad Gita 11.51

1. Parth.
2. Parth.

Arjuna asked Krishna to show him His original nature, and when Krishna revealed the Supreme Reality which is the original nature of us all, Arjuna babbled in fear. He pleaded with Krishna to return to his gentle, heavenly form of Vishnu (see p. 136). Immediately Krishna does so Arjuna declares that his mind is composed and he is back to *his* original nature. What he means is that he has returned to his material nature as a rajasic (active, desiring) person, worshipping Krishna as the material being Vishnu. This limited form is familiar to Arjuna, loved by him but separate from his own being. His material nature stays intact. Once everything is back to 'normal', Arjuna is appeased.

No rajasic person, suddenly experiencing the full glory of the Brahman, out of the blue as it were, could stand it. The little self, the ego, is still there and liable to panic. The point is that, even from a relative point of view, if we take in more spiritual knowledge than our nature can assimilate, we frighten ourselves. Knowledge has to be given in careful doses by someone who has understood it, a guru – the gentle form of God – so we can digest it and make it our own.[1]

1. Parth.

8 Sannyasa – Renunciation

118.

I am the strength of the strong, devoid of desire and attachment...
                                         Bhagavad Gita 7.11

True strength comes only when we are rid of all desires and attachment.

Take the mechanic who is solicited by a beggar on his way to work. The beggar desires money from the mechanic. The mechanic desires nothing from the beggar. In this situation the mechanic is strong, the beggar weak.

When the mechanic reaches his workplace he goes to see the manager. He wants a rise so he can afford to marry. He is dependent on the boss because of this desire. There is nothing he has which the boss desires. There are plenty more mechanics where he comes from. Now the mechanic is weak and the employer is strong.

The shifts of power in this story illustrate that strength is not an object we possess, it is a relationship between us and the world. If we desire something from the world, we are weak; if we do not, we are strong. To be truly strong, require nothing of the world. Desirelessness is a state of tremendous power.[1]

1. Parth.

119.

... I am the desire which is not incompatible with dharma.
Bhagavad Gita 7.11

Desire for the pleasures of the world is, by definition, contrary to
your dharma (true nature). In this situation you are seeking the
world instead of your Divine Self. The only desire not
incompatible with dharma is the desire for the Self which will
lead you to Its very threshold before dissolving into the Self.[1]

120.

*The Blessed Lord said: O Son of Partha, when a man casts all
desires from his mind and is satisfied in the Self [Atman] alone by
the Self, then he is said to be in pure consciousness.*
Bhagavad Gita 2.55

Desire is personified in all religions as the devil, standing
between man and God: Satan to the Christians, Shaitan to the
Muslims, Mara to the Buddhists, Asura to the Hindus. It is one
and the same. It is that which entangles us in the world of objects
and beings so we do not discover our own godhood. When
Christ, on the Mount, told Satan, 'Get thee behind me, Satan,'
he was banishing the desires which were coming between him
and his own godhood. So we have to cast out desire that attaches
us to the world – but there is a rider to this.

We are told to give up desires *and* take up the Supreme Self.
Renunciation is the process of spiritual growth which goes on
throughout life as we give up something to take up a higher
pleasure. We see this in the case of two brothers.

One day, the elder boy calls his brother and says, 'My dear
brother, here are all my marbles for you.' The young boy is
shocked at the renunciation of his elder brother. 'Such a
wonderful thing you have and you are giving it away?' But the

1. Parth.

elder brother is not giving up anything. He is taking up something higher. He has discovered billiards.

Similarly, as long as we are attached to the world we are shocked by the Self-realized man who has renounced the world. But that man has taken up something far, far greater – the Infinite Self – so he is totally satisfied, full of infinite bliss, infinite power, infinite knowledge.

It is a matter of taking up the higher values, then the lower values automatically drop away. You don't give them up. They give you up. As the flower emerges into the fruit, the petals drop away of their own accord. If you want to get the fruit more quickly and start pulling off the petals you will have no fruit at all. Similarly, it's no use tugging out your desires before the higher values have begun to emerge. Educate yourself to higher and higher values. Understand that beyond the body is the mind, beyond the mind is the intellect, beyond the intellect is the Atman. When you get to the highest level of growth and realize the Self, automatically all your desires will fall away.[1]

121.

> . . . *By renunciation of this may you enjoy* . . .
>
> Isavasyopanishad 1

The path to the ultimate awakening is 'by renunciation of this', that is, renunciation of this world. Renunciation does not mean going without. Renunciation is giving up something to take up something else. The emphasis is on 'taking up' for no one gives up anything until there is something better in his sights. The child gives up its toys when it takes up the interests of adolescence and these, in turn, fall away in favour of adult interests. Renunciation is the mechanism for personal evolution to higher states. But people get stuck. In extreme cases, we see adults who have never let go of their childhood toys. More frequently, it is money, wife, family, friends to which a person has become attached. As long as you are attached to these you can

---

1. Parth.

only imagine higher enjoyment as more of the same, just as the child can only imagine adulthood as the freedom to buy as many candies and dolls as she wants.

On the other hand, renunciation does not mean running away from objects. It is a matter of disentangling the self from those objects so that their true value, not their black-market value, is realized. To renounce this world is to understand its mortal, material nature. Everything – your spouse, children, reputation, money, power, your body – will die. You must not attach yourself to them for this can only cause suffering – the constant fear of loss, the constant attempt to secure the insecurable and then the inevitable loss itself. Just as a stockbroker can enjoy playing the stockmarket because it is not 'his' money he uses, so can you enjoy material objects when you do not identify them as 'mine'. Enjoyment comes when you have no vested interest.[1]

122.

The Blessed Lord said: I am the mighty destroyer, Time, now engaged in annihilating the worlds. All these worlds are now in the process of destruction.

Therefore, arise. Conquer enemies and enjoy this wealthy kingdom...

Bhagavad Gita 11.32–33

This is very important. Here is the Supreme Soul telling us to act and to enjoy the wealth those actions bring. In Arjuna's immediate context Krishna is telling him to conquer his opponents on the battlefield and enjoy the kingdom he wins back. But the wider context concerns every individual and the worlds we inhabit. We have to conquer our own areas of challenge and enjoy the wealth, whether it be financial, emotional, intellectual or whatever. Nowhere are we being told to limit ourselves. We are reminded first, however, that the worlds are in a state of destruction (see pp. 30–31). Destruction is constant as is its alter ego, creation. They are the constant process of change – of time – which is inherent to material existence and

1. Parth.

which makes attachment to anything in this world a lost cause.

The point made throughout the Gita is to act and enjoy without attachment. You can be very, very rich, but with no attachment to that wealth, or you can have very few possessions, providing you with scarcely a scrap of enjoyment, and be totally attached to them. Attachment to those miserable possessions will do you more harm than all the riches of the world will do a millionaire who is not attached to them.[1]

123.

Having controlled all his senses and fixed his mind on Me as the Supreme, a man is well established in perfect wisdom.

Bhagavad Gita 2.61

To realize the Supreme, your senses must be controlled so your mind is not hauled away by the lures of the world. Only when the mind is available is it possible for you to focus on the Supreme Self.

Whenever Krishna uses the first person singular – Me – he means the all-pervading Self. The greatest blunder made in all religions today is that this is taken to mean the personality speaking. Christ, Muhammad, Krishna all said, 'Come to Me, I will save you.' But they were not talking about their little self, their ego, they were talking about the Atman, the Eternal 'Me' that is in you as much as in them. The only difference between the prophets and you is that they have realized that all-pervading Self, you haven't.

Krishna means 'dark' in Sanskrit. He is the Atman in us which is dark in the sense that It is unknown to us. It is the spark of life which is blacked out by our fixation on the body, mind and intellect. One of the images of Krishna is that in which his right hand holds the staff he used to drive his cattle to pasture while the left hand joins the index finger to the thumb to form a circle. This is the symbol of wisdom showing the ego, your bundle of desires, bowing to meet the Atman and thereby forming Infinity.

These two hands of Krishna are the two ways in which our

1. Parth.

eternal spark can work. They represent your capacity to fix your
little self – your ego – on that great Self so you can take your
senses under control to their pastures – the sights, sounds,
smells, tastes and sensations of the world – that feed them.[1]

124.

*But a self-controlled person who is free from all likes and dislikes
and moves among the objects with his senses restrained attains
peace.*

Bhagavad Gita 2.65

The first principle of self-control is to act freely, without
prompting from likes or dislikes.

The second principle is to act without creating fresh likes and
dislikes. Self-control is not refusing what is offered to you. You
can enjoy anything without losing control. You only lose control
when you linger mentally in that enjoyment beyond the actual
point of contact, thereby creating a fresh ripple of desire.

This is beautifully indicated by Lord Ganesha (the elephant-
headed god of success) who sits with one leg on the ground and
one leg folded under him to indicate that one aspect of his person
walks in the world, talks in the world, dines and wines in the
world, while another aspect of him is in constant contact with the
Atman within.

If you see a picture of Lord Ganesha you will see plenty of food
spread around, signifying prosperity at his heel. There is a small
rat on the ground near his foot, looking up with a piece of food in
its mouth. That rat represents desire. Ganesha does not kill the
rat, but the rat looks up to him as if asking for sanction – 'May I
have it?' So nothing in the world is carried out without the
sanction of the discriminating intellect. Desire is not crushed
underfoot but is only allowed fulfilment when the intellect
sanctions. It looks up to the law.[2]

1. Parth.
2. Parth.

125.

*There is no possibility of one's becoming a yogi [spiritual person],
O Arjuna, if one eats too much or eats too little, sleeps too much or
does not sleep enough.*

*He who is regulated in his habits of eating, sleeping, recreation
and work can mitigate all material pains by practising the yoga
system.*

Bhagavad Gita 6.16–17

In the spiritual life, extremism of any kind is discouraged. We
must moderate our life in such a way that we can fulfil the various
functions of the body without becoming attached to them. To
regulate our activities is essential, not allowing ourselves to
become subject to the whims of the mind, but setting a plan. The
words 'disciple' and 'discipline' are linked. We have to become
disciples of self-control.

The body is an instrument and the soul is secured in the body.
The human body is a wonderful machine because it can be used
to reach our ultimate destination. So the purpose of yoga is to use
the body perfectly. To be a yogi we must know how to utilize the
body, neither to be too involved with it, nor to neglect it. If we try
to neglect it we become more attached to it and so cause distress
to the soul. The soul is linked to the body, so if we cause pain for
the body, then the soul is also troubled.[1]

126.

*[Arjuna said:] O God of Gods, abode of the Universe, have
mercy, I am delighted to have seen what I have never seen before,
yet my mind is laden with fear. Show me, O abode of the
Universe, only that previous form.*

Bhagavad Gita 11.45

1. Char./Das.

Having asked for the Divine vision of Ultimate Reality, Arjuna then becomes terrified. He begs Krishna to resume the familiar face of the god Vishnu, a sublime but nevertheless material expression of the Atman (Supreme Self). The message here is not to overstep your capacity in the spiritual life. The moment you overstep you get into trouble. You must prepare. You must slowly develop your self-sufficiency, not renounce the world with a grand gesture that strikes terror into your own heart.[1]

127.

Be not afraid or bewildered, having seen such a terrible form of mine as this; with your fear dispelled and your gladdened heart you will now behold my former form.

Sanjaya said: The God of Gods, having thus spoken to Arjuna, pacified him by showing him his gentle form.

Bhagavad Gita 11.49–50

We become attached to the burdensome world we have created. Arjuna's response to a glimpse of the Absolute Reality is echoed in the parable of the man toiling along the roadside with a huge load. As he struggled along the old fellow prayed to the god of death, 'O Lord Yama, when are you going to take me so I am free from all this?' His prayer was so intense that Lord Yama appeared as the man was resting the load on a stone.

Lord Yama said, 'Yes, I have come to relieve you.'

The man said, 'No, no, I only wanted somebody to put it on my head. That's all, then you can go.'

We have got so accustomed to agitation that we don't feel happy without it. We are so acclimatized to ignorance that we don't feel happy gaining knowledge.

1. Parth.

9   Moksha – Eternal Release

128.

As a lump of salt dropped into water becomes dissolved in water and cannot be taken out again, but wherever we taste, it tastes salty, even so, my dear, this great, endless, infinite Reality is pure Knowledge. Arising out of these elements one vanishes into them. After attaining this there is no more knowledge.

Brhadaranyaka Upanishad II.4.12

When we reach the highest stage of spiritual evolution, individuality disappears like a lump of salt in water. Just as the lump disappears but saltiness pervades the water, so our ego disappears but we are everywhere. This allays our fears that, by merging into the One, we cease to be. Our self, squeezed as it has been into a tiny personality, is far from lost, it is everywhere. It is Infinite.[1]

129.

The prophets were not unique, they were men like you and I. They were great yogis. They had gained this super-Consciousness and you and I can get the same. The very fact that one man ever reached that state proves that it is possible for every man to do so. Not only is it possible, but every man must eventually get to that state – and that is religion.

Swami Vivekananda

1. Bhav.

When we constantly contemplate the divine qualities of God, we become engrossed in God. We see Him everywhere and in everything. We realize our true nature is the eternal and immortal Brahman. The Supreme Divinity resides within us.

By knowing and realizing the true Self, the knower escapes the fear of death. It ceases to be relevant. The boundless happiness of God's presence is experienced in life and will continue to be so in death. When the body of a realized person perishes, the soul ascends to the divine, eternal abode of God. This is the highest goal, the final release. The soul resides eternally in the presence of God as a river which has merged with the sea.[1]

130.

As rivers flow into the sea and disappear, losing name and form, so the enlightened one, delivered from name and form, enters into God the highest of the high.

Mundakopanishad III.2.8

The individual soul of the enlightened person goes to God the Universal Soul and flows into Him, losing all individuality and becoming one with the Divine Being. Hindus believe that individualism bolsters the ego and maintains isolation and separation from other parts of the Divine Soul, also imprisoned in bodies. The intrinsic yearning for unity of all souls which exist in all living creatures may occasionally be glimpsed during moments of close physical contact between mother and child, husband and wife. The five shells (anatomical, physiological, logical, intuitive and blissful) around individual souls prevent union on earth. It is only when they have been purged of their load of sin and have themselves become loosened and finally stripped off that the liberated individual soul can return to God, its source, there to become unified with its origin.[2]

1. Panch.
2. Chand.

131.

That which illumines the world of waking, dreaming and deep sleep, that Brahman am I. Thus realizing, one is liberated from all bonds.

Kaivalyopanishad 17

What is that which illumines the waking, dreaming and deep-sleep states?

'I'. 'I am the waker,' 'I am the dreamer,' 'I am the deep sleeper.' You have a narrow concept that you are the waker, but the waker will die and the dreamer will be born, the dreamer will die and the deep sleeper will be born. This goes on in continuous waves, but the illuminating principle, pure Consciousness, beyond the knowing of waker, dreamer or deep sleeper, will never die. 'That Brahman am I.'

When you cease to identify as the waker, dreamer or deep sleeper you will cease to be fettered to the appetites of the body, agitations of the mind, plans and schemes of the intellect. Repeating 'I am the Brahman' from the heart, not the lips, will de-hypnotize you from this illusory world. You are then free to become that Brahman.[1]

132.

[Arjuna said:] Just as many rivers flow towards the ocean, so do these men enter the flaming mouth.

Bhagavad Gita 11.28

When Krishna reveals his true Eternal Self Arjuna sees the great protagonists of the Mahabharata battle flowing into His mouth, like rivers inexorably flowing to the ocean. Any number of obstacles will not prevent the river getting to the ocean. If the terrain blocks it, it changes its course, going around or under hills. If there are small pebbles it crushes them as it runs over them. This is the autobiography of all rivers, gathering more and

1. Parth.

more water, overcoming all obstacles, moving with the single purpose of reaching the sea. Similarly, each one of us is like a river and our destination is realization of our own godhead.

From the moment of birth each one of us is constantly after this elusive thing called happiness or bliss. Why are you reading this book? Because you find some happiness in reading it. Why aren't other people reading it? Because they find some happiness in not reading it. Whatever we are doing, wherever we go, we are after this happiness. The only people who have cried, 'Stop, enough,' are the people who have realized the Self. They want nothing from anybody because they have reached Totality, Absolute Bliss.[1]

133.

Just as moths rush into a blazing fire, only to perish, even so all the world seems to be rushing into your mouths to perish.

Bhagavad Gita 11.30

Why does the moth go round and round the flame? Because it's enchanted. Its love is so great for the flame that it identifies with it. Out of sheer love for the flame, the moth embraces the flame and is destroyed. But what has the flame done? The flame gives light to the moth and, in so doing, destroys itself by burning its fuel. Both the moth and the flame merge in the spirit of love and sacrifice.

Sacrifice will take you into the Totality. Every one of you will do this. The whole world has to do it. It's only a question of time. That desire to reach the Atman is inherent in us. That is the call for peace, for happiness. The best and the worst of us, there is no difference – we all want this peace. We will never compromise. Similarly, the pressure keeps pushing us. This pressure shows that we are not in our original state. Constantly we want to be other than we are at the moment. We want to wash ourselves, we want to feed ourselves, we want to rest ourselves, we want to exercise ourselves, we want to entertain ourselves. We are driven

1. Parth.

like cattle. The wants go on. Only when we reach the original
state will the pressure stop. Only those people who have realized
the God in them have stopped and are at peace. They tell us again
and again, 'There is no pleasure, there is only Bliss.'[1]

134.

*Devouring all the worlds on all sides with your flaming mouths,
you are devouring it. Your fierce rays, filling the whole world with
radiance, are burning, O Vishnu.*

Bhagavad Gita 11.30

In the vision of the Absolute Self which Krishna reveals to
Arjuna the whole world is burning because just as any object that
enters the fire becomes the fire so anyone who enters the Atman
(Supreme Self) becomes the Atman. Thereafter there is only
burning, meaning there is only Atman.

There is an incessant demand for this ultimate culmination.
Everybody wants it. But you have got to pay the price. The moth
gave its life (see above) – you give your desires.[2]

135.

*It is higher than heaven, shining resplendent in the cave of your
heart. Those who strive for it enter into it.*

Kaivalyopanishad 3

The teacher indicates where and how to find the Ultimate Self,
Brahman. It is higher than heaven. *Nakam* is translated here as
'heaven' (literally, 'non-sorrow'). We are all born with unmanifested desires (vasanas) from our previous lives. If we didn't have
them we wouldn't have been born. As we grow up these vasanas
manifest themselves and we become agitated and aggrieved,

1. Parth.
2. Parth.

cultivating more and more desires. When we reach a distress-free pocket of existence, that is called heaven – non-sorrow – even if it is only temporary.

So what is higher than non-sorrow and shines resplendent in the cave of our hearts?

Positive Bliss. That is what lies at the very core of our being, but it is so buried in desires that until we start to clear them away we hardly know it is there. Only we can discover the Self for ourselves. The journey is not easy but when we arrive we will enter the Self as a river does the ocean, becoming one with it.

136.

That do those ascetics enter who are well established in Vedanta wisdom. Those ascetics whose minds have been purified through the path of renunciation [dwell] in the worlds of Brahma. At the end of time, being one with the Immortal, they are all liberated.
                                                    Kaivalyopanishad 4

To be an ascetic is to exercise self-control so the soul may be freed of worldly entanglements. The ascetic cares for his body, mind and intellect as equipment which needs to be kept in good condition, but he does not allow them to get attached to worldly pleasures – sensual, emotional or intellectual.

There are two types of ascetics in this verse. The first are 'well established in Vedanta wisdom'. This means they have fully assimilated knowledge of the Self which only arises through deep reflection on the scriptures. Such ascetics enter 'That', the pronoun used throughout the Upanishads to refer to the One Reality. They become the Brahman, the eternal Bliss.

The second type of ascetic has travelled far spiritually through renunciation. From birth the mind is muddied by desires so, to purify it, the path of renunciation must be followed (see pp. 90–97). Some ascetics lead such a life but, nevertheless, their meditations do not bring them to realization during that lifetime. These people are said to go to the Brahma-heaven where they enjoy the fruits of their good actions before they ultimately Self-realize at 'the end of time'. Time ends when the ego, i.e., desires, ends, for at that point we leave this world of time, space and causation and merge into Eternal Bliss.[1]

137.

He is all, what has been and what shall be: the Eternal. Knowing him one transcends death. There is no other way to liberation.

Kaivalyopanishad 9

He is the definition of Reality – that which persists in all time. Liberation from the cycle of birth and death into the changeless Reality can only happen through knowing Reality. If a child sees a post and thinks it is a ghost, no amount of action and agitation will drive that ghost away. Only knowledge of the reality of the post will drive away the ghost.[2]

138.

... The wise, having renounced and risen above this world, become immortal.

Kenopanishad 1.2

Mortality means death. Death means birth. There cannot be death without birth or birth without death. Together they make change. The day dies, the night is born, summer dies, autumn is born, childhood dies, adolescence is born. The process of change is the process of birth and death, the process of material existence.

Here, right now, we are changing factors – breathing in, breathing out, emotions and thoughts rising up and dying in an endless stream. Only Consciousness is unchanging, so when we shift the focus of attention from the constantly changing objects of action, perception and comprehension and focus on their subject – 'the mind in the mind' – we become that changeless

1. Parth.
2. Parth.

Reality. We become immortal, God, a Self-realized person. We free ourselves from the cycle of birth and death that returns us again and again to this world.[1]

139.

> . . . *I think I have known Brahman.*
> *I do not think I know well. Not that I do not know. I know too.*
> *He among us who knows It knows It. He among us who does not know It also knows It.*
>
> Kenopanishad 2.1–2

A student has realized Brahman – become Self-realized. His words, trying to describe the state, read at first like babble. But, taken sentence by sentence, we begin to see the sense if we keep in mind that realizing Brahman is realizing the Self. Brahman is the subject (experiencer) in everything so that the subject-object distinction of this world dissolves.

The second sentence, 'I do not think I know well', seems a retraction of the first but in fact it is a clarification: the student does not intellectually comprehend It as he would maths or chemistry. The Self is not an object of comprehension. It is the subject of comprehension.

The following sentence, 'I know too,' is best understood by imagining for a moment that your name is Mr Gupta and you are at a party. Someone comes up to you and asks, 'Do you know Mr Gupta?' You might answer, 'No,' but then add, 'Well, yes I do . . .'. The difficulty comes because a subject does not *know* itself in the way that it knows another object. A subject *is* itself. To say it knows itself implies it experiences itself as an object other than itself.

The last two sentences of the verse make the point that you are the Self whether you know it or not. Imagine you are a courier who goes from Delhi to Varanasi to deliver an important document to a Mr Mavani. When you arrive the train is late and the office is closed so you have to wait till the next morning to

1. Parth.

deliver the document. That evening you go to the park where you overhear two gentlemen chatting about the political situation. You join the conversation and are waylaid talking for more than an hour without ever finding out the men's names, so embroiled are you in the topic of conversation. The next morning you take the document to Mr Mavani's office. You walk in and see before you one of the men you spoke with the previous evening.

Now on that evening, as the three of you were talking, if Mr Mavani's friend had been asked, 'Do you know Mavani?' he would have said yes. If you had been asked you would have said no, and yet you were sitting there talking to him. So – he who knows Mavani knows Mavani. He who does not know Mavani also knows Mavani.[1]

140.

[*Teacher:*] *To whomsoever it is not known, to him it is known. It is unknown to those who know it. It is known to those who do not know it.*

Kenopanishad 2.3

There are two types of 'knowing' involved in this verse: to know objectively and to know subjectively. Brahman cannot be known as an object of thought, but only as the subject – the absolute 'I' – behind all thought. The verse can be paraphrased: he who does not conceptualize It becomes It. He who conceptualizes It does not become It. To the realized person It is not known as an object of thought. To the ignorant person It is only known as an object of thought.[2]

141.

He who is able to realize It has lived a life of Truth. If you have not realized the Self, it is the greatest of losses. He who is able to

1. Parth.
2. Parth.

concentrate on the Atman in every living being, rising above the world, he attains immortality.

Kenopanishad 2.5

Your only purpose in life is to realize the Self. If you haven't done that, you haven't fulfilled yourself, your life is meaningless. In every perception, thought and action, if you constantly focus your attention on the Self which is the ultimate source, you raise yourself from the world of birth and death to the changeless, immortal Self. You can gain the Self or you can gain this worldly life, which has no meaning. As you think, so will you become – it is a law.[1]

142.

Truly, he who knows it thus, having destroyed sin, he is established in that boundless, highest and blissful Truth. Yes, he is established in it.

Kenopanishad 4.8

Sin means agitation. Your mind will be free of agitations when you are no longer dependent on the world. The world will, in turn, cease to be agitated by you for your actions will not be driven by the passions of the ego. Once you are established in the highest, boundless, blissful Truth, you can go about in the world enjoying it while being free of it.

The relationship of a Self-realized person to the world can be understood through the story of a village flood. One man managed to climb out of the torrential flow onto a branch of a tree. An angry gale clawed at the branch pulling it this way and that, so the man clung shivering, fearing that any moment the branch would break and he would plunge to his death in the churning waters. Nearby, a bird perched singing on a branch as it was buffeted in the wind.

What is the difference between the man and the bird?

If the bird's branch breaks, it simply flies away. Even though it

1. Parth.

is sitting on the branch, it is really sitting on its wings. But the man is dependent on the branch. If it breaks, he breaks.

All the scriptures, all the prophets in all religions say, 'Grow your wings and sit on the branch. You've got that capacity. Get established in the Truth and live in the world.'[1]

143.

For he that is realized, all beings having become the Self, what delusion, what grief can there be for this seer of the unity of existence?

Isavasyopanishad 7

When we have *seen* the Self in all beings we have crossed the first barrier of delusion in our spiritual evolution. When we *become* the Self in all beings we have crossed the second and last barrier.

There are many prophets and saints who crossed the first barrier but far fewer who crossed the second. In the first instance, what happens is that the person understands material existence as the mirror of Brahman. He recognizes in the qualities of the world the reflected qualities of Brahman. Nevertheless, the seer's individuality is still lingering as the one who perceives the Truth but has not yet become the Truth. There is an 'I' and a truth. When a person crosses the second barrier of delusion he becomes one with the Truth just as the snake dissolves into the rope when its true identity is realized.

'He that' subtly communicates the transition from a personal self *who sees* the Truth to an impersonal self *that is* the Truth.[2]

144.

He is all-pervading, resplendent, without a body, unscathed, without muscles, pure, untainted by sin, seer, omniscient,

1. Parth.
2. Parth.

transcendent and self-existent. He has allotted the respective duties to the eternal years.

Isavasyopanishad 8

This verse applies to the Self-realized man and the Brahman for they are one and the same. It brings assurance to those who imagine realization means becoming irrevocably gloomy. To be 'resplendent' is to be full of fun and frolic, love and affection – bursting with limitless energy. The light of knowledge is also the light of humour. This is the example that Lord Krishna set us. In the many stories of his life he never left his mother or wife alone. He was always up to something, always enjoying and providing enjoyment.

He is 'without a body, unscathed, without muscles' because he is free of his gross (physical) body. He is not bound by sensory experiences. This is the point where most of us are stuck.

He is 'untainted by sin' because his mind and intellect – that is, his subtle body – is not agitated. To sin is to act so as to agitate the mind with thoughts and desires.

He is 'pure' because without desires, known as the causal body, there is no fuel for the cycle of karma (action and reaction). He has no karma.

He is the 'seer' because he understands everything. He is 'omniscient' for he is the pure Consciousness in everything. He is 'transcendent' because he has crossed beyond the objects, emotions and thoughts of the gross, subtle and causal bodies. He is 'self-existent' because the Atman (Self) is the Totality.

All objects and beings in all time, poetically described as 'the eternal years', derive their duties or nature from the Atman. The Atman is the strength in the strong, the light in the sun, the wetness in water and so on.[1]

145.

The face of Truth is covered by a golden disc. O sun, remove that covering so as to be seen by me who is of the nature of Truth.

Isavasyopanishad 15

1. Parth.

The student, on the verge of realization, addresses the Atman (Supreme Self) symbolically as the sun. He is saying: I am the Atman, so let me see the Atman.

'The face of Truth' (the Atman) is said to be 'covered by a golden disc' because gold represents wealth. Wealth is the accumulation of material objects. So when the student commands the sun to remove the golden disc he is calling to the Atman to discard the last accumulated vestige of the material world.

The last vestige is thought because thought is the subtlest aspect of the material world. As the spiritual seeker discards his or her material sheaths, the thoughts and desires are whittled down until they converge on a single thought such as the mantra 'Aum' or 'Krishna'. This is called single-pointed meditation. What covers the face of the Atman, for the student on the verge of realization, is this last mantra. After that last thought has ended the thoughtless state remains. That is realization. He is the Atman.

We can bring ourselves to the single point of the last thought and then we can't do anything else. The devotional person says the Lord takes it out. The intellectual knows the thought can't stand by itself. It thins out like a gold bar being stretched thinner and thinner until it snaps.[1]

146

O Sun, nourisher, sole courser, controller, acquirer, son of Prajapati [Lord of Creatures], remove your rays and gather up the dazzle that I may behold the form of yours which is most auspicious. I am That Being.

Isavasyopanishad 16

The student has exploded into Self-realization. He addresses the Atman (Divine Self) symbolically as the sun. It is the nourisher of everything. It appears to move but it is the sole mover of everything else. It is the Absolute controller for it makes all laws

1. Parth.

- physical, chemical, psychological, social. It is the 'acquirer' because nothing can be gained physically, emotionally or intellectualy without Atman. It is the son of Prajapati, meaning it is an expression of Brahman.

In the previous verse (see 145), the student called for the golden disc (the last thought) to be removed. When this is done, the Truth is revealed. He is dazzled by it as we are when we come out of a dark room into the light.

The student asks that the dazzle may be withdrawn so he can see the Truth. But just as our eyes eventually adjust to the sunlight, so does his consciousness adjust to the Absolute Truth and the 'dazzle' ceases.

'That Being am I', he realizes. He is the Atman.[1]

147.

Then Maitreyi said, 'Just here you have bewildered me, venerable Sir, by saying that after attaining [Oneness] the Self has no more consciousness.'

Yajnavalkya replied, 'Certainly I am not saying anything bewildering, my dear. This is enough for knowledge, O Maitreyi.

'For when there is duality, as it were, then one smells another, one sees another, one hears another, one speaks to another, one thinks of another, one knows another. But when everything has become the Self, then what should one smell and through what, what should one see and through what, what should one hear and through what, what should one speak and through what, what should one think and through what, what should one know and through what? Through what should one know that owing to which all this is known - through what, my dear, should one know the knower?'

Brhadaranyaka Upanishad II.4.14

Maitreyi is confused by the concept that there is no knowledge where there is pure Knowledge. Yajnavalkya explains that when

1. Parth.

the individual self merges with the Supreme Self there is nothing
to experience, either physically or mentally.

In Sanskrit, life is defined as *anubhava dhara* (literally, 'stream
of experiences'). An experience is a unit of life consisting of three
factors: the subject, the object and the experience. The subject is
the experiencer. The object is that which is experienced. The
experience per se is the product arising from contact between
these two factors. All experiences, whether they are seeing,
hearing or knowing, require these two factors. So when the Self
becomes everything this duality is dissolved. The Self is the all-
embracing subject with nothing left outside of it to be an object
of experience or knowledge.[1]

148.

*Abandon all other dharma and come unto Me alone for refuge. I
will free you from all sins. Do not grieve.*

Bhagavad Gita 18.66

This is the most well-known declaration in the Gita. There is no
single English world for dharma. It signifies duty, nature, law.

In its material expression, dharma varies from person to
person according to our past karma which has shaped our
personality and destiny (see pp. 52–4). But, behind all laws, all
natures, all duties, is the One Reality. In its pure form dharma is
a deep feeling of love. That is our goal, our refuge. Krishna is
telling us that if we come to the Eternal Self ('Me') we are going
direct to the source. We no longer follow dharma because we are
dharma.

As long as we are thwarted from our true goal we agitate
ourselves by pursuing the world. This state of agitation is sin.
When we have fulfilled our true duty we are freed of desire and
attachment and therefore free of sin and sorrow.

1. Parth.

149.

Now let my immortal air merge with the total air. Let this body be reduced to ashes. Aum. O mind, remember what has been done. Remember mind, remember what has been done, remember.

Isavasyopanishad 17

The previous two verses (see above) dealt with the death of the ego which occurs with realization. This verse deals now with the death of the body. It is the last will and testament of the Self-realized man.

First he bequeaths back to the total air the quantity of air he has taken for his body to function. Then he bequeaths his body back to the earth from which it has come. Of course, this will happen anyway. But the attitude is important. It is a gesture of abrogation of the personality.

Last of all, the dying man says, 'Remember, mind, what has been done.' The rites of Consciousness have already been done in his life through realization. His individual mind has merged with the Total Being so he is bequeathing what has already been bequeathed.

But, you may ask, how did he function in his life between the death of his ego when he Self-realized and his bodily death? The topic requires much discussion. Some understanding can be gained, however, by imagining a car driving along a road at 60 mph. The engine cuts off. What happens to the car? It keeps going because the momentum is already there although the propulsion has switched off. This is the same as the man who Self-realizes. He has a momentum which will continue to move him through life. But once the body brakes, he will never start up again in this world because he has switched off the propulsion – desire.[1]

1. Parth.

150.

*He who goes everywhere unaffected by whatever good or evil
happens to him, neither praising it nor despising it, is a man of
perfection and steady wisdom.*

Bhagavad Gita 2.57

Krishna is answering Arjuna's question, 'How does he [a man of
perfection] speak?'; in other words, 'How does the Infinite
express itself in the finite?' Krishna makes the point that the
God-realized person goes everywhere, dispelling any delusions
we might have of a fat swami sitting in a corner of a cave. The
man of perfection is out and about, full of energy, activity and
enthusiasm. That is Krishna.

The man of perfection has a wonderful time because he is
detached from the good and evil which might befall him. He is
steadied by a greater Knowledge. It is like when you go to a tragic
movie. You meet your friend afterwards and say to him, 'Have
you seen that picture? It's a beautiful picture, don't miss it. The
only thing is, I took one handkerchief. You'd better take three.'
Comedies, tragedies, horror films are all fun because we are
detached. We experience the emotion but we are not affected by
it.

But don't misunderstand. Detached does not mean loveless.
All the prophets were totally detached but they had all the love in
the world. It's only when you are attached that there is no love
(see p. 146).[1]

151.

*In the Puranas there is a story of Narada, the great seer and
jester, on his way to heaven as was often his inclination, when he
passed a sage meditating in the mountains. The sage greeted
Narada and asked where he was going.*

*'I'm on my way to heaven,' replied Narada. 'Is there anything
you want while I'm there?'*

1. Parth.

'*Well, yes,*' said the sage. '*Could you find out for me please how many more lives I have before I Self-realize.*'

Narada promised to find out for the fellow and went on his way. Before long he came to a second meditating sage. The conversation went the same way as the earlier one and Narada left having made the same promise.

In a few months he returned from heaven and met the first sage.

'*What news, Mahatma?*' called the sage.

Now this sage was a very highly developed spirit and was on the verge of realization, but Narada said to him, '*Not so good, my friend. You see that tamarind tree [known for their multitude of tiny leaves]? Count the number of leaves on that tree and you have the number of lives you have yet to live.*'

The sage clasped his hands in joy. '*I am so happy. Now at least I have only a finite number of lives before I Self-realize.*'

Then Narada came to the second sage who called out, '*What news, Mahatma?*' Now this sage was a long way yet from Self-realization and had many, many lives to go. But Narada said to him, '*Very good news. This is your last generation and you're off, free for ever.*'

The sage's eyes nearly popped out of his head. '*O my goodness. Let me pack quickly and leave for the city while there's still time. So much to do, so much to see.*'

A. Parthasarathy

Aham Brahma Asmi – I Am Brahman
Statement of Experience

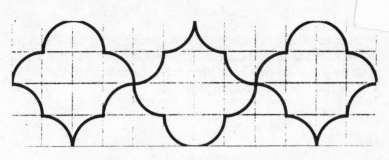

10 Aham Prakritim Asmi – I Am This World

152.

. . . The entire Universe is pervaded by you. You have infinite forms.

Bhagavad Gita 11.38

Wherever there is a reflecting surface in the world, there is a reflected sun. Even a dewdrop reflects the sun. Millions of reflecting surfaces produce millions of suns. Similarly, there are millions of reflected forms but there is only one all-pervading entity and that is the Brahman.[1]

153.

In Me alone, all is born. In Me all exists, in Me all dissolves, that non-dual Brahman am I.

Kaivalyopanishad 19

If the ocean were speaking about the relationship between itself and the waves and froth continuously rising and dissipating on its surface, it would use these exact words. You and I are different, like the bubbles that foam up out of the ocean, but we are also part of the ocean that is an indivisible One. Both the bubble and the ocean are water. The person who understands the water in the bubble understands the water in the ocean and all

1. Parth.

water everywhere. Similarly, Consciousness is one and the same in the microcosm and the macrocosm. Discover this essence in your own Self, then all the pluralistic phenomena of the world will merge into that eternal Self.[1]

154.

I am subtler than the subtlest, I am greater than the greatest. I am the manifold universe. I am ancient. I am the Purusha [primal being] . . .

Kaivalyopanishad 20

This verse deals first with space, defining the Supreme Self as reaching beyond its limits in both directions – 'subtler than the subtlest', in other words, tinier than the tiniest, and 'greater than the greatest'.

The next reference is to time. 'I am ancient,' that is, 'I am the first.' The first is, by definition, before time. Just as space lies between two points, time lies between two experiences. In both cases, a second is required. The Atman is the most ancient, so it is before a second, before time.

The third reference is to cause. The Purusha is the Being out of which all beings are born, not in the sense of a first cause superseded in time by its effects, but in the same sense that the ocean is the *cause* of all waves while *being* all waves.

Thus the three constituents of the gross world (the same three dealt with by modern science), space, time and causation, are used to indicate the Brahman.[2]

155.

. . . *I am the Lord. I am golden. I am the auspicious form.*

Kaivalyopanishad 20

1. Parth.
2. Parth.

Having described the Brahman in terms of the gross world (see above), the teacher now describes It in terms of the subtle world. He is the 'Lord' because he is the ruling power without which nothing happens. He is 'golden', in this context meaning brilliant, the source of all knowledge. He is auspicious, the source of all joy. These are the three things we seek in the world: power, knowledge, happiness. Brahman is the seat of all three. And you are Brahman if only you realized It.[1]

156.

O son of Kunti [Arjuna], I am the taste in the water, the radiance in the sun and moon, the Aum in all Vedas, I am the sound in space, I am the strength in humanity.

Bhagavad Gita 7.8

Water is tasteless, yet anything dehydrated has no taste. We need water, even if it is no more than our own saliva, before we can taste food. Just as water is tasteless yet is the source of all taste, the Brahman does not act or think yet is the source of all thoughts and activities.

The Brahman is the essential being in all beings. It is their nature (dharma). This is beautifully conveyed here by a list that can be added to endlessly.

It is the direct and indirect light principle in the sun and moon respectively. It is Aum, the ultimate message of the Vedas (see pp. 3–4). It is sound, the only perceivable aspect of space (see p. 138). It is the vitality in humanity. That strength is our ability to think – to judge and conceptualize. If we do not use it we deny our own divine nature.

That Divinity is all these without being any of these, just as electricity is the heat in the oven, the cold in the refrigerator, the movement in the fan, the light in the lightbulb, but is none of those things.[2]

1. Parth.
2. Parth.

157.

I am the sweet fragrance in the earth. I am the brilliance in fire. I am the life in all beings and the austerity in all ascetics.

Bhagavad Gita 7.10

He is the living principle in all beings. He is that which makes anything itself. There are people all around the world going to the temple, to the mosque, to the church, praying, chanting, ringing bells, sending up sweet smells so that God might glance down and notice them. They beg Him, 'Here I am God, please see me, care for me.' But they are ignoring Him. He is everywhere saying, 'Here I am, please see me, care for me.' We don't see Him. We don't care for Him. We do our utmost to blur the expression of Him.

'The sweet fragrance in the earth' refers to the pure smell of the earth, unmuddled with other smells. The concept of purity is the crucial point here. The essence of anything – that which is itself and nothing else – is God (Brahman) made manifest. If we can learn to apprehend the pure form in everything, we bring ourselves one step closer to apprehending the pure formlessness. We need a purity of vision at the terrestrial level before we can hope for it at the transcendental.[1]

158.

Among horses know me as Uccaihsrava, nectar-born. Among lordly elephants I am Airavata and among men I am the monarch.

Bhagavad Gita 10.27

In the Vishnu Puranas the story is told of the gods and demons using a mountain and snake to churn the milky ocean which consumed the world; poison was the first by-product. Then came many wondrous objects and beings, including the winged

1. Parth.

horse Uccaihsrava and the elephant Airavata. The final thing to emerge was nectar.

Essentially the myth is about an individual enlisting both his spiritual and material nature to get hold of his ego (the snake) and his experience (the mountain) so they can be used to churn his consciousness until it releases its poisonous desires. When the desire is out, material well-being follows and then, ultimately, the nectar of Self-realization. Uccaihsrava and Airavata are two of the symbols of material well-being. So Krishna is saying here that not only is the Supreme Self spiritual opulence but It is also pure, unadulterated material opulence.

In the same vein he is the king among men, that is, he is the ultimate state of material opulence which can befall a soul.[1]

159.

Of all weapons I am the thunderbolt...
Bhagavad Gita 10.28

If Krishna were speaking today he would say, 'Of all weapons I am the nuclear missile.' Whatever the object, the Eternal Self is the very soul of it. If the subject is destruction then the Self is the pure form of destruction, symbolized by the best object of destruction.

People today think that the world has fundamentally changed because of the nuclear age. But in every age there is a tremendous fear of some terrible means of destruction devised by humanity. First, there were bows and arrows, then poison arrows, then catapults, then gunpowder, then aerial bombs, and now nuclear weapons. Ultimately, whatever the weapon, the fear is the same – that the weapon will kill us. So what we are afraid of is our own mortality. All these weapons we devise to frighten ourselves are simply the manifestation of that fear. We create weapons to protect us against death and then we fear death from their hand. It is no accident that the cultures which have developed nuclear

1. Parth.

weapons and have the biggest arsenals are the most materialistic cultures in the world. Their Divinity has taken fright.[1]

160.

I am all-devouring death and I am the origin of all to be born. Of the feminine, I am fame, fortune, eloquence, memory, steadfastness and forgiveness.

Bhagavad Gita 10.34

The very definition of material existence is change through the endless cycle of birth and death. They are the necessary prerequisite of each other. One moment dies so another is born. The inseparable nature of birth and death is recognized in Hinduism by its embodiment in single deities such as the dark and naked goddess, Kali. Giver and taker of life, she is time dressed only in the black robe of space.

The qualities of material nature are feminine. The finest of them are listed here. They are all worldly qualities which conserve and preserve. They are the maintenance arising out of the constant flow of birth and death.

These qualities must not be confused with feminine in the biological sense. The masculine qualities of outwardness, exploration, daring, thirst for the unknown, which take people beyond the known material world, are as likely to be found in a woman as the feminine qualities are in a man.[2]

161.

I am the gambling of all frauds. I am the splendour of the splendid. I am victory. I am determination. I am the sattwic of the sattwa.

Bhagavad Gita 10.36

There is nothing that is not Brahman (the Eternal Self). Truly to

1. Parth.
2. Parth.

understand Brahman we have to be able to see It not only in the beautiful song or the wondrous landscape, but in every name and form. Of all frauds, gambling is the worst and that is Brahman, just as the alcoholic's craving for whisky is Brahman and the lecher's craving for women is Brahman. Now please don't understand this as a recommendation to take up these addictions as religious endeavours. Addiction is a state of agitation which prevents you apprehending our own Serene Self. But recognize that others whom you judge as godless are simply too agitated to know themselves. In reality they are no different from the splendid. They are you and you are they. We are all dreamers in the dream world which will dissolve into the One when we awaken.

Determination and a sattwic (non-desiring) nature are the qualities we should develop as the expression of the Brahman which leads to It, just as the desire to gamble leads away. Through determination and sattwa comes victory. We achieve the goals, both relative and ultimate, which we set for ourselves.[1]

162.

> ... [*Arjuna said:*] *I see you with infinite arms. The sun and the moon as your eyes, the burning fire your mouth, heating this Universe with your radiance.*
>
> Bhagavad Gita 11.19

Many people ask why the Hindu gods have so many arms. The symbolism is that arms equal power. This equation is a common one. 'Many hands make light work,' 'Could you give me a hand?' etc., are talking about needing more power. So Arjuna says to Krishna revealed as the Supreme Self, 'I see you with infinite arms,' meaning 'You have infinite power.'

The sun and the moon are the worldly illuminators and energizers, powered by Brahman, the Absolute illuminator.

The burning fire is the boundless energy of the Infinite Self. The moment we have infinite expanse, there is play. If we have a

1. Parth.

bucket of water there is no play, if we have a puddle there is no play. But when we have the ocean there is play – the crash and splash of the waves. But if you have ever seen films of the ocean depths you will know that it is perfectly still down there. It is that serenity which creates the surface ferment. This is called the Lord's play. This is why Krishna is known as a playful god.

This divine energy is burning everywhere. It is the cause of the Universe, it is the cause of the hunger pangs we feel every three or four hours.[1]

163.

All beings exist in Me. I do not exist in them. All this world is pervaded by Me in my unmanifested form.

Bhagavad Gita 9.4

Everything is nothing but Brahman, God, the Atman, whatever you wish to call It. The entire world is a projection upon the Brahman as a dream is a projection upon the dreamer's mind. The world is the illusory manifestation of the unmanifest Brahman. We are all figures in the dream of the Brahman, so we exist in It, we are pervaded by It. But although the Brahman is every part of us It is not contained within us any more than the figures in our dreams contain us within them. They are mere rays of us reflected out. They become as great as us only when they awaken to us. Similarly we become the Infinite Brahman only when we awaken to that highest plane of pure Consciousness.[2]

164.

The nonexistent was not, the existent was not...

Rig Veda X.129.1

The Absolute is beyond the existent and the nonexistent,

1. Parth.
2. Parth.

because it is beyond time. We can only catch a glimmer of this through analogy.

You don't understand the concept of mud so I find three mud pots to show you. Their substance is mud, and only mud, given form. You look at these three pots and your concept of mud is round hollow shapes. You say, 'Now I understand.' But I see you don't. I break the pots to show you that when this form of mud ceases to exist there is still an existing substance. So you look at these pieces of mud and say, 'Now I see.' Then you are standing in a field of mud and a friend asks you to explain mud to him. You take him ten miles to the broken pots!

You understand the existent and nonexistent aspects of mud pots but you don't understand the mud that is beyond the existent pot, beyond the nonexistent pot.[1]

165.

The biggest among the big, and the subtlest among the subtle.
Kathopanishad I.2.20

God is described as subtler than the subtlest and greater than the greatest. The Vedas and Upanishads have enlightened us with the knowledge of God. We are nothing compared to this Infinite knowledge. Science now speaks of His tiny manifestation, the atom. God is present in an atom even if it is split a thousandfold. He is the greatest because He is the creator of countless universes. God sustains each and every soul. He is the cause and the world, with its countless universes, is the effect. As Albert Einstein has said, 'Everyone who is seriously involved in the pursuit of science becomes convinced that a spirit is manifest in the laws of the universe – a spirit vastly superior to that of man, and one in the face of which we, with our modest powers, must feel humble.'[2]

1. Parth.
2. Panch.

11 Aham Devan Asmi – I Am the Gods

166.

They speak of Indra, Mitra, Varuna, Agni
And there is the Divine winged Suparna.
The wise call the One Being by many names as Agni, Yama,
*   Matarisvan.*

Rig Veda I.164.46

In the Vedas, various deities are worshipped through various hymns: Indra, Mitra, Varuna, Agni, Suparna, Yama, Matarisvan and so on. Each of the deities is described as the Highest Deity in his respective hymns. At the same time, there are hymns that declare that all these deities are one and the same – the different aspects of the Ultimate Reality is praised in different names.

There is no real contradiction in saying 'I believe in one God' and worshipping several deities. A diamond has many facets and different facets look dazzling from different angles. We see from our own angle and the facet facing us appears as the brightest. But we know in our mind that all the facets are equally bright and it is the whole diamond which possesses the dazzling quality.[1]

1. Choud.

167.

Then Vidagdha, the son of Sakalya, asked him, 'How many gods are there, Yajnavalkya?'...

'As many as are indicated in the Nivid [sacred verses] of the Visvadevas [hymns to the gods] – three hundred and three and three thousand and three.'

'Very well,' said Sakalya, 'how many gods are there, Yajnavalkya?'

'Thirty-three.'

'Very well,' said the other, 'how many gods are there, Yajnavalkya?'

'Six.'

'Very well,' said the other, 'how many gods are there, Yajnavalkya?'

'Three.'

'Very well,' said the other, 'how many gods are there, Yajnavalkya?'

'Two.'

'Very well,' said he, 'how many gods are there, Yajnavalkya?'

'One and a half.'

'Very well,' said Sakalya, 'how many gods are there, Yajnavalkya?'

'One.'...

Brhadaranyaka Upanishad III.9.1

The exchange takes place at the great debate regarding Absolute Reality which was held at the court of the spiritual seeker, King Janaka.

Three thousand and three is a poetic way of expressing Infinity. The gods are infinite in number because they are part of the One Infinity. Yajnavalkya's enumeration of the gods is akin to describing a wood as having ten million parts (leaves), a million parts (branches), a hundred parts (trees), one part (the wood). The former description is always pervaded by the latter. The leaves are within the branches which are within the trees which are within the wood. Similarly, the hierarchy of gods takes us closer and closer to the unifying factor of the world, arriving at last at the Infinite which is all of it and more.

168.

'. . . Which are the two gods?'
'Food and the vital air.'
'Which are the one and a half?'
'This that blows. On this, some say, "Since the air blows as one, how then is he one and a half? Because in him, all this grew up."'
'Which is the one God?'
'The vital breath. He is Brahman. They call Him That.'

Brhadaranyaka Upanishad III.9.8–9

In the verses immediately preceding this one, Sakalya's interrogation (see above) had continued, prompting Yajnavalkya to name the thirty-three principle gods governing the main aspects of time, space and causation. The sequence of multiples of the mystical number three is broken when he reaches the two gods, matter and spirit. The third is the One Brahman which encompasses them both. In the Upanishads, the physical world is described as food, differentiated into two categories: that which has the vital breath and therefore eats (animate) and that which doesn't (inanimate). Our modern terms for 'food' and 'vital breath' are, therefore, 'matter' and 'spirit'.

The vital breath is 'one and a half' because the splendid illusion of the world arises from it. It is one and a half in the sense that the rope, mistaken for the snake, is 'one and a half'. There is the One Totality (the snake) and then there is the lesser form, the illusion, which comes out of it, without diminishing the Totality. This is poetically phrased as 'one and a half'. In reality, the snake is within the one rope, just as the visible world is within the invisible Brahman. This unmanifest Brahman is known as 'That' throughout the Upanishads, indicating that, although It is all 'this', It is also beyond it.

169.

When the sun cannot emphasize It,
Nor the moon, stars or lightning
How can the fire do any better?

For brightened is the world by Its brilliance –
The sun, the moon, stars and all.

Mundakopanishad II.2.10

Brahman (the Ultimate Reality) is like a lamp with a lampshade that has different coloured sides. The colour of the light appears to be different depending upon where people stand. One person may see it as red, one as green, another as yellow. Similarly, everyone has their own conception of Brahman – as Krishna, Shiva, Kali and so on. The viewer of the light knows that behind the coloured light is the brilliant central light which has no colour but contains all colours. Similarly, we should realize that the one Brahman has no qualities but contains all qualities which are understood as the gods of the different natural phenomena.

Here, as in most hymns, the Ultimate Reality is referred to as 'It', whereas the different manifestations of the Ultimate Reality are given a masculine or feminine identity.[1]

170.

Those deprived of wisdom by various desires approach other gods, resorting to various rites according to their own natures.

Bhagavad Gita 7.20

Hinduism has long been questioned, if not condemned, for its proliferation of gods. Everybody else gets by with one, why do we need hundreds? Nevertheless, we are also acknowledged as the world's most spiritual society. There is a direct relation between the two phenomena.

To reach God, we have to bring our mind to single-pointed concentration. Therefore, all religions have some form of meditation. The rosary is to help focus the mind but, as long as the mind is saturated with desires, it is going to run helter-skelter after the world. If you were just to pick up the rosary and start chanting you would only polish the rosary, not your mind. It takes ten minutes to explain meditation but ten years of constant

1. Choud.

effort to shed the desires that prohibit it. If you try to force your desire-saturated mind, you will only destroy it.

The great rishis (sages) understood this, so instead of asking people to focus their mind on the single point of God, they planted God wherever there was an object of desire. People have a tremendous desire for wealth so they planted the goddess Lakshmi as the goddess of wealth. For those after knowledge there is Saraswati; for success there is Ganesha; for strength there is Hanuman and so on. Every material aspect of the world is divinized, so as the mind chases the objects of the world, it is also chasing God. Wherever there is a desire there is also a worship to be performed according to one's nature.[1]

171.

As the same fish is dressed into soup, curry or cutlet and each man has his own choice of dish of it, so the Lord of the universe, though one, manifests Himself differently according to the different likings of His worshippers and each one of them has his own view of God which he values most.

Sri Ramakrishna

Each one of us is God (Atman). Nobody is deprived of this. When we realize our Infinite Self we are replete. There is nothing more to desire. But as long as we do not recognize our own Divinity, we have a yearning. It is a yearning for our divine Self but, blinded by the maya (illusion) of the world, we mistake this yearning as desire for material pleasures. So desire for wealth, fame, knowledge are all, in truth, desire for God. Hinduism acknowledged this displaced desire by planting a god at the goal of every desire. So even in our delusion we are reminded of our true love. This constant reminder of Divinity has the capacity to turn that desire back to its true goal.[2]

1. Parth.
2. Parth.

172.

God has form and, again, He is formless. Once upon a time a sannyasi [man of renunciation] entered the temple of Jagannath. As he looked at the holy image he debated within himself whether God had a form or was formless. He passed his staff from left to right to feel whether it touched the image. The staff touched nothing. He understood that there was no image before him. He concluded that God was formless. Next, he passed the staff from right to left. It touched the image. The sannyasi understood that God had form. Thus he realized that God has form and is also without form.

Sri Ramakrishna

In Hindu imagery, the left is symbolic of the transcendental, the right of the terrestrial. So when the sannyasi tries to contact God, starting from the transcendental, he discovers that God is formless. When he tries to contact God starting from the right – the material world – he encounters God as a form. As long as we are focused on the material world God has form, just as the dreamer's mind has all the forms in his dream. When the dreamer awakens the dream forms dissolve. His mind has no form.

The many forms of God which, between them, control all aspects of the world are the projection through our mind of the formless Divinity. They are the intellectual capacity to control our attraction to the material world and, ultimately, to recognize these desires as God desiring God. It is the God within us that enables us to desire. It is the God within us that we truly desire. By facing a god – Lakshmi, Shiva, Brahma or Krishna – wherever there is a desire, we face ourself whether we recognize it or not. Whatever we ask of them, we ask of ourselves. The restraining power that their constant presence has on our desires is the restraining power of our own intellect. By reining in the senses we gradually move back and back from the material world towards the Divine Self.[1]

1. Parth.

173.

Whoever worships whatever form with faith, I make that faith unswerving.

Bhagavad Gita 7.21

Whenever a person takes up something, whether a god in heaven or an earthly fad, he develops a taste for it. He or she wants more and more. They get into a deeper and deeper groove.

Why?

Because everybody wants infinite joy. We will not rest content until we get it. So when we experience some happiness through an object or activity we keep pursuing it, trying to get more. We are like a six-foot coiled spring which has been compressed underfoot to six inches. There is great pressure in that spring, pushing upward, wanting to return to its original form. If the spring is released to two feet high there is less pressure, but still the spring is not content. It will not stop pushing up until it reaches its full stature.

The joys of the world release some of the internal pressures pushing towards the full stature of Infinite Bliss. So we go towards anything we identify which releases some of this pressure, becoming devoted to it unswervingly. The key is discrimination in the direction we choose. We have the capacity to go to God 'as the crow flies' or to take off in the opposite direction and have to go around the world before we arrive.[1]

174.

Endowed with that faith he seeks the worship of that god and from him he fulfils his desires. These are truly decreed by Me alone.

Bhagavad Gita 7.22

Sraddha, translated as 'faith', is the ability to reflect deeply on knowledge so that we go to its very essence and make that essence our own. It becomes our inspiration, our genius. There is a saying, 'Genius is 10 per cent talent, 90 per cent hard work.' Deep reflection is hard work. It requires a consistency of purpose

1. Parth.

which is the secret of all achievement.

We can achieve anything once we have set our sights and are not distracted from following through to the end. This applies to the relative (limited) goals of material existence as well as to the Absolute goal. If we worship the god of music, knowledge, business, physical ability, or whatever, with utter consistency of purpose, we will achieve our desire.

Ultimately, all desires are 'decreed by Me' – empowered by the Eternal Self – as the means by which we work our way back to that Self.[1]

175.

Finite indeed are the fruits accruing to those of little intellect. The ignorant pursue limited goals and achieve limited fruits. Those worshippers of gods go to the gods. But devotees reach Me.

Bhagavad Gita 7.23

Desires to be a great industrialist, a prime minister or to run an ashram (religious retreat) are all limited goals. There is nothing wrong with these goals or their fruits, but they are less than what we are capable of. If we worship god in the form of Lakshmi, as the goddess of wealth, or Ganesha, as the god of success, and we devote ourselves to that goal with consistency of purpose, we will achieve it.

But as long as we worship the world there is never a point at which we will have satiated our desire for Infinite Bliss. There is never a time when we will turn around and say, 'Thank you, no more money, I've got enough money,' or 'Thank you, I've got enough knowledge now.' After the brilliant scientist Einstein discovered the theory of relativity, he responded to the flood of acclaim by saying, 'I am grateful that you appreciate my discovery of the theory, but still I do not know who put that theory in the atom.'

If we extend our devotion beyond the forms of god to the formless God which is our Ultimate goal, we will reach that.[2]

1. Parth.
2. Parth.

176.

This form of mine which you have seen is very difficult to behold. Even the gods ever long to behold this form.

Bhagavad Gita 11.52

The gods are the subtlest, most perfect expressions of Divinity in the material world. They are true to their own natures. Lakshmi does not desire wealth, she is wealth. Ganesha does not desire success, he is success. And so on. The gods are our own bodies, minds and intellects, cleansed of all desire but to realize the Self. They are any person who is of a sattwic (non-desiring) nature. Even they must still work for realization of their greater Self, performing tapas (austerities), studying and meditating until that last desire is itself dissolved into the Oneness of Brahman.

177.

[Arujna said:] I see you with your crown, mace and discus, a mass of radiance, shining everywhere. You are difficult to behold, blazing all around like the sun, dazzling and inconceivable.

Bhagavad Gita 11.17

To Arjuna Krishna reveals his Divine form as the god Vishnu. In one hand Vishnu has the lotus, in the other he has the conch, in the third he has the mace and in the fourth he has the discus. The significance is applicable to us today in everyday life. Vishnu is our own state, our own form.

The lotus represents the infinite peace of God-realization. That peace comes from the core within, represented by the conch. This is the voice, the whisper deep inside calling us to that Divine experience. We know it as the conscience. Even the worst of us know what is right and wrong, whether we follow it or not.

If you do not heed that call within you get the knocks and shocks of life, represented by the mace. Whenever you get the hard edge of life, understand that it is the gadha (mace) warning you against the wrong direction that you have taken.

If you still do not respond to that call, you face the chakra (discus), annihilation. In other words, you will destroy yourself.

There is no God anywhere punishing you. You are punished by your own actions. You are denying yourself the kingdom of heaven that is within you.[1]

178.

... Among the yakshas [sprites] and rakshasas [demons], I am the Kuvera [god of wealth]...

Bhagavad Gita 10.23

Kuvera is described in the Puranas (see p. xxvii) as a monstrous creature. He is three-footed, fat, with a small head and eight protruding teeth. He is grounded in the three aspects of the material world – body, mind and intellect – and the three planes of consciousness: waking, dreaming and deep sleep.

He is bloated by his consumption of the world to feed the insatiable appetite of his eightfold (see p. 27) material nature. In the process his intellect has diminished.

This does not mean that every rich person is an avaricious monster. King Janaka was a very rich man but he was also a spiritual man. He was willing to give away all his wealth to know the Truth. The Brhadaranyaka Upanishad says that wealth accumulates in the mind, not in the treasury. Those who are obsessed by wealth, planning how to acquire it or hang on to it, are the personifications of Kuvera. They are the worst of the demons of desire, but they are still the Atman. Desires of this world are the perversions of our inherent desire for the Self. So the ugliest of desires is simply the greatest perversion of the Self desiring Itself.[2]

179.

... Of the vasus I am Fire...

Bhagavad Gita 10.23

The vasus are gods of the elements. The greatest of these is the

1. Parth.
2. Parth.

fire god Agni because he is the god of sacrifice. His is the flame
which liberates us by burning our offerings, symbols of our
material trappings. In ritual, his flames symbolize that eternal
energy which burns within us, desiring the world and desiring
the Self.

Fire is worshipped in all religions because it is the subtlest
element that is visible. Space is the subtlest element of all because
it can be contacted by only one sense (hearing) when sound
moves through space. Air is the next in subtlety because it can be
contacted by two senses: hearing and touch. Next is fire which
can be heard, felt and seen. Seeing is believing so, as the subtlest
element to be visible, fire is a very potent idol. Water and earth,
the other two visible elements, are grosser than fire because they
can be contacted by four and five senses respectively. Therefore
they make cruder symbols of the Divine.[1]

180.

... Of the gandharvas, I am Citaratha...

Bhagavad Gita 10.26

The gandharvas are celestial singers of whom Citaratha was the
finest.

Music is the most sublime type of sound, which is itself the
most sublime element in the physical world (see above).
Through music we experience many of the qualities that are
indicative of Brahman. Pitch is an expression of space (the pitch
of a note is a direct result of size); rhythm expresses time; and
melody is the causation which conditions the texture of both.
Thus we have the three fundamental constituents of music –
pitch, rhythm and melody – reflecting those of the Universe:
space, time and causation. The musical harmony arising out of a
mathematical balance of pitch, rhythm and melody reflects the
harmony – dharma – which unifies the Universe.

1. Parth.

181.

... Of causes for procreation I am Kandarpa...

Bhagavad Gita 10.28

Kandarpa is the god of sexual love. Because it feeds all the senses sex is the total sensual experience. Therefore Kandarpa is the best cause of procreation. As long as we identify with our ego sexual love is the greatest desire and the greatest satisfaction, although, like all desires for the material world, it can never be satiated. It is because of our unrecognized Divine nature that we chase after it so voraciously, mistaking it for that Infinite Love and Bliss.[1]

182.

He who is without beginning, middle or end, One, all-pervading, who is formless, knowledge and bliss, wonderful, who has Uma as his companion, the highest Lord, the controller, who is three-eyed, blue-necked, tranquil, by meditating on him the sage reaches the womb of all beings, the witness of all, who is beyond darkness.

Kaivalyopanishad 7

The Brahman is deified here as the god Shiva. Shiva, meditating in his traditional lotus position, represents the supreme state of perfection in humanity – realization. This is only reached through the 'marriage' of meditation with revealed Truth, the scriptures. Shiva's companion, Uma, is the symbol of the scriptures (see also pp. 271-2).

In the form of Shiva, Brahman is three-eyed to symbolize the divine vision of the realized person which is beyond physical vision. Where we see a dualistic world he sees the infinite, indivisible Reality. Shiva is blue-necked because, in a story told in the Vishnu Puranas of poison churned out of the primal milky ocean, Shiva swallows the poison to save the world. Uma grabs him around the throat to prevent the poison running into his

1. Parth.

system. It remains in his throat, staining it blue. It is a symbolic story of the personality churning out all desire through meditation. These desires are not let loose on the world but are swallowed by Consciousness and then arrested, through the wisdom of the scriptures, between head and heart. Thus the poison of desire affects neither the thoughts nor the emotions of the God-realized person. He is at peace.

By meditating on the pure Consciousness the sage reaches that Consciousness which is the source of all beings. It is the witness because, although it is the power enabling the eye to see, the legs to walk, the intellect to think, etc. (see pp. 6–8), it remains totally detached from all perceptions, actions and thoughts. It is as totally essential and unrelated to the world as electricity is to the air-conditioner, heater, washing machine, etc. To reach this Self is to step out of the dark shroud of ignorance.[1]

183.

He is Brahma, he is Shiva, he is Indra, he is imperishable, supreme, self-luminous. He is Vishnu, he is life [prana], he is time, he is fire, he is the moon.

Kaivalyopanishad 8

This verse describes the Supreme Self (Brahman) in terms that encompass the three aspects of the material world: gross (physical), subtle (mental) and causal.

Brahma, Shiva and Vishnu are the three gods worshipped by Hindus who represent the fundamental phenomena of the world. Brahma represents creation; Vishnu, maintenance; and Shiva, destruction. The entire physical world is nothing but an expression of creation, maintenance and destruction. All are one and the same and are, therefore, also shown as the three-faced god, Lord Dattatreya. There cannot be one without the others.

For example, if I break a cane, what have I done? I have destroyed one cane. I have created two canes. In other words, the destruction of one is the creation of another and that is possible

1. Parth.

only when the cane is maintained. These examples are everywhere. The death of the morning is the birth of the afternoon and so on through evening, night and back to morning in an endless chain of birth and death in which the day is maintained. The death of your babyhood is the birth of your childhood and so on through adolescence, adulthood, old age and back to babyhood in an endless chain in which you are maintained.

So the Supreme Self (Brahman) is Shiva, Brahma, Vishnu because He is the entire phenomena of the gross world.

He is the god Indra who, as Lord of the Senses, is the symbol of the mind and intellect. So He is the subtle world.

He is imperishable because He is the substratum out of which all this perishable world arises, as clay is the (relatively) imperishable substratum which creates perishable pots. So He is the causal body.

But He is supreme because He is beyond all of this.

He is life and time, in other words, birth and death. The description ends with fire and the moon, terrestrial and heavenly symbols respectively of the many-formed unchanging light of Reality.[1]

184.

If you think 'I've understood Brahman', then you have understood very little. The form of Brahman whom you have known in the way that you have felt and understood is also the form of the deities. Therefore, you should enquire further about Brahman...

Kenopanishad 2.1

The teacher warns his students not to mistake the sense of intellectual comprehension or divine inspiration as knowing God (Brahman). Such feelings belong to the terrestrial plane as do the multitude of deities ascribed to the heavens. Both are expressions of the highest material existence, but they are not God-Consciousness.

1. Parth.

God-Consciousness is the fourth plane of Consciousness, beyond the waking, dreaming and deep-sleep states (see pp. 33–6) which constitute our material existence. As long as we are in one of these three material states we cannot be in the fourth state, any more than we can be in the waking state when we are dreaming or dreaming when we are in the deep-sleep (dreamless) state. Whatever state we are in, the laws of that state apply and we cannot understand or experience another state simultaneously.[2]

1. Parth.

12 Aham Tvam Asmi – I Am You

185.

You are man, you are woman; you are youth and maiden too. You are an old man who totters along leaning on a stick. You are born with faces turned in all directions. You are the dark blue butterfly and the green parrot with red eyes. You are the thunder cloud, the seasons and the oceans. You are without beginning and beyond all space and time. You are He from whom all worlds have origin.

Shvetashvataropanishad IV.3–4

God exists beyond the Universe as well as within the Universe, where He is present in people and things. Although the Creator of space and time and all that exist within them, He is beyond such limitations. Nevertheless, all living creatures and natural phenomena are manifestations of Him.

Hindus may show deep reverence for persons, things or places; but this must not be misconstrued as deification of persons or things. It should be understood as devotion to God's presence in the object of worship. Hindus reserve such extreme reverence for those persons, places and things which they feel intuitively have the ability to concentrate and project the spirit of God. Thus for certain ceremonies or festivals, images or objects may be made and consecrated for visual use, to concentrate the presence of God and to multiply it by the attendance of many devotees. When the ceremony or festival is over, however, the object may be thrown away in a river as a discarded empty container that has fulfilled its purpose.[1]

1. Chand.

186.

Lo, verily not love for all is dear, but for love of the soul all is dear.
Brhadaranyaka Upanishad II.4.5.

Deep love brings us to our own immortality. The presence of the
Lord in our husband or wife, parents, siblings and children
makes them dear to us. Once the Divinity leaves a body, it is the
memory of that Divinity which we love, not the body. Indeed,
when the soul departs from the body of a woman's beloved
husband she is afraid of remaining with the body of the man
whom she loved so well. If the shrouded presence of our Lord in
each person makes them lovable how much more lovable is the
Lord Himself fully realized?[1]

187.

*May all be happy, may all be free from disease, may all realize
what is good and may none be subject to misery.*
Rig Veda I.89.1

These prayers echo the innermost feelings of the ancient rishis
(sages). Prayer is the most powerful form of energy we can
generate. It is an expression of love, the very foundation of
ancient Indian culture. Love arises when we understand what
the great rishis understood. The world is one family. The entire
Universe is a manifestation of the Divine which is found in the
heart of each and every human being.

Where there is love, there is brotherhood, harmony, tolerance
and freedom. This is why the rishis never developed weapons
although they had an intuitive knowledge of the laws of physics.
This is why tolerance and freedom are the essence of Indian
culture. It is unique as a society which respects and wishes well
all religions. Every religion in the world has flourished in India.
At the Chicago Parliament of Religions, Swami Vivekananda

1. Panch.

(see pp. xxxvii–xxxviii) said, 'I am proud to belong to a religion which has taught the world both tolerance and universal acceptance. We believe not only in universal tolerance but we accept all religions as true.'[1]

188.

That Brahman is well known as the adorable being, the Atman of all, which is to be meditated upon as the worshipful Self in all beings. All beings love Him who knows it thus.

Kenopanishad 4.6

The person who hates another being is like the dog in the parable of the Maharajah and the mirrors. The Maharajah had a room which was mirrored on all sides so that he could stand in the middle and see himself from all angles. Normally this room was kept closed but, one day, the Maharajah went out leaving the door ajar. The palace guard-dog found the door, entered the room and discovered to his rage that there was another dog in the palace and, what is more, it was brazenly blocking his path.

The guard-dog barked and so did the other dog and so did another dog to his right and left. The guard-dog realized he was surrounded by dogs all barking, jumping, crouching and snapping whenever he did so. The guard-dog flew into a frenzy, throwing himself biting and snarling at his opponents.

When the Maharajah returned he found his dog dead in a pool of his own blood, surrounded by shattered glass. The mirrored room which had been the means for the Maharajah to see himself better was the means of destruction for the dog because he was ignorant. He did not know it was his own reflection that he saw. We are like this dog because we do not understand that the world we experience is our own reflection. We bark, it barks, we bite, it bites. We are in a pool of our own blood.[2]

1. Panch.
2. Parth.

189.

There is a well-known saying, 'As a man thinks so he becomes.' We should therefore expand our circle of oneness and unity to the greatest possible extent in order to increase our resulting collective strength. When our unity or oneness with the Universe is complete in thoughts, words and deeds, we become one with Him, the Universal Self, or nature. Our acts become the acts of nature or God and we develop unlimited power and authority. It depends, however, upon the intensity of our conviction of the truth of universal unity.

Swami Rama Tirtha, Universal Unity

Love is not something we fall into. Love is what we rise to. It is not the selfish attachment to a handful of individuals at the expense of all others. It is identifying yourself with all beings in the world. When we accept that all the world is the One Supreme Self, we must love all beings literally as ourselves.

Your spouse and children have taught you to love, but the home has become the boundary of your affection. The home should be the centre of affection which radiates out to all the world. At the moment you can't feel beyond your family. 'My wife, my children, my parents – and the rest of you can drop dead.' If this is the way you are feeling there can't be any spiritual progress. You don't need to love your family any less, but don't stop there. No one is asking you to give your property. That you can give to your family as your first obligation. It is finite. But love is infinite. Give love and attention to others as to the family. Be happy for them when they have a new car, a well-paid job, a great success. Feel for them when they suffer. If you don't love your fellow human beings you don't love God.[1]

190.

Brahminhood [spiritual ascension] deserts him who knows brahminhood in anything else than the Self. Kshatriyahood

1. Parth.

[leadership] deserts him who knows kshatriyahood in anything else than the Self. The worlds desert him who knows the worlds in anything else than the Self. The gods desert him who knows the gods in anything else than the Self. The Vedas desert him who knows the Vedas in anything else than the Self. The beings desert him who knows the beings in anything else than the Self. All desert him who knows all in anything else than the Self. This brahminhood, this kshatriyahood, and these worlds, these gods, these Vedas, all these beings, these all are the Self.

Brhadaranyaka Upanishad IV.5.7.

When there is duality one sees another, one smells another, one hears another and so on. From this we create individuality. The ego develops and the dualistic world is created and maintained in orbit around the ego. This world of maya (cosmic illusion) is a very subjective world, based on highly individual perceptions and associations which, in turn, are based on our past actions (karma). Placed at the centre of it, the ego fattens and becomes complicated. It does not love, it only desires. Spiritual life is the effacement of this ego. We should never underestimate the ego's appetite. It fattens on holiness as much as on unholiness, on poverty as much as on riches. It misses no opportunity to grow fat. By spiritual disciplines which acknowledge the Self in all things, the ego is thinned out and the individual merges with pure Consciousness which is pure Love.[1]

191.

Whatever is here, that is there. Whatever is there, that too is here. Whoever perceives plurality here goes from death to death.

By mind alone is this to be obtained. There is nothing of plurality here. Whoever perceives anything like plurality here goes from death to death.

Kathopanishad II.1.10–11

All things in this world are in love because the true and universal

---

1. Bhav.

Self of our own particular self is all around whether we recognize it or not.

Before we know God we learn our lessons of unselfish love at home. What we don't realize is that in all these loving expressions we are really loving God Himself. What is lovable in a person is not his or her face or intelligence or sweet disposition. All these factors are changing. But our love doesn't change for its roots are much deeper.

Everything in this world has three dimensions – asti, bhati and kriya. Asti means 'is'. Everything *is* here. Furthermore, it is bhati – shining – with life. There is a glow about it which makes it kriya – lovable. These three are the nature of God, the Atman, in this world. He is glowing here and he is lovable. We can't help but love the leaves on the plant in springtime. There is a great joy we feel at the sight of them. The object of love for everyone is the real Self. Love of anything or anyone is a mixture of sweetness and bitterness until we have developed an insight into what it is we love. If we only love the leaves and not the Self, which is the source of their glow, we hate them by autumn when they are clogging our gutters.

Only when we turn to the underlying Reality is the love marvellous for then it is pure.[1]

192.

Common be your prayers.
Common be your end.
Common be your purpose.
Common be your deliberations.
Common be your desires.
United be your hearts.
United be your intentions.
Perfect be the union amongst you.

Rig Veda X.191.3–4

Human beings live in this world not only as individuals but as

1. Bhav.

members of families and society. To bring prosperity to family, nation and humanity as a whole, we need to have a unity of purpose. We need to see the interests of others as our own. Otherwise we tear ourselves apart with our conflicting desires.

This prayer is offered communally to God and society to help create an attitude of harmony, love and shared direction. Perfect union at all levels is the secret of success.[1]

193.

When the lyre is played upon, it brings out a similar note from another lyre placed opposite it. When you strike a chord on one instrument a similar chord on the opposite instrument begins to vibrate. Similarly, on a theatrical stage, when an actor weeps, the eyes of receptive persons in the audience also get moist. Rama has noticed, while lecturing, that when he laughs the audience also starts laughing. Why so? It is so because of the law of continuity . . . Science has proved that if a body is to act upon another body, there must be continuity between the two. It is because of this law of continuity that we are all united to one another psychologically. If you smile at a baby he smiles. If you put up an angry face he weeps. If you sing, others also start singing.

Swami Rama Tirtha, *Universal Unity*

1. Bhav.

13   Aham Avataras Asmi – I Am the Divine Incarnations

194.

*[Krishna said:] Of the descendents of Vrsni, I am Vasudeva
[Krishna], and of the Pandavas I am Arjuna. Of the sages I am
Vyasa and among the poets I am Usana.*

Bhagavad Gita 10.37

'I am me, I am you, I am the teller of this tale...' The Eternal
Self is not the god Krishna, as distinct from everything else. In
this verse, Krishna says in one breath that he is his present
incarnation, Vasudeva (the personal name Krishna inherited
from his worldly father); he is Arjuna to whom he is speaking; he
is Vyasa, the great sage, who recorded these very words as the
Bhagavad Gita; and he is Usana, one of India's finest
philosophers.

How can Krishna be different people? The whole point is that,
whenever he is talking about 'Me', he is talking about the all-
pervading Reality, Brahman. Krishna was a historical figure who
had achieved the highest achievement – Self-realization. When
you reaches this plane you merge with the Self, the Brahman, the
Atman, God, whatever you want to call It. So Krishna, having
become That, is trying to tell us that, whoever we be, whatever
we be, once we reach that fourth plane of Consciousness we
become one with It. The whole Bhagavad Gita is trying to get
that across to us.[1]

1. Parth.

195.

[Krishna said:] Although I am unborn and my divine form never deteriorates and although I am the Lord of all Creation, I still appear in every age in my original state.

Bhagavad Gita 4.6

Krishna was God-realized as were all the great prophets and saints of all nations and times. They had all become the Divine Self and were simply trying to show us that capacity in ourselves. Krishna's incarnation has had an immeasurable impact on Indian civilization. Every aspect of his life is profoundly symbolic and an unending source of inspiration for Indian religion, philosophy, mysticism, poetry, painting, sculpture, music and dance.

Krishna is blue-skinned and wears yellow clothes. Blue is the colour of the sky and the sea, two recurrent images of Divinity. Yellow is the colour a colourless flame becomes when it is bedded in sand. Thus these colours represent the Infinite Reality shrouded in human existence – God on earth. But Krishna's entire life, beginning with his birth in a prison and instant release when the doors miraculously flew open, is a sign to us that the Infinite is never really limited by its human form.

Krishna plays a flute, a hollow tube symbolizing the body emptied of desire. Out of it comes beautiful music which enchants all who hear. After Krishna killed a serpent which had regenerating multiple heads he danced on its crushed heads playing his flute. He is the man who has crushed the self-generating heads of egocentric desire and revels in the Infinite Bliss of Self-realization.[1]

196.

[Krishna said:] Whenever and wherever there is a decline in religious practice, O descendant of Bharata [Arjuna], and a

1. Parth.

predominant rise of irreligion – at that time I descend Myself.
                                                    Bhagavad Gita 4.7

Multiple divine incarnation is fundamental to Vedic religion.

This world affords the opportunity for the expression of love and sacrifice but, at the same time, it is full of trials and difficulties which test our souls severely. Only through honest striving can we improve ourselves. We know plenty of theories but it is example which makes an impression on us. So, at times of great disharmony, the divine power is drawn out in human form. God comes down to set an example. Out of great compassion he takes birth to strengthen and guide people in the right direction when they have reached an impasse.[1]

197.

To deliver the pious and to annihilate the miscreants, as well as to re-establish the principles of religion, I Myself appear, millennium after millennium.

One who knows the transcendental nature of my divine birth and activities will not be born again when he leaves his body. He attains me.

                                                    Bhagavad Gita 4.8–9

Lord Krishna is the omnipotent controller of the material world, so when there is a decrying of religion he comes as a king comes when there is trouble or a revolt in some part of his kingdom. It is as easy for Krishna to do this as for the king to visit the prison. When the king goes to the prison he doesn't become a prisoner. Simlarly, Krishna can visit the prison of material existence without becoming a prisoner. As prisoners, our actions are directed by the law of karma (see pp. 52–4), but that principle does not apply to Krishna. No law can touch him. Nevertheless, like the king who is above the law, he does not break the law. The purpose of his coming is to establish religious principles, in other words, the law of the Lord.

Krishna comes to reclaim us by displaying his identity to us,

1. Bhav.

but we may choose to remain blind to it. To some he will appear only as an ordinary person. When we understand that his birth and activities are divine we become free from material bondage and the karmic cycle.

In past ages he would literally kill the miscreants – those who did not abide by him – but in this age he came as Lord Chaitanya (the fifteenth-century Krishna-bhakti saint) who destroyed the demonic tendencies of atheism with love.[1]

198.

[The gods said to Vishnu:] We shall set a task for you, Vishnu, for the sake of the welfare of the worlds. There is the king of Ayodhya, Dasaratha, who is virtuous, generous and his power equals that of the great sages. O Lord Vishnu, please divide yourself into four parts and be born as the sons of the three wives [of Dasaratha] who are like Modesty, Beauty and Glory. Then you will become a man. And then please destroy Ravana, who has grown like a thorn in the world.

Ramayana I.15. 19–21

In the Ramayana epic the god Vishnu is sent down to earth by the gods to conquer Ravana, the demon desire.

Vishnu, the god of maintenance, forms a trinity with Brahma and Shiva. *Vish* means 'to pervade'. Brahma and Shiva effect the cycle of Creation and destruction with Vishnu as the all-pervading Reality, sustaining these changes. He is the Atman at the core of our being which manifests through body, mind and intellect.

This Atman has three 'mothers'. It is 'born' in the body through the modesty of self-control in all actions. It is 'born' in the mind through the beauty of pure love for all beings. It is 'born' in the intellect through righteous discrimination which is the glory of the human species.

Thus Vishnu is the God of all avataras (divine births). He is every man who is God-realized – who has 'four sons': body,

1. Char./Das.

mind, intellect and pure Consciousness (Atman). Rama and Krishna are the two most beloved of Vishnu's avatars.[1]

199.

In an auspicious moment, Kausalya gave birth to a son, Rama, Lord of the world, worshipped by everybody. He bore the sign of divinity. He was one half of Vishnu, a great person who was the joy of the Iksaku people.

Ramayana I.10.11

Kaikeyi had a son named Bharata who was truly a great warrior; he was one quarter of Vishnu incarnate and had all the virtues.

Then Sumitra bore two sons, Lakshmana and Satrughna; they were valorous, skilled in all weapons, consisting of the two halves [of one quarter] of the incarnation of Vishnu.

Ramayana I.18. 13–14

King Dasaratha performed a sacrifice and was blessed with four sons by his three 'wives', who represent his body, mind and intellect respectively.

The 'four sons' make up a God-realized human being. Lakshmana and Satrughna are the mind and body, skilled in the ways of the world. Bharata is the intellect, seat of virtue, which is separate from but incorporates the mind and body as the separate quarter incorporates two eighths. Rama is the Atman which, as the all-pervading Reality, is separate from but incorporates the body, mind and intellect, as the separate half incorporates one quarter and two eighths.

200.

[Lord Shiva said to Parvati:] Parvati, the qualities of Lord Hari are unaccountable, his names are innumerable, his greatness is unfathomable. I shall relate them as far as I can. Please listen

1. Parth.

carefully. Whenever dharma is in danger, the wretched demons get stronger and perpetuate all kinds of immoral and sinful acts, and when brahmins, cattle, gods and the whole earth become desperate in frustration, Lord Hari then assumes various forms to remove the burden of sorrow.

 Rama has been born as a human being for three reasons: to protect the gods by killing the demons, to keep the flow of the Vedic religion uninterrupted – the Vedas which he himself created – and to spread his spotless glory all over the world. The devotees cross the ocean of samsara [cycle of birth and death] by praising his glory. Rama, therefore, assumed the human form for the purpose of doing good to the people.

Tulsidas, Ram-carit-manas, I.129

Tulsidas describes here the purpose of the incarnation of Rama. Lord Vishnu has incarnated himself as Rama to lessen the burden of sorrow and sin on earth. This is connected with the religious doctrine of the ten different incarnations of Lord Vishnu to save the earth from sinking into immoral, irreligious disorder. Rama is one of the incarnations. Lord Shiva is relating this story to his wife, Parvati. Shiva is represented here as the highest of the devotees of Rama. In Tulsidas's faith, Rama is the highest god, god of gods, the ultimate Brahman and therefore Shiva, being a god himself, becomes a devotee of Rama.[1]

201.

By knowing Him one can cross the Ocean of Death; no other path exists for such a crossing.

Shvetashvataropanishad VI.8

To go through the process of birth and death among the 8,400,000 different species of living beings is the greatest misery and tragedy of the soul. Liberation is possible only when we attain human life for only then can we attain knowledge. But knowledge of whom and what? The Hindu scriptures testify that

1. Mat.

the person who has known the visible human form of God in all His glory, divinity and infinite powers is a man of perfect wisdom. God incarnates Himself in human form to liberate humanity, but to recognize God in human form is very difficult.

A person may have studied all the scriptures in the world and not be a man of wisdom. In the Mahabharata epic (which includes the Gita), it is Arjuna's firm belief in Lord Krishna as God that earns him the grace to see the Divine form. Arjuna then fights the battle undaunted by fear of sin. On the other hand, Yudhishthira, his elder brother, who never faltered in any moral injunction, does not recognize the human form of Lord Krishna. He relies only on his own understanding of the scriptures and so, overwhelmed by the horrors of war, believes he will never be redeemed.[1]

202.

On the self-same tree a person immersed [in the world] is deluded and grieves on account of his helplessness. When he sees the Other, the Lord who is worshipped and His greatness, he becomes freed from sorrow.

                                        Shvetashvataropanishad IV.7

The Supreme Self is so close to us that we don't recognize it. It has to be separate from us before we see it. The life and character of a divine incarnation introduces the ideal man and shows us the power within the limited world. It is the sacrifice of Brahman to show us the gateway out and set the example for us to take and cherish in our heart. Every generation has to discover an incarnation in itself. But, ultimately, that power is within us. The incarnation is a projection to help us and show the way back to our Self. The incarnation can tell us where to go, but going is our business. If a person understands and uses a divine incarnation to experience the Reality in him- or herself the purpose of incarnation is achieved.[2]

1. Panch.
2. Bhav.

203.

You must have marked that when there is an itching sensation in some part of your body, your hand automatically finds the exact spot to relieve you of some irritation... It is so because your real Self is pervading throughout your own body. It is here, there and everywhere in your body. It is on the itching spot and also in your hand which relieves you of your itching sensation. It proves the unity and all-pervasiveness of 'I' in the body.

So too is the case with this universe, wherein the all-pervading force [power, energy, God or Atman] is present and inter-penetrating throughout... the common object is to safeguard the security and welfare of the whole. It is to implement this law that the avatars [incarnations], the prophets and the saints come down for the common good of all.

Swami Rama Tirtha, *Universal Unity*

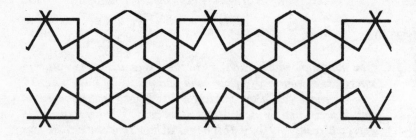

14 Aham Gurus Asmi – I Am the Spiritual Teachers

204.

The spiritual seeker must find proper instruction at the feet of a guru who is well-versed in the Vedas which lead to the knowledge of God.

Bhagavatam II.3.21

There are three types of people who investigate the world so you and I can eke out happiness in it – the scientist, the economist and the politician. There are three sets of relationships they take in hand: you and the physical environment, you and wealth, you and society. Subsequently, the world has changed beyond recognition, yet humanity is sitting in this wonderful world weeping.

What has gone wrong?

They have dealt with the object – the world – but never the subject – you.

Another set of investigators, however, has investigated you, the subject. They approached the subject in a scientific manner, taking material from the world, studying it, experimenting with it and drawing conclusions which they formulated as laws of the subjective world. Just as there are laws pertaining to the external world so there are laws pertaining to the internal world. We all follow the external laws because we know we suffer otherwise. Put a hand in the fire and the fire burns it. It's a law. But we do not heed or even know the internal laws. We are constantly conflicting with them, creating stress and suffering for ourselves.

So you need to go to these investigators of the subject, you. They are the prophets and saints, the munis, rishis and mahatmas of religion. They have gone to the heart of their subject and communicated as much as possible to the world. Through study and reflection at their feet, i.e., in total devotion, we can learn from these great souls or from the teachings revealed by them in the books.[1]

205.

Arise and awake, approach the excellent and experienced ones and learn to realize the Truth. Narrow is the path and difficult to tread, sharp like the edge of a razor. But success is sure to those who dare and do.

Kathopanishad I.3.14

For ultimate redemption, the Upanishads direct us to a guru.

Who is awake? One who rises from the slumber of ignorance and attachment to material objects is indeed genuinely awakened. It is the guru who lights the path of a stranger lost in the darkness of the unknown. The guru is a powerhouse of divine energy. He nurtures the budding divinity in the heart of the disciple. By his grace material attachments are cleansed from the disciple's thoughts and deeds. Only when this internal dirt and debris have been removed can the disciple perceive the divine beauty and light. Total faith in, and commitment to, the guru is essential for liberation.[2]

206.

If a person who is deeply attached to the body and bodily relations is similarly attached to a God-realized saint, the doors of redemption will be opened for him.

Bhagavatam III.25.20

1. Parth.
2. Panch.

We cannot hope to achieve permanent liberation (moksha) without a deep spiritual attachment to a saint. A genuine saint is kind, patient, compassionate, calm; devoid of anger, malice, worldly possessions and worldly desires; egoless; full of spiritual wisdom and active in spreading that wisdom.

Just as an ageing king who becomes a father loves his child with patience and forbearance whatever the child's mistakes, so the guru is loving and tolerant of his disciple's ignorance. And just as the child loves his father without question or criticism, so the disciple loves and obeys his guru.

The glory and greatness of the saint are our inspiration on the path to realization of God.[1]

207.

He who has the supreme devotion to God and the same for a guru,
only that great soul attains the highest good.

Shvetashvaropanishad 6.23

The scriptures emphasize that complete surrender and service to the guru are essential for redemption. The Lord abides in a true saint and therefore devoted service to such a saint is as good as serving the Lord in person. The guru has obtained the highest knowledge by honest effort, the grace of God and the guidance of his own guru. Having understood the truth, he does not shut himself into a cloister or retire into a forest. He brings the message to our doorstep.

A disciple must be like clay in the hands of a sculptor. The guru moulds him into the finest medium for the Divine Power to manifest. If the guru and disciple are welded together by divine affection, the guru will transform the disciple into another touchstone of Divinity.[2]

1. Panch.
2. Panch.

208.

Just try to learn the truth by approaching a spiritual master. Inquire from him submissively and render service unto him. The Self-realized souls can impart knowledge unto you because they have seen the truth.

Bhagavad Gita 4.34

We have to approach a qualified teacher, one who is conversant with spiritual life and the scriptures. We must approach him with an attitude of submission and service. Receiving knowledge is very dependent on sincere inquiry.

Transcendental knowledge is such that it is not received by the mind or intellect, but induced in our spiritual hearts by the mercy of the spiritual master. The knowledge is actually there in us because we are all spiritual entities, part and parcel of the Supreme Knower. But it is the covering of ignorance that has made us forget, like a lightbulb that is on but coated in black paint so no light can radiate. The heart is full of material grime, lust and desire, but when we remove that dirt, then the knowledge is automatically remembered. By receiving the mercy of the spiritual master we can remove that grime covering our hearts. The spiritual master knows the process, because his heart has been purified.[1]

209.

Sukesha, son of Bharadvaja, Satya-kama, son of Shiba, Gargya, grandson of Surya, Kausalya, son of Ashvala, Bhargava of the Vidarbha country, Kabandhi, son of Katya, these truly devoted to the lower Brahman, intent on the lower Brahman, seeking the highest Brahman, approached the revered Pippalada with sacrificial fuel in their hands, thinking: 'This one will explain all to us.'

1. Char./Das.

> *To them that seer said, 'Live [here] another year with
> austerity, brahmacharya [chastity] and faith. Then ask us
> questions according to your desire and if we know we shall indeed
> tell you all That.'*

Prasnopanishad I.4

In ancient times dedicated students found their way through the
Himalayan jungles to the great rishis (sages) of the Upanishads.
The word *Upa-ni-shad* means 'near-below-sit', indicating the
position of devotion and receptivity the students adopt at the
guru's feet. They are sitting at the feet of knowledge.

The students' journey was made more difficult by the
firewood they carried as an offering to the guru, a practical gift in
the cold Himalayas and a symbol of the material world they
renounced so that they might uncover the flame of their own
Atman (Eternal Self). When they arrived and asked to be taught
the true knowledge, the guru sent them away for a year to reflect.
This was the acid test of the students' devotion and a time of
preparation for them to understand better what they asked.
Without true devotion, the knowledge would be meaningless to
the students – or worse. It could be devastating.

So the students whom the sages were teaching in the
Upanishads were first-grade students. They had undergone
extreme physical and mental endurance: seeking out the gurus,
living the austere life in the mountains, studying and
contemplating deeply. This is why the language of the
Upanishads is so superbly condensed and poetic. It did not have
to be spelt out. There was already a bedrock of knowledge in the
students that the teacher was able to build upon. This is the
difference between the Upanishads and the Gita, where Krishna
is teaching a fine but spiritually unschooled human being.[1]

210.

> . . . *[Arjuna said:] You are to be worshipped. You are the greatest
> guru. None is equal to you. How then can anyone excel you in these*

1. Parth.

three worlds, O being of incomparable power?

Bhagavad Gita 11.43

With his completely unfolded Divinity Krishna boosts Arjuna's personality. He temporarily lends him the feeling and thinking of God-realization.

When people go to a mahatma (great soul) in a state of distress, the mahatma is able to give solace to them. For a while they feel relieved. They have a sense of Divinity which they experience through the guru. That feeling will not be sustained until they have discovered it in themselves. It is not possible for one person to unveil the Atman (Eternal Self) for another. We must each do it ourselves through our own dedication, discipline and single-pointed contemplation. All a teacher can do is inspire us on that path through his understanding and love.

In Arjuna, Krishna is dealing with a fine human being, but Arjuna has no real grounding in the science of religion. He is the man in the street. Krishna speaks to Arjuna as his lifelong and dearest friend. The devotion he draws upon to teach Arjuna is the devotion Arjuna has for him as a friend. This, in its sincerity, is enough to teach the art of practical living, which is what Arjuna wants. It is circumstances – an impending battle against his own friends and relatives – that push Arjuna into spiritual searching and he learns within the framework of this need.[1]

211.

Whatever I have importunately said from carelessness or love, addressing you as 'Krishna, my friend', please forgive me.

In whatever way I have been disrespectful to you for the sake of fun, when we were at play, lying, sitting or at meals, when alone and in company, I implore forgiveness, O infallible One.

Bhagavad Gita 11.41–42

Arjuna is begging the forgiveness of his lifelong friend, Krishna,

---

1. Parth.

for not recognizing him (before circumstances demanded it) as
the mahatma (great soul) who could be his guru.

You have to be very alert. You could have a Krishna next to
you and be so wrapped up in your little self that you miss Him. In
Hamlet, Polonius advises his son Laertes, 'Give ear unto all but
few thy voice...' Now we have a tendency to give voice to all but
ear to none. We must learn to hear others. Talk when you are
asked, not otherwise.[1]

212.

*The Supreme form has been shown to you by My own yoga
[spiritual] power, full of splendour, primeval, infinite, universal
form which none other than you has ever seen.*

Bhagavad Gita 11.47

Krishna is Arjuna's guru. He reveals the Divinity in himself so
that Arjuna can experience It in himself. Krishna lends Arjuna
spiritual vision. A mahatma (great soul) can do that in a relative
sense. He can take away agitations so our mind is perfectly still.
Then we see the Divinity which underlies the world. The same
thing can happen if we study the Gita or any of the scriptures.
We become relatively calm and catch a glimpse of Reality.

When Krishna says: 'None other than you has ever seen [the
Supreme form],' the 'you' he is referring to is the Supreme Self.
It is all, there is no other, so there is no other that can see It. Only
the Self sees the Self. That Self is 'Me', it is 'You'.[2]

213.

God Himself is the guru.

Sri Ramakrishna

A prophet is a person who is able to communicate the knowledge

1. Parth.
2. Parth.

of the Eternal Self to us. The extent to which a person has unfolded the Atman (Self) is the extent to which he or she can communicate It. When a person is completely unfolded he or she can communicate the entire Atman to any who are open to It. It is not dependent on erudition or oratorical skills. The Atman speaks.

A typical example is Ramana Maharishi, a realized soul who died in the middle of this century. People used to flock to his South Indian village. He would sit there for hour upon hour in silence, occasionally changing position. But people came back from there inspired and fully charged. When you reach that state even silence speaks.[1]

214.

When going to a strange country, one must abide by the directions of the guide who knows the way. Taking the advice of many would lead to utter confusion. So in trying to reach God one must implicitly follow the advice of one single guru who knows the way to God.

Sri Ramakrishna

1. Parth.

Ayam Atma Brahma – The Self Is Brahman

Statement of Practice

15 Svadharma – Personal Law

215.

Better to do one's own dharma imperfectly than the dharma of another, however well discharged. Better is death in one's own dharma. The dharma of another is fraught with fear.

Bhagavad Gita 3.35

There are many angry people in the world. Everything makes them angry – the children are too noisy, their dinner is overcooked, their boss is incompetent, their subordinates are lazy. They are individuals thwarted from following their dharma. Their natural path of action has been blocked, perhaps by parental, economic or social pressure. In the wrong field of activity they are starved of satisfaction and in constant fear that they cannot do the job properly. Thus they are constantly angry.

There is no single English word which embraces the concept of dharma. It is your essential nature, law, duty, path. The unifying dharma of all of us is the Atman, but each one of us has an individual dharma because of our vasanas (unmanifested desires – see p. 48).

The tiger must hunt, the nightingale must sing, the cow must yield. Similarly, there are tigers among men, nightingales among men, cows among men. We must act according to our dharma if we are to have any peace in this life. In the words of the Shakespearean character, Polonius, 'Be true to thyself and it must follow as night follows day, thou canst not then be false to any man.'

Self-realization may be many lives away, but if we have been

true to ourselves, to our own dharma, we will die having
advanced some way towards the Eternal Self.[1]

216.

*Having seen your mighty form with so many mouths and eyes, O
maha-baho [mighty-armed one], with many arms, thighs and
feet, with many stomachs and terrible tusks, the worlds are
terrified and so am I.*

Bhagavad Gita 11.23

Who are the people who terrify us? Who are the people whom we
dare not disobey?

The person we respect is one who is honest and straightforward, upright, disciplined, wise and unselfish. We have a
reverence for such a person. On the other hand, someone who
does not have these qualities may have a very powerful position
but we neither respect nor fear them. How did a person like
Mahatma Gandhi command so much reverence? It was his total
commitment, selflessness and love. A mahatma (great soul) does
not interfere with people, he does not try to force them to do
anything, yet they speak to him in whispers. They are terrified of
him. Even in an office, a boss who is just and principled
automatically commands respect and obedience.[2]

217.

*[Arjuna said:] On seeing you touching the sky, shining in many
colours with mouths wide open with large fiery eyes, I am terrified
at heart and I find neither courage nor peace, O Vishnu.*

*Have mercy, O Lord of Lords, O abode of the Universe.
Having seen your mouth fearful with tusks, blazing like cremation
fires, I know not the four quarters, nor do I find peace. I'm
finished.*

Bhagavad Gita 11.24

1. Parth.
2. Parth.

Who are the people who have no courage? Those who are not living up to the standard. In an office, the manager is feared by a person who does no work. This person is always watching and worrying about what others are doing. But a person who does his work meticulously with sincere commitment doesn't care who the manager is or what he does. He does not fear the manager. In fact, the manager fears and respects him.

This is a law of life. If you are not performing your obligatory duties, if you are not upright and straightforward, you have fear.

Now Arjuna is on the battlefield with an army waiting for him to lead them. At the last moment he becomes emotional, lays down his bow and arrow and refuses to do his obligatory duty. It is a righteous war and he is a kshatriya (warrior-king). As long as he does not do what he knows he must do, he fears. The sight of the pure Righteousness (dharma) terrifies him.[1]

218.

Therefore, bowing down, I crave forgiveness, O adorable Lord. Please treat me as a father treats a son, as a friend to a friend, or a lover tolerates a partner.

Bhagavad Gita 11.44

Now it was on Arjuna's request that Krishna revealed the higher Truth; this then sent Arjuna into paroxysms of fear and guilt. But God is not to be feared. As long as we follow the eternal laws we are protected. We are God, the Supreme Law of all laws (dharma). We are the custodians of the laws. We are the protector of the laws. If we fear the law of karma we are like a Supreme Court judge who is frightened of the police. He is the last person who should have any need to fear them.

The problem in our life is that we fear what is not to be feared and we do not fear what is to be feared. We are fearless of the senses. But, given half a chance, these senses will bring about our

1. Parth.

downfall. Yet we play with them as if they were our dearest
friends and fear the One that loves us most.[1]

219.

*Therefore, without attachment, perform your duty for by working
without attachment a person attains the Supreme.*

Bhagavad Gita 3.19

After completing his explanation of the path of karma-yoga
(sacrifice and service) Krishna tells Arjuna, quite bluntly, 'Get
on with it, man.' As long as a person is not Self-realized he has
duties to perform which are his karma-yoga (spiritual action).
Arjuna is a kshatriya (warrior) and so it is his dharma to fight for
the righteous cause.

All of us have duties to ourselves, our family, society, country,
humanity and all living creatures, in accordance with the birth
we have taken. When we perform our duty we should not have
the attitude, 'I am the doer.' Such people make much fuss for
very little result. They imagine themselves to be indispensable.
They become attached to their duties. All duties must be done
with grace and sincerity in the true spirit of sacrifice. Only then
will we be free of the desires which bind us to the chain of action
and reaction.[2]

220.

*Of all rulers I am the sceptre. Of those who wish to conquer I am
righteousness . . .*

Bhagavad Gita 10.38

Whether we are rulers on the spiritual plane, governing our own
desires, or rulers on the material plane, governing other people,

1. Parth.
2. Parth.

the Atman is the power which enables us to 'conquer' – to achieve our goals. It is pure power which acts according to the medium processing it.

To draw upon the power we must understand the operating instructions of its transmitter. In other words, we must understand the dharma of our personality and our world. Dharma is one law which manifests as all laws – the laws of nature, morality, religion, psychology, sociology and so on. If we flout dharma, the Eternal Power will not be harmed but the transmitter will inevitably short-circuit. We will be agitated and damaged. We will not 'conquer' either our own ego or the world.[1]

221.

Abandoning all duties, come to my shelter only, I shall release you from all the sins. Grieve not.

Bhagavad Gita 18.66

Lord Krishna advises the perplexed Arjuna that it is his duty (dharma) as a kshatriya (warrior) to fight on the battlefield – even if it is against his relatives, elders and his guru. But, more importantly, he should do it in compliance to the wishes of the Eternal. He should renounce his own will and perform without expectations or concern for the fruits of his action.

Living a life within the bounds of duty to God elevates us spiritually. Arjuna's part (to fight a battle in the Mahabharata war) was, on the surface, wrong. But because he acted according to the Lord's wishes, his actions became pure and justified. If he had fought for a kingdom through his own will then he would not have gained any spiritual merit. It is only when we lead a life according to God's wishes that we experience peace and happiness.[2]

1. Parth.
2. Panch.

222.

[Arjuna said:] My dear Krishna, O infallible one, my delusion is destroyed. I have regained my memory through Your grace. I am firm. I am free from doubt. I shall act according to Your instructions.

Bhagavad Gita 18.73

Krishna has finished his advice and Arjuna speaks for the last time. He is completely transformed by the message of the Lord. He surrenders his individuality and accepts the command of the Lord as his highest duty. His delusion has been removed. Until then he had identified himself as his mind and body and therefore doubts crept into his mind. God can be realized only by the knowledge inspired by Him and not through the senses, mind, intellect or ego, which are evolved out of maya (delusion).

Arjuna did not awaken spiritually through his own effort but through the Lord's mercy. When the Lord is pleased with us he blesses us with a discriminating intellect – our soul remembers the dharma (universal law). Arjuna has understood the meagreness of human effort and the greatness of the grace of the Lord. His ignorance is removed. He is now a man of steady wisdom.

We may wonder how God himself can encourage his disciple to fight a war. It was God's plan to destroy the demonic rulers in the world. Arjuna was merely an instrument to serve the purpose.[1]

223.

Wherever there is Krishna, the master of all mystics, and wherever there is Arjuna, the supreme archer, there will certainly be victory, welfare and morality, such is my firm conviction.

Bhagavad Gita 18.78

When two energy streams, the energy of God and the energy of

1. Panch.

practical efficiency, flow together in a human being, there is righteousness and success. Divine grace and human effort lead to liberation. This is the message of the Gita.[1]

224.

Whatever action a great man performs, common men follow. And whatever standards he sets by exemplary acts, all the world pursues.

Bhagavad Gita 3.21

There is a great need in society for exemplary behaviour. It is the natural tendency of people to follow a leader. So even if a person is engaged in the perfect duty of serving the Lord, he doesn't stop acting but continues to lead by personal example. In modern society we find that the personal lives of heroes and idols leave a lot to be desired. Examples at all levels are needed from parents, teachers, politicians, anyone who can lead another – and that is, in fact, all of us.[2]

225.

As Bharata was prostrating himself before Rama and pleading for his return, the charming prince [Rama] still decided not to go back, for the mind of mighty and great Rama was well set to obey the command of his father. The people [of Ayodhya], having seen this unparalleled firmness of mind, were both delighted and sad. They were sad because he would not return to Ayodhya, but glad to observe his firmness to keep his promise [made to his father].

The priests, expert in Vedic lore, and the mothers, overwhelmed with grief and tears, praised both Rama as well as Bharata, who was repeatedly asking Rama to return.

Ramayana I.77.26 & 29

1. Panch.
2. Char./Das.

Rama's younger brother, Bharata, had been appointed heir to the kingdom of Ayodhya because of a promise their father was forced to make by Bharata's mother. As an ideal son Rama did not challenge his father's promise but went into the forest. Bharata, showing the character of an ideal brother, went into the forest to bring Rama back. Rama, of course, would not budge an inch from the promise he had made to his departed father and thereby showed that keeping a promise is equivalent to keeping the Truth of dharma intact – this is one of the ideal moral virtues.

Bharata did not lack sincerity, neither did Rama. The people of Ayodhya were both delighted and sad. It is a perfect example of a situation of moral conflict where one duty takes precedence over another, although the agent feels pain and regret for being unable to do both (for both were morally recommended). It is a pity that, in an actual situation, one cannot perform one duty without neglecting another.[1]

1. Mat.

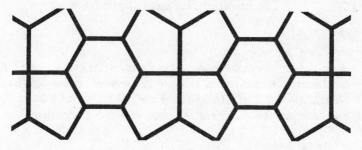

16   Varnashrama Dharma – Social Law

Varna – Caste

226.

*When they [the gods] divided the Purusha, into how many parts
did they arrange him? What was his mouth? What his two arms?
What are his thighs and feet called?*

*The brahmin [priest] was his mouth, his two arms were made
the kshatriya [warrior-king], his two thighs the vaisya
[trader/farmer] and his feet the sudra [labourer].*

Rig Veda X.90.11–12

The Purusha, the Immortal Being who is One and Infinite, gives
Itself to be divided by the forces of material nature – the gods –
into the pluralistic world.

The four divisions of society are described symbolically as the
very limbs of the divided Purusha which, although divided,
remain an integrated whole.

These four divisions are the broad categories of human ability
and activity which are all essential for a whole and healthy
society. Each is dependent on the others and depended upon by
the others for survival as are the various parts of the body. No one
is fit for everything. To be a politician requires a certain quality.
To be a teacher another and to be a coalminer another. People are
happy and suited to performing different duties. All should do
their duty according to their nature for the collective welfare, and
in the process build up their inner spiritual life.[1]

1. Bhav.

227.

*According to the three models of material nature [gunas] and the
work associated with them, the four divisions of human society are
created by Me. And although I am the creator of this system, you
should know that I am yet the non-doer, being unchangeable.*

Bhagavad Gita 4.13

There are four divisions of human society – intellectuals;
administrators and fighters; traders and farmers; and workers.
This applies to all societies. All have their thinkers who are more
concerned with the higher Truth and who are more detached
from material existence. Then there are those who are concerned
with running and protecting the society. Next are those who are
not very powerful but are involved in material activity and
catering to the material demands of the society. Finally, there are
those who are not inclined to act independently but will abide by
other instructions. In Sanskrit they have been termed as
brahmin, kshatriyas, vaisyas, and sudras.

According to the predominant tendency (guna) in their nature
which arises from their past actions (karma), people fit into these
four classes. Those who are mainly in the mode of goodness
(sattwa) are in the philosophical, spiritual class. Those within
whom the mode of passion (rajas) predominates are warrior-
kings. They want to enjoy nature so, therefore, they are also
inclined to protect it.

The traders and farmers have a balance of passion (rajas) and
ignorance (tamas). They want to enjoy material existence
because of their passion but lack direction because of their
ignorance. This makes them less powerful than the warrior-
kings, who are able to attain what they want on the material plane
through wider vision and discipline.

Those who are in the mode of ignorance (tamas) work under
the guidance of others because they are not inclined to think for
themselves or take responsibility.[1]

---

1. Char./Das.

228.

The humble sages, by virtue of true knowledge, see with equal vision a learned and gentle brahmin, a cow, an elephant, a dog and a dog-eater [outcast].

Bhagavad Gita 5.18

The brahmin (priest) is situated in the most elevated position in Hindu society, above the king. The cow as a symbol of sacrifice is the most sacred of all animals. The elephant is a symbol of material wealth and success and the dog is the lowest of animals, representing ignorance. Those who were dog-eaters were classed as outcasts because of their disregard for the accepted standards of Vedic society. But a person situated in true knowledge is not swept along by the delusions of the material world. He sees the Divine spark in all things.[1]

229.

This is the gist of all worship – to be pure and to do good to others. He who has served and helped one poor man, seeing Shiva in him, without thinking of his caste or creed or race, or anything – with him Shiva is more pleased than with the man who sees Him only in temples.

Swami Vivekananda

The caste system places highest value on the brahmin (preacher/teacher), followed by the kshatriya (warrior), then the vaisya (trader/farmer) and finally the sudra (labourer). But if we accept that every human being is divine by nature, having the spark of Brahman (the Supreme Soul) within them, then we have to accept that all human beings are equal in spirit. How can a sudra (labourer) be condemned as being lower than the other three castes? Diversity in occupation should not demean the intrinsic equality of humanity.[2]

1. Char./Das.
2. Choud.

230.

What good is it if we acknowledge in our prayers that God is the
Father of us all and in our daily lives do not treat every man as our
brother?

                                                    Swami Vivekananda

The Untouchable (which, in fact, is a wrong translation from the
Hindi word for 'fifth') is a historical aberration from the proper
organization of a society. It is a common failing throughout the
world where a group of people become marginalized, such as the
North American Indians, the New Zealand Maoris, the
Australian Aborigines and so on. In India, this is being slowly
corrected through education and social integration into the
society.[1]

231.

... Of all warriors, I am Rama...

                                                    Bhagavad Gita 10.31

Rama is the great hero of the Ramayana epic (see pp. 75–80). He
represents the ideal personality whom all Hindus try to emulate.
He was a kshatriya (warrior-king) but this does not mean we
must all be warriors to be perfect people. What made Rama
perfect was not his caste but how he performed his duty as a
member of that caste. It's not what you do but how you do it. As
the ideal warrior Rama always protected dharma. He only killed
for righteousness and the benefit of all. He was not only an ideal
warrior but an ideal man because he performed all his duties as
husband, son, brother, friend, king, citizen and so on, to
perfection.

1. Bhav.

232.

O Bounteous Ones, we surely establish now our brotherhood with equality in the mother's womb.

Rig Veda VIII.83.8

There is a law laid on each one of you in this land by your ancestors, whether you are Aryans or non-Aryans, rishis [sages] or brahmins [priests], or the very lowest outcasts. The command is the same to you all, that you must make progress without stopping and that, from the highest man to the lowest pariah, every one in this country has to try to become the ideal brahmin.

Swami Vivekananda

The highest spiritual life is open to all classes of people. The only thing preventing a person from being God-realized is him- or herself. You cannot be a brahmin through family name or wealth or career. It is the highest stage of spiritual development for a human being. It is to India's credit that it put spiritual, rather than material, conquerors at the top of its social hierarchy. It is to India's discredit that it then cursed itself by making this system hereditary. Anyone can become a brahmin through rooting themselves in the Supreme Truth.

Ashramas – Stages of Life

233.

The youth should be of good character, learned, ambitious, full of self-confidence and strong. The earth will be full of prosperity for one who possesses such qualities.

Taittiryopanishad II.8.1

Affluent societies are facing problems of despair, restlessness and crime among their youth. Lack of character, permissiveness and a doctrine of maximum profit for minimum effort are at the root of these evils. Worldly pleasures can never provide total satisfaction. They are simply petrol feeding the fire of dissatisfaction and restlessness. Self-realization in these circumstances becomes impossible.

Ancient Indian culture placed strength of character above all other human achievement. Youth has a tremendous amount of energy, vigour, dynamism and enthusiasm. The swift flow of a river looks devastating. If a dam is built, however, the flow is harnessed to produce beneficial energy. Similarly, if young people's energy is properly channelled for constructive work, a great deal of good can flow. If they are taught moral conduct they will help others. If they study well they will be full of ambitions – nothing will be impossible for them, life will not be a problem. They will eagerly seek bigger challenges in life. They will be motivated to finish the work they take on. They will be the vanguard of peace and spirituality in the world.[1]

234.

Having taught the Veda [knowledge], the teacher instructs the pupil. Speak the truth always. Perform your dharma [obligatory duties]...

Taittiriyopanishad I.11.1

This is the beginning of the advice given thousands of years ago to brahmacharis (students) on completing their studies with the great rishis (sages) in the Himalayas. The advice stands today as the blueprint of Indian morality. It continues to be given to the young when they are about to enter the world for the second stage of life.

A Hindu's lifetime from initiation to death is divided into four stages or ashramas:

The first is a period of continence, austerity and intense instruction known as brahmacharya.

The second is the stage known as the householder or grihastya, in which, within marriage, there is the pursuit of pleasure and wealth, but also of virtue and liberation from rebirths.

After this comes the vanaprasthya or life of retirement. Here

1. Panch.

the householder gives over all family responsibilities to his now grown-up children and retires to a secluded place (such as a forest) where he can worship and meditate in peace and quiet.

The final stage, known as sannyasa or renunciation, calls for meditation, living on alms and the observance of purity, good conduct and control of the senses.

The teacher's advice to the brahmachari is, essentially, to be true to the self in word and deed. In so doing, he will unveil his Eternal Self, which is the duty behind all duties, the law behind all laws, the dharma behind all dharmas.[1]

235.

> ... *Let there be no neglect of the scriptures. Give the teacher his due. Take care that the line of your family is not broken. Do not neglect truth. Do not neglect what is proper [dharma]. Do not neglect welfare. Do not neglect prosperity. Do not neglect study and teaching of the Vedas. Do not neglect worship of the gods and spirits of the ancestors.*
>
> Taittiryopanishad I.11.1

This verse sets out some of the instructions passed down by a teacher to his young student after initiation (see also pp. 182–5). The emphasis is on good work and conduct as a discipline to ennoble actions and personality, so that illumination ultimately may be obtained. Asceticism is for those who have chosen a monastic life or for the later stages of secular life. The householder is therefore expected to marry, have children, acquire wealth and enjoy life, although always through actions which remain moral and ethical. It is thus a legitimate goal of householders to seek prosperity, but without transgressing the rules of righteous conduct and action.

Study and teaching of the scriptures help understanding and assimilation of the text, and develop powers of thought and memory which will be of value in maturity and old age. Sharing

1. Chand.

knowledge is a responsibility of all to their society. The Truth will glow more clearly within them and in their society.

The worship of God and ancestors is a reference to the five prescribed daily devotions: prayers to God; to ancient saints and teachers; to the spirits of ancestors; and service to one's fellow men, the poor and the afflicted; and care of the environment including animals, plants, places and things.[1]

236.

... Let your mother be a god to you. Let your father be a god to you. Let your teacher be a god to you. Let your guest be a god to you ...

Taittiryopanishad I.11.2

These three lines are a cornerstone of Indian culture.

Hindu families are traditionally closely knit and this is partly due to the feelings children have for their parents. Children, by nature, love their parents, but Hindus ask for more – respect and reverence for the presence of God in parents which impells them to extraordinary sacrifices on behalf of their children.

Teachers of moral precepts are also specially revered, as the spirit of God is considered to be specially strong and active in such good men.

Guests, by custom, must be accorded every hospitality and reverence is prescribed. Stories abound in the scriptures about saints, sages, kings, manifestations of God even, appearing incognito as uninvited guests at the dwelling of householders. Welcoming rituals may include washing the feet of the guest, garlanding him and providing the best available in food and drink.[2]

1. Chand.
2. Chand.

237.

*... Perform deeds which are above reproach, not others. Respect
the deeds of ours that have been well done, not others.*

*Whatever brahmins there are superior to us, they should be
comforted by you with a seat.*

*Give with faith, not without faith. Give in plenty, with
modesty, with reverence, with sympathy.*

*Then, if you are in any doubt regarding conduct, you should
behave as the brahmins – who are competent to judge, not led by
others, not harsh, lovers of virtue [dharma] – would behave in
such cases.*

*Then, as to the persons who are spoken against, you should
behave as the brahmins – who are competent to judge, not led by
others, not harsh, lovers of virtue – would behave in regard to such
persons.*

*This is the command. This is the teaching. This is the secret
doctrine of the Veda. This is the instruction. Thus should one
worship. Thus indeed should one worship.*

                                        Taittiryopanishad I.11.2–3

This completes the advice of the teacher to the brahmachari
(student) as he prepares to re-enter the world (see pp. 182–5).

Respect for dharma – righteousness – is the key to living a life
of worship. This begins with deference to one's betters – those
who are spiritually and morally advanced. Such people are
brahmins. They are to be role models and advisers.

The respect shown to brahmins should be shown by youth to
their elders who have studied longer under the great teacher,
Life. The ability to be silent and listen when their elders and
betters are speaking is the ancient art of youth too often
disregarded in the modern world.[1]

1. Bhav.

238.

The father protects the woman in childhood, the husband protects her in youth, the children protect her in old age, a woman should never be independent.

                                                  Manusmriti 9.3

In Hinduism a woman is looked after not because she is inferior or incapable but, on the contrary, because she is treasured. She is the pride and power of society. Just as the crown jewels should not be left unguarded, neither should a woman be left unprotected. No extra burden of earning a living should be placed on women who already bear huge responsibilities in society: childbirth, child care, domestic wellbeing and spiritual growth. She is the transmitter of culture to her children.

Marriage and family life have always been an integral part of spiritual growth, not a means of self-gratification. It is the second stage in the four stages of life leading to perfection, following that of the celibate student and preceding retirement and full renunciation. Therefore, the romantic view of marriage is not accepted. The couple are spiritual partners, each supplementing the other as they proceed towards the ultimate goal (see pp. 98–115). Marriage is lived in a spirit of discipline, duty and service.[1]

239.

The God [Agni] is the wife at home, hastening to help all.

                                                  Rig Veda I.66.5

Lord Agni is the god of sacrifice. Wives and mothers are the divine embodiment of sacrifice. This is why women in Indian homes do not eat until they have fed everyone else. She feeds all even if it means sacrificing her own portion to a guest who turns up at the last minute. In some houses it is the custom for the mother to go outside before she eats and see if anyone is sitting

1. Panch.

hungry in the street. Treating others as gods, she must herself be recognized as god.[1]

240.

He is not a friend who does not give to a friend, a fellow being, who comes pleading for food. Let him leave such a man – his is not a home . . .
Let the wealthy man satisfy him who seeks help, looking upon a longer pathway. Wealth revolves like the wheels of a chariot, coming now to one, now to another. In vain does the foolish man acquire food. It is – truly – the death of him who does not cherish a fellow being or friend. He is a sinner who feeds only himself.

Rig Veda X.117.4–6

It is fundamental to Indian homes that what you have you share with relatives and guests, giving to them before yourself. You may have a lot or a little, the relative may be a parent or a distant cousin, the guests may be invited or uninvited, but you share.

The householding stage in life is particularly important for paying our debts to family and society for supporting us in the first twenty-five years of life as a brahmachari (student). In this second stage, we are in a position to support others as we ourselves have been supported and will be supported again in old age.[2]

241.

Gifts must be made with sincerity, never unwillingly. Gifts should be related to possessions. A gift should be given without ostentation and with diffidence. A gift must take an approved form.

Taittiryopanishad I.11.23–28

Giving is an essential feature of Hinduism, but the manner in

1. Bhav.
2. Bhav.

which the gift is made is important. The idea of giving is bound up with hospitality, with ceremonies and with duty.

At religious ceremonies consecrated sweet foods are given to devotees as well as an ensuing meal of savoury dishes, prepared in prescribed traditional ways. At weddings there is a special ceremony around the bestowing of a daughter in marriage and around the offerings of dowry to give the couple a good start in life. Members of a caste of beggars regard it as their duty, no matter how wealthy they may be, to put on simple clothes and go begging for alms at least once a week. Gifts to such a mendicant, when given in the right way, not only help the receiver to work off some portion of his load of karma (see p. 52), but also yield virtue to the giver. In the final stages of life for a Hindu there is increasing dependence upon gifts of food and basic necessities which must be made in the proper prescribed manner.

A gift not only benefits the receiver, but the gain for the giver must only be spiritual, not material, and unintended and unsolicited. Gifts must be made in humility and in an atmosphere of harmony but also with detachment. Expectation of a return of worldly favours, such as recognition by the community or honours from the State, is forbidden. The need for organized charitable institutions is small in Hindu societies since every householder is duty-bound to give to the needy in proportion to the wealth possessed.[1]

242.

Divinely inspired, the wandering sage is at home in both eastern and western oceans. Treading the path of the apsaras and the gandharvas [heavenly dancers and singers] and of the wild animals, the long-haired man comes as a dear friend, bringing joy.

Rig Veda X.136.4–6

The fourth stage of spiritual life is as a sannyasin (man of renunciation). Having withdrawn from life in the vanaprasthya (retirement) stage, such a person has gone on to total

1. Chand.

renunciation. These men are revered in India as gods, for renunciation is the stamp of Divinity, just as possessiveness is the stamp of material bondage.

The eastern and western ocean symbolize the light and dark forces of life, as do the heavenly entertainers and the wild animals. Being one with God, the wandering sage is content and unruffled in all situations. He brings with him the joy of Eternal Bliss.[1]

243.

Truly those who take to the forest, dwelling in penitence and faith, free from passion, devout and living on alms, they indeed become cleansed of sin and depart by the portal of the sun to Him who is imperishable and immortal.

Mundakopanishad I.2.11

Full renunciation of the world is the fourth stage of life (ashrama). If this state of mind is reached – the physical situation is only a means – the final release will be achieved. The 'portal of the sun' leads souls to higher abodes after death. Unlike lower abodes (such as the portal of the moon) which lead to rebirths, the higher abodes involve no return of souls to earthly existence. Nevertheless, the ultimate fusion of the individual soul with God, the Universal Soul, requires time in the lower abodes – the heavens – for the gradual eradication of ignorance and realization of the true nature and essence of God.[2]

244.

I tell you the truth: there is nothing wrong in your being in the world. But you must direct your mind towards God, otherwise you will not succeed. Do your duty with one hand and with the other

1. Bhav.
2. Chand.

hold to God. *After the duty is over, you will hold to God with both hands.*

Sri Ramakrishna

17 Narinam – Women

SARASWATI
(From Moor's *Hindu Pantheon*)

245.

Ahalya, Draupadi, Sita, Tara and Mandodari – these five
should be remembered daily. Remembering them will destroy all
sins.

Daily mantra

This verse, which informs the mind of Hindu girls from an early
age, lists five great heroines who should be their models in life.

Who were they? There is no saint among them and, but for
Sita, no goddess. They were devoted wives and mothers who
sought, with single-minded devotion, the grace of the Lord
which all received. Therefore all had lives which were full of
meaning.

Ahalya had transgressed in her loyalty to her husband but,
through tremendous love for Lord Rama, an incarnation of the
god Vishnu, was redeemed. Rama turned her back from stone to
human flesh.

Draupadi, the wife of the five Pandavas, was insulted and
humiliated by their opponents, the Kauravas, before the great
battle of the Mahabharata epic. She was dragged by her hair to a
crowded hall and an attempt was made publicly to strip her.
Draupadi prayed to Lord Krishna and as her humiliator,
Dushasana, pulled her sari away, another one appeared.
Dushasana kept on pulling away the saris and another kept
appearing until there was a pile of 1000 saris and Dushasana was
exhausted and defeated.

In the Ramayana epic (see pp. 75–80) Sita went through the
furnace of fiery trials after her husband Lord Rama banished her
for infidelity of which she was not guilty. Yet she entertained no
ill feelings for Rama. On the contrary, she said, 'O Rama, may
you be my husband birth after birth.'

Tara and Mandodari were both wives of Lord Rama's enemies
in the Ramayana. Tara was married to the monkey Vali (see p.
78) and Mandodari to the rakshasa (demon) king Ravana. Both
women were loyal and loving to their husbands at the same time
as trying to dissuade them from the evil path they had taken.

All these women showed great devotional love to God in his

human forms of Krishna or Rama, acting only according to his wishes.[1]

246.

She is given as a collaborator in the performance of duties which a householder ought to perform. She is to inspire and stimulate and she is to lead you on in the path of dharma (the Eternal Law).

Marriage vows

These words are recited by a father when he gives away his daughter in marriage. The various creation stories of the scriptures tell us that a wife and husband are equal parts of the One Being.

A wife's relation to her husband is that which Saraswati, the goddess of knowledge, has towards Brahma, the god of Creation; that Lakshmi, the goddess of fortune, has toward Vishnu, the god of sustenance; and that Parvati, the goddess of this mortal world, occupies towards Shiva, the god of destruction. In each case, the partners are inextricably linked. They are each other's prerequisite.[2]

247.

My dear Krishna, your lordship has protected us from the poisoned cake, from a great fire, from cannibals, from the vicious assembly, from sufferings during our exile in the forest and from the battle where great generals fought... I wish that all those calamities would happen again and again so that we could see you again and again, for seeing you means that we will no longer see repeated births and deaths.

Bhagavatam I.8.24–25

1. Panch.
2. Panch.

In this prayer Kunti, the mother of the Pandavas, is asking for more suffering. She did not beg for removal of her pain like an ordinary person. She felt that her suffering increased her devotion to the Lord.

Furthermore, Kunti is considered a sati (revered woman) even though she was an unmarried mother. Draupadi, the wife of the Pandavas, is also considered a sati despite having five husbands. There is no orthodoxy in Hinduism. These women are given the highest place in Hindu religion because of their knowledge, ability, virtue and strong character.

The notion of a sati as a woman who dies in the funeral pyre of her husband comes from the time of the Muslim rule which preceded British rule in India and lasted for 650 years (from the eleventh to the mid-eighteenth century). During this period purdah was introduced in North India, followed by a general decline in attitudes to women. Nevertheless, women remained strong. Many heroic women not only fought against the invaders but, when defeated, immolated themselves on burning fires in order to save their honour from the lust of their enemies. If they could not live with honour, they died with honour. This custom, which became an expedient means of dealing with widows who had no one to care for them and caused terrible hardship for Indian women, fortunately is no longer practised. Through the hardships they suffered every time the social and economic fabric was disrupted Hindu women have emerged like the lotus out of the mire.[1]

248.

Go to the house as the mistress of the household. A ruler of the house, you [the bride] will address the vidhatha [religious assembly].

Rig Veda X.85.26

1. Panch.

No religious activity in Hinduism takes place without the presence of a wife. When Lord Rama was performing a yagna (sacrifice) while Sita was in the jungle, he made a golden statue to represent her.

In Vedic times (2500–500 BCE), the highest education was open to men and women and Vedic sacrifices were offered jointly by both sexes. The upanayan ceremony, an initiation ceremony which marks a child's spiritual rebirth, was given to both boys and girls. When this equality was lost in the following era, women continued to practise spiritual life through bhaktivad (devotion to a personal god), fasting, worshipping, chanting hymns and reading the scriptures. No matter what society has imposed upon them, Hindu women have always been bastions of spiritual life.[1]

249.

Where women are worshipped there the gods love to dwell.
Manusmriti 3.56

In ancient times in India, women were worshipped as the harbingers of material and spiritual prosperity. Where the gods dwell there is harmony and happiness. In modern India, this understanding continues. When a man regards his wife only as an object of physical satisfaction, disaster befalls the family. Without the gods, all work and religious practice is fruitless.

Woman is the goddess of fortune, Lakshmi, and the goddess of knowledge, Saraswati. She is also Durga, the goddess of destruction. Even this terrible face of the goddess is worshipped because it is only through destruction that there can be new life and evolution of the soul.[2]

1. Panch.
2. Panch.

250.

The shining harbinger of youthful vigour has appeared. The brilliant one has opened the doors. Rousing the world she has shown us riches. The Dawn has awakened all living things.

Generous Dawn sends off the sleepers, one to enjoyment, one to wealth, another to worship, that those who see little may see widely, the Dawn has awakened all living things.

One to win power, one to [spiritual] glory, one to his profit and another his labour, all see their different occupations, the Dawn has awakened all living things.

Rig Veda I.113.4–6

The Vedas are full of hymns and praises to feminine power, as in these beautiful verses from a hymn to Dawn, wife of the Sun. Hindu women give and do not demand. Like Dawn, a wife and mother lights the way so that her family may see and pursue its own nature, achieving success in whichever of the four occupations – spiritual life, leadership, business or labour – they choose. The mother is the first contact all children have to help them awaken to their true Self. 'She is the first of the endless Dawns to come' (I.113.8).

251.

Mira's Lord is Giridhar Nagar. I have found a perfect bridegroom.

Poems of Mirabai

Mirabai, a sixteenth-century princess, is the most famous woman poet-saint of Hinduism (see also p. 231). In her married life she suffered much injustice and many attempts were made to kill her. Widowed young, she suffered many obstacles from her in-laws to her devotion to Lord Krishna, yet she remained a steadfast devotee of God. Her early poems are about the pain of separation from the Lord. Later on she sang of joy and union with Lord Krishna. When she died she merged with an image of Lord Krishna.

Hindu women obey a man if he is honourable, but by no means are they meek or docile when challenged by injustice or wickedness. They have played a significant and vital role in building and preserving Indian culture. They have maintained the sweetness of Indian homes and a beneficial influence upon men. But Hindu women have also served as queens, teachers, administrators, philosophers, mystics, scholars and poets. In these positions of responsibility they have exhibited calmness, patience, dignity – indeed, all the virtues associated with family life.

While most of the gods are portrayed with moral lapses, the goddesses are endowed with remarkable personalities, full of grace and dignity, resplendent with the fullness of life. The goddesses seem to have blessed Hindu women with this richness of character.[1]

252.

Why, to the women of this country I would say exactly what I say to the men. Believe in India and in our Indian faith. Be strong and hopeful and unashamed, and remember that, with something to take, Hindus have immeasurably more to give than any other people in the world.

Swami Vivekananda

The Vedas are full of praises to the feminine principle in the world. The status of women has fluctuated with the tide of economic and political conditions in India. Successive foreign rulers have brought her great suffering through war and imposed social values which corroded the high esteem and freedom afforded women in the Vedic period. Nevertheless, the scriptures have continued to be filled with women of distinction who were neither saints nor virgins but housewives. They displayed a courage and serenity in the midst of worldly hardship which has been the inspiration of millions of Hindu women.

It may be asked why Hindu women suffer today in the eyes of

1. Panch.

the world. It is not lack of achievement on the women's part but the world's ignorance of their achievements.[1]

1. Panch.

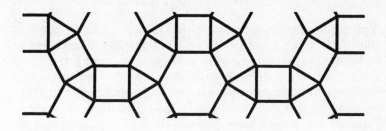

18   Yoga – The Spiritual Paths

253.

There are as many paths to God as there are faiths.

Sri Ramakrishna

Hindus never claim that they are the 'chosen people'. They lay no claim to superiority over other faiths but declare equality among all faiths. If we believe that every one of us can realize God in our own way then we also have to accept that our way to God cannot be the 'only' way or the 'best' way. Every individual has his or her own way to God and that is the right way for them. Moreover, it is not right to force our beliefs on another. This perspective of tolerance helps overcome sectarianism. In a Hindu festival honouring a particular deity, it is common to find various sects – Vaishnavas (devotees of Vishnu), Shaivas (devotees of Shiva), Shaktas (devotees of Kali), etc., all worshipping together.[1]

254.

Never quarrel about religion. All quarrels and disputes concerning religion simply show that spirituality is not present. Religious quarrels are always over the husks. When purity, when spirituality goes, leaving the soul dry, quarrels begin and not before.

Swami Vivekananda

1. Choud.

The major religions in the world tend to make exclusive claims to the whole truth but there is no need for any controversy or feelings of superiority or inferiority. We can't grasp the whole truth. Different people grasp different aspects. There is no need to impose our own path on others or to fight with them when they do not accept it. Religion is not busying yourself with others' business but, rather, attending to your own. All seek peace yet forsake that very goal because others do not share their approach.

Life is a pilgrimage to perfection. All forms of religion and systems of thought can be used for improving our own spiritual personality. Progress in spiritual life depends upon a healthy and positive response to a steady life. The different religions are but different paths appropriate to a particular time and place, trying to teach us the higher reality. Step by step people travel from the truth that is lower to the truth that is higher. We discover harmony, synthesis and unity. When we reach the highest we realize that, for all his different names, God is one.[1]

255.

Each soul is potentially divine. The goal is to manifest this divinity within by controlling nature, external and internal. Do this either by work or worship or psychic control or philosophy – by one or more or all of these – and be free. This is the whole of religion.

Swami Vivekananda

To a Hindu 'religion', 'spirituality' and 'philosophy' are one and the same. All end in Self-realization – realization of the Self's unity with the Supreme Soul, Brahman.

Because we each identify with our physical self, the oneness among all souls is difficult to realize, but it is not impossible. This realization comes through constant contemplation, meditation and control of desires. Gradually, we develop a sense which reaches beyond external forms and is able to comprehend the oneness behind it.

1. Bhav.

Despite Western misconceptions Hindu religion does not simply mean ritual. Nevertheless, rituals are not to be underestimated and abandoned altogether. They have their merits on a different level. They serve as the first steps for disciplining the mind and redirecting it away from material thoughts. Moreover, people of emotional nature do not care for abstract definitions of Brahman. To them God has to be tangible and real. The path of ritual suits their temperament and is right for them.

No matter which path we follow, whichever faith or sect, as long as it leads to realization it is the right path for us.[1]

256.

[Arjuna said:] O Janardana [protector of people], Keshava [demon-killer], if you think knowledge is superior to action why are you asking me to plunge into this terrible action?

You confuse me with these equivocal words. Tell me one word for certain by which I may attain perfection.

The Blessed Lord said: O flawless one, as I said before, in this world there are two paths. There is the path of knowledge for the intellectuals and the path of action for the active people.

Bhagavad Gita 3.1–3

In the previous verses Krishna has explained the value of detaching oneself from the world of the senses and looking inwards for knowledge, but he also told Arjuna he should go out and fight on the battlefield. This has confused Arjuna. He is a soldier, a man of action. He is used to unequivocal commands so he wants an unequivocal command from Krishna.

With love and patience Krishna reiterates what he has said before. There is no single mode of behaviour which is right because people are not all the same. Their spiritual illness takes different forms. You cannot administer one medicine for all ills.

Broadly speaking, human beings can be divided into two classes: introverted, philosophical personalities and extraverted,

1. Choud.

active personalities. These personalities arise through vasanas (unmanifest desires) which are the accumulated reaction to all past actions. The fewer vasanas they have the less active they *need* to be. This doesn't mean they *are* inactive, only that they are not driven into action by desire (see p. 52).

In effect, the two types of personality are a matter of degree. There is a continuum from total introversion to total extraversion. The path to the Supreme Reality must be from each person's starting point. Therefore, there can be no single correct route.[1]

257.

O best of bulls [Arjuna], there are four kinds of pious people who worship me – the distressed, the seeker of knowledge, the seeker of wealth, the wise.

Of them, the wise person who is ever united with me in single-pointed devotion is the one to whom I am supremely dear as he is dear to me.

Bhagavad Gita 7.16–17

The first kind of spiritual seeker is the person who is after *emotional* solace. He is catering to his mind. These people are swept away in religious ecstasies.

The second kind of spiritual seeker is the person seeking *intellectual* pleasure. These people will devour the scriptures, ask many questions, but will have no time to sit and reflect.

The third kind of seeker is after *physical* benefit. These people go to the temple to pray, make offerings and then put in a request. This sort of person makes God a business partner.

The fourth seeker is the wise who seeks the Atman through all paths – body, mind and intellect – but these do not become ends in themselves. The fourth plane of Consciousness is always his goal, always his thought. Of the seekers, only he will become one with the Eternal Self.

(Krishna addresses Arjuna as the best of bulls because, in

1. Parth.

Hindu society, the bull is symbolic of sacrifice and service. It puts in maximum effort for minimum profit to itself.)[1]

258.

Brahma, the grandfather, said to him, 'Know it by the joining of faith, devotion and meditation. Not by action, not by birth or wealth, but by renunciation.'

Kaivalyopanishad 2

The student has asked Brahma (god of Creation) how to rejoin the Eternal Self, Brahman, and is told to practise sraddha-bhakti-dhyana-yoga. This can be roughly translated as 'faith-devotion-meditation-joining'. It is essential to understand these concepts.

Sraddha is, according to the great sage Sankara (see pp. xxxiii–xxxiv), the capacity to reflect, to understand, to assimilate and make things one's own. Faith is not blind. The poet Tagore described faith as 'the bird that feels the light and sings while the dawn is still dark'. The bird knows the sun even before it sees it – the dawn always comes.

Bhakti, or devotion, is the highest form of love. It is the love of student for teacher, the seeker for the Truth.

Dhyana, or meditation, is complete concentration on any action without being distracted by thoughts of what has been, what might have been and what might be. Brahman fills every moment of time if the mind is only still enough to realize it. This tranquillity through all action, not action per se, is what will rejoin us with the Ultimate Self.

Most of us are trained to act out rituals as a means to spiritual elevation. But, by mechanically reading the Gita, Bible or Qur'an, we only maintain, rather than elevate, ourselves. While action is essential to existence, the key is not to get involved in it, i.e., to remain unconcerned with the fruits of action.

Birth, referring, in this context, to social class with its trappings of education and wealth, will be of no use. Only renunciation of infatuation with the material world – its

1. Parth.

sensations, feelings and ideas – will free us to return to the Brahman.[1]

259.

The foundation of the Truth is self-restraint and dedicated work. The Vedas are all its limbs. Truth is its abode.

Kenopanishad 4.7

In their search for stimulation the ever-restless senses drag the mind and intellect away from the spiritual path. So the first injunction here is to practise self-control. Self-control is not self-denial. The person who abstains from all pleasures of the flesh because he or she fears them is no better off than the person who indulges wantonly in them. Sense objects must not be feared as a slave fears the master. Sovereignty must be shifted from objects to the intellect. But it's no good simply denying your body sensual pleasures as your mind returns again and again to the object in sheer frustration. That is still slavery. We need to be able to enjoy the world of the senses and yet remain detached from it.

The second injunction is to perform dedicated service. This means action (karma) for the higher ideal, not for personal gain. It is the attitude, not the action itself, which marks it as dedicated service. Physically, emotionally and intellectually we should give to others.

Unless a spiritual seeker observes these two principles: self-control and self-sacrifice, his or her search is a waste of time.

Having established ourselves in the attitude of giving to, rather than taking from, the world, knowledge (Vedas) is the means by which we move forward. In this context knowledge refers not only to the Vedic scriptures but to all aspects of knowledge – chemistry, maths, history, knitting, boat-mending and so on. Each is an expression of Brahman. They are the branches which lead back to the root: Truth.

Brahman is situated in Truth. Until we are consistently true to

1. Parth.

ourselves and, therefore, true to the world, we can never reach Divinity.[1]

260.

Who acts for me, who keeps me as the goal, devoted to me, free from attachment, without enmity to any creature, he will reach me, O Pandava [Arjuna].

Bhagavad Gita 11.55

Realizing the Self is seeing It clearly reflected in the personality we have now. It is the vasanas (unmanifest desires) which prevent us so doing. The great sage Rama Tirtha explained them as being like the algae on a lake. There are two ways of seeing our own image. We can push the algae aside but it is so thick it moves back across in no time. We only get a glimpse of our own reflection. It passes away. This is what usually happens in the spiritual field. This is what happened to Arjuna, he caught a fleeting glimpse.

The other method is to take a little of the algae from the lake and put it on the shore. Then keep on gathering it. You don't see the reflection immediately because the algae always moves back again, but every time you take another handful you are making the mantle thinner and thinner. If you keep on doing it a time comes when you take a handful, making it so thin it separates by itself. Then you get a perfect, permanent view of your own self.

What is that removing? It is the three disciplines given in this verse: karma-yoga, bhakti-yoga and jnana-yoga. Physically, we act for the higher Self; emotionally, we are filled with love for that higher Self; intellectually, we peg our concentration on that higher Self.

Freedom from attachment and hatred, the positive and negative aspects of desire, is the yardstick of progress. How free from likes are you? How free from dislikes are you? If you do not discard likes and dislikes, you are not developing on the spiritual path.[2]

1. Parth.
2. Parth.

261.

[Krishna said:] Not by study of the Vedas, nor by yagna
[sacrifice], nor by charity, nor by rituals, nor by austerities can I
be seen in such a form in the world of men by any other than you, O
great hero of the Kurus.

Bhagavad Gita 11.48

The mind has a tendency to become attached to whatever it does. Religious people are attached to religious objects, just as worldly people are attached to worldly objects. Having taken up a spiritual stance we become attached to the enchanting aspects of spiritual life which are far more enchanting than those of the world. We get stuck with the temples, gurus, deities, even the very thoughts and ideas, instead of unfolding the Self. We stay put with the means, never reaching the end.

At the last, we must let go of yogas as the pole-vaulter lets go of the pole that takes him right up to the bar he wants to cross. Without that pole he couldn't reach those heights. But if he hangs on to it, he won't clear the bar.

Krishna is talking to Arjuna while Arjuna is in a state of realization. In this state of unity with the Eternal Self, 'me and you' are one and the same. So when Krishna says 'nor . . . can *I* be seen . . . in the world of men by any other than *you*', he means 'you', the Eternal Self, and 'I', the Eternal Self. Only the Self and the Self alone can take us to realization.[1]

262.

If you are unable to fix your mind steadily on Me, then seek to
reach Me by devotional service, O Dhananjaya.

If you are unable to practise the regulations of devotional
service, be intent on acting for My sake; even by performing
actions for My sake you shall attain perfection.

If you are unable to do even this, then try taking refuge in union

1. Parth.

with Me, self-controlled, renounce the fruits of all actions.
                                                    Bhagavad Gita 12.9–11

The capacities and abilities of human beings vary and yet unvaried Divinity (Atman) is innate in all of us. Like electricity it is endless and unchanging but it manifests differently. The low-wattage bedroom light is dull in comparison to the bright living-room light and that is dull in comparison to the brilliance of football-field floodlights. Yet in the case of all three it is the same electricity – neither weaker nor stronger nor in any way differentiated – which sheds that light. The Atman in us is like that electricity. We are all different because our equipment is different as the lighting equipment is different. But we are not our body, mind and intellect any more than electricity is that low-wattage bulb. The bulb is merely the equipment for shedding the light of electricity. The problem is that we have conditioned ourselves to identify with that heterogeneous equipment rather than the homogeneous Atman which is the true Self in each and every one of us.

To return to our true Self, we must follow the path which is most suited to our particular set of equipment. Therefore Krishna advises Arjuna that, if he is unable to concentrate his mind on the Truth which lies beyond it, he should try devotional service. This involves rituals such as songs, prayers and offerings to Krishna. If Arjuna cannot manage this, then he should try acting for 'My sake', in other words, performing actions with the thought always of returning to the True Self. If he cannot manage this, he should try self-control so, at least, he never acts in such a way that he moves further back from his final goal. To do this, he must act without concern for the fruits of his actions.[1]

263.

Those who worship avidya [ignorance of Brahman] enter into blinding darkness. Those who delight in vidya [knowledge of Brahman] enter into greater darkness.
                                                    Isavasyopanishad 9

1. Parth.

Worshippers of avidya are those who are attached to the material world. These people are plunged into darkness because they have turned away from the source of all knowledge, Brahman. So why does this verse tell us that those who delight in vidya, knowledge of this ultimate Truth, are plunged into greater darkness?

To understand we must consider the route to Truth which can be divided, broadly speaking, into three paths: karma-yoga (the path of action); bhakti-yoga (the path of devotion/emotion); jnana-yoga (the path of the intellectual). On your journey to Truth you can use all three – action (body), emotions (mind) and thought (intellect) – in the combination best suited to your personality.

The difficulty begins, however, once a person treads on his or her personal path; the path itself is so enchanting that 99 per cent of travellers get stuck on it. They anchor themselves to the joy of active service, devotional ecstasies or religious studies.

Such people are in greater darkness than those who are simply attached to name, fame, wealth or family because the spiritual paths are so much more enchanting. Therefore the attachment is much stronger. The path becomes the end in itself instead of the means to a higher end.[1]

264.

They say the result reached by vidya [knowledge of Brahman] is totally different from that reached by avidya [ignorance of Brahman]. So we have heard from the great masters who explained It to us.

Isavasyopanishad 10

This verse may simply be saying that those who devote themselves to knowledge reach a totally different goal from those who devote themselves to pursuit of worldly pleasures. The former eventually reach moksha (eternal release), the latter sink deeper into the mire of desire and agitation.

At another level, the verse may be comparing the destination

1. Parth.

of those who use their spiritual path as a means and those for whom it becomes an end in itself. The paths themselves – active service, devotion and intellectual thought – are worldly pursuits. They are part of avidya, so if, instead of leaving the path behind when it has run its course, we keep pacing up and down it, we have opted for avidya. We may be doing great service to humanity in the name of Brahman or spending all our days chanting and singing His praises or studying the scriptures, and we will indeed experience relative happiness in worldly terms. That, however, is a totally different happiness from the bliss of moksha (eternal release from the world). That can only be reached by blending these three paths of action (for they are all forms of action) with contemplation which eventually dissolves all thoughts and desires so that the ultimate Truth, vidya, may be realized.[1]

265.

[*Krishna said:*] *Neither by the Vedas [scriptures], nor by austerities, nor by charity, nor by sacrifice can this form be seen as you have seen.*

Only by single-pointed devotion may men see and know Me in Reality and merge with Me, O mighty-armed one.

Bhagavad Gita 11.53–54

We do not get realization by appointment. What we have to do is aspire to getting onto the path through study, self-control, sacrifice and service. These will be of no help, however, unless we maintain a constant commitment to that supreme goal. If this ultimate knowledge is our goal in all our thoughts and actions it is only a question of time until we reach it.

By dedicated study and reflection we will live a peaceful and meaningful existence, coming ever closer to the Brahman (Supreme Self). Realization may be many lives away but whatever knowledge we achieve of the Self we will take to the

1. Parth.

210   *The Essential Teachings of Hinduism*

next life. The wealth and family to which we are so attached cannot be taken – they are not our achievements.[1]

266.

One who has indomitable faith and controls his senses attains divine knowledge. Having obtained this knowledge he quickly attains the supreme spiritual peace.

Bhagavad Gita 4.39

A disciple may not make rapid progress because of lack of adequate faith in the goal. We must have faith. As Mahatma Gandhi has said, 'Faith is not a delicate flower which would wither under stormy weather. Faith is like the Himalaya mountains which cannot possibly change. No storm can possibly remove the Himalaya mountains from their foundations ... And I want every one of you to cultivate that faith in God and religion.' For the development of spiritual knowledge it is essential to cleanse one's heart of all material dirt and control the senses. The time taken to gain knowledge varies from person to person. One must realize that nothing can be mastered overnight. Through practice and perseverance the apparently impossible can be accomplished.[2]

267.

Let me tell you how powerful faith is. A man was about to cross the sea from Ceylon to India. Vibhishana [the saintly brother of the demon Ravana] said to him, 'Tie this thing in a corner of your wearing-cloth and you will cross the sea safely. You will be able to walk on the water. But be sure not to examine it, or you will sink.' The man was walking easily on the water of the sea – such is the strength of faith – when, having gone part of the way, he thought,

1. Parth.
2. Panch.

'What is this wonderful thing Vibhishana has given me, that I can even walk on water?' He untied the cloth and found nothing but a leaf with the name of Rama written on it. 'Oh, only this!' he thought and immediately sank.

Sri Ramakrishna

19   Karma-Yoga – The Path of Action

268.

All the work you do is done for your own salvation, is done for your own benefit. God has not fallen into a ditch for you and me to help Him out by building a hospital or the like. He allows you to work not in order to help Him but that you may help yourself. Do you think even an ant will die for want of your help? Most arrant blasphemy! The world does not need you at all . . . Cut out the word help from your mind. You cannot help; it is blasphemy. You worship. When you give a morsel of food to a dog, you worship the dog as God. He is all and is in all.

Swami Vivekananda

Selfishness can corrode our inner being. We all have the spiritual qualities of gods and goddesses but we practise them in very small measures. If we can only expand on them through action, worshipping the Divinity in others, then we become Divine ourselves. The collective welfare is an essential dimension to good action. If desire dominates let our desire be for a nobler purpose, the good of humanity. If anger dominates let it be against ourselves for our lapses.[1]

269.

By 'detachment' I mean that you must not worry whether the

1. Bhav.

desired result follows from your action or not, so long as your motive is pure, your means correct. Really, it means that things will come right in the end if you take care of means and leave the rest to Him.

Mahatma Gandhi

Do the job that you have to do but do it without expecting rewards from it. Expectation brings disappointment. Disappointment leads to unhappiness. If we do not crave for rewards we have no reason for frustration. This does not mean that we lose our motivation to work. When we talk of rewards and results we interpret these according to our personal perspective, conditioned by ideas of profit and loss, power and prestige. To get a clearer, more objective perspective we have to step aside from our personal involvement to an impersonal level of detachment. Detachment is not indifference or apathy. It means putting action (karma) into a broader perspective, away from petty gains. Carry out karma for its own sake with single-pointed effort (yoga) and you will be free to enjoy total job satisfaction.[1]

270.

You have a right to perform your prescribed duty, but you are not entitled to the fruits of action. Never consider yourself the cause of the results of your activities, and never be attached to not doing your duty.

Perform your duty equipoised, O Arjuna, abandoning all attachment to success or failure. Such equanimity is called yoga.

Bhagavad Gita 2.47–48

We all are by nature actors. We have to act at every moment – to breathe, we have to act, to eat we have to act – but, unfortunately, our actions are motivated by a desired reaction. Krishna tells us that we should not act in the hope of a favourable outcome. If we do, we only become frustrated when we don't get the result we want. The best way to act is on behalf of the Lord, leaving the

1. Choud.

result to him. Whatever we receive we accept as a mercy of the Lord.

If we want to be at peace with ourselves, the key is to take pleasure in doing our duty, not in getting results in this world. It is enough to know that we are doing our duty, whatever comes or doesn't come.[1]

271.

One should aspire to live 100 years performing actions without desire. There is no other path for you to be free of evil deeds as long as you are involved in your human life.

Isavasyopanishad 1.2

We are not all philosophers. If our nature is to be doers in the world, contemplation cannot play the dominant role. This verse speaks to those who are involved in the hurly-burly of human activity. Such people should aspire to follow their own nature for the full lifespan of 100 years, but in the direction of Self-realization.

Action (karma) driven by desire will not take us in that direction. It is desire which provides the shroud over our own Divinity and whips us into a frenzy of activity which can never be satisfied. Action driven by desire creates desire, creates action and so on, through bigger cars, bigger houses, more of this, more of that.

So we must learn to act without desire. But how does one act if not at the prompting of desire? The first and last step is to consider a higher ideal, a good that is beyond the pleasure-seeking of body, mind and intellect. If the concern is beyond personal gain we will cleanse ourselves of desire. Rather than being the perpetrator and accomplice of desire, action becomes the scourge of desire and, ultimately, the scourge of itself. When the desires are finally washed away, the higher state beyond action can be realized.[2]

1. Char./ Das.
2. Parth.

272.

A person does not gain the state of perfection by abstaining from action to free himself from reaction, nor by mere renunciation.

Bhagavad Gita 3.4

There is a great misunderstanding that the spiritual life is one of inactivity. Too often genuinely committed people declare, 'That's it, no more action, no more business, no more family, I'm off to sit in the forest and find God.' You can retreat to the Himalayas but, as long as you have vasanas (unmanifested desires), you should not be surprised to find yourself organizing trekking tours, feuding with other sannyasis or looking for something to read, having finished the scriptures. Your vasanas will show themselves.

Vasanas are the seed of personality remaining from the fruit of actions in past lives. As your vasanas are, so are your actions. It is these vasanas, not action or contact with objects of the senses per se, which stand between you and perfection.

To free yourself of the need to act you have to get rid of your vasanas. To get rid of your vasanas you have to act. Action can free you of action. We dig a thorn out of our flesh with another thorn, fight fire with fire, stop disease in our body by injecting that disease into our body. In each case the difference between the problem and the antidote is that the former was out of control, the latter is under control.[1]

273.

He who restrains his organs of action but sits thinking of the objects of the senses is called a hypocrite.

Bhagavad Gita 3.6

There are two ways of being a slave to the material world: physical and mental. This verse deals with the latter, the hypocrites who physically restrain themselves from an activity

1. Parth.

but then mentally indulge. He is the husband who is faithful to his wife in body but fantasizes about other women. He is the swami who renounces all and then envisages himself behind the wheel of a large, shiny Mercedes. She is the woman who declares she will buy no more jewellery and then thinks all day about the beautiful gold bangles in the shop window.

Trying to reach perfection instantly from a starting point of physical obsessions is like trying to leap from the bottom of a valley to the top of a mountain. You will lose your footing on the slope of mental obsessions. The only way up is to climb slowly and steadily.[1]

274.

He who controls the senses with his mind while engaging in action without attachment performs karma-yoga. He excels.

Bhagavad Gita 3.7

This is the key to life and the very essence of the Bhagavad Gita – action without desire, action in which we are in control. Nothing is prohibited. We contact the sights, sounds, smells, tastes and touches of the world, but we are not prey to their magnetism.

Imagine yourself on your way to a meeting with a very dear old friend whom you haven't seen for many years. You are driving along the main road and you come to some roadworks. There is a diversion sign which you follow and find yourself winding through country lanes. You are aware that the countryside is very pretty, but you are not distracted by it. You don't decide to spend the day out there in the country lanes. Your attention is on getting back to the main road which will take you straight to your friend. This is how we are when on the path of realization. We act without becoming distracted or attached to the pleasurable diversions of the world. We pass through them without lingering or losing sight of our destination.

Therefore we excel in our actions because they are direct and

1. Parth.

efficient. We excel in ourselves because we come closer and closer to our true Self, the Atman.[1]

275.

Perform your obligatory duties for action is superior to inaction. Even the maintenance of the body would not be possible through inactivity.

Bhagavad Gita 3.8

Each one of us is in this life because we have an unfulfilled duty to ourselves to free our self of the desires separating us from the one true Self, Brahman. To fulfil this duty we must cast off our particular vasanas (inherent desires) through appropriate action performed without desire, whether it is as a soldier, musician, farmworker, athlete, philosopher, etc. This path automatically has duties – to ourselves, our community, country, the human race, all living beings. Some are regular duties, such as those to our family. Some are occasional, such as feeding a starving animal. They are all part of experiencing the Self as something greater than the body, mind and intellect we keep mistaking for our self.

Duty is the cornerstone of Indian society. Husband to wife, wife to husband, child to parent, parent to child, householder to guest, guest to householder and so on – everybody knows their duty. It's not a culture of rights, it's a culture of duty.[2]

276.

This world is bound by actions which are performed other than for the sake of yagna [sacrifice]. Therefore, O son of Kunti [Arjuna], perform actions free from attachment.

Bhagavad Gita 3.9

1. Parth.
2. Parth.

Yagna simply means surrendering egocentric interest to the greater good, the higher ideal. Any action performed without the spirit of yagna binds us to our ego, thereby binding us to this world.

The yagna ritual, performed throughout India and one of the oldest in the country, encapsulates this spirit of sacrifice although, as is so often the case with religious practice, most Hindus do not themselves understand the symbolism of the ritual.

For the ritual a mud or brick trough is built, stoked with firewood and lit by priests who then sit around it chanting mantras. As the congregation gathers, grain or ghee offerings brought by each person accumulate into a large pile. When the time comes to make the offerings each person takes a handful from the pile and throws it on the fire. The fire is nourished and flairs up in response. This is taken to be a blessing from Lord Agni, god of fire and sacrifice. When the fire has burnt itself out, the ashes are distributed to everyone. They smear them on their forehead in three stripes and then go to the temple.

The trough represents any field of activity. The fire is the higher ideal, the highest of which is the Infinite Self, Brahman. The offerings are the faculties of the people arising out of their vasanas (unmanifested desires, see pp. 47–8).

The communal pile of offerings from which each person takes a handful is essential to the yagna. It is this which makes it an act of cooperative endeavour and benefit, rather than one of personal gain with each person offering what they brought and being personally blessed accordingly. Whether they bring grain or not, whether it is a lot or a little, they are able to make an offering to the fire on behalf of everyone and receive the ashes along with everyone else. The worship is performed in a spirit of sacrifice to the common purpose and the higher ideal. Each person's action becomes one of spiritual purification. Their vasanas which bind them to this world are consumed by the higher ideal, symbolized by the fire burning the offerings.

The three stripes of ash smeared on the forehead are a declaration that the person has transcended the three types of vasanas: sattwic, rajasic and tamasic (see p. 81). Entering the temple signifies a return to their own godhood.[1]

1. Parth.

277.

In the beginning, having created humanity together with sacrifice, the Creator said, 'By this sacrifice you shall propagate. Let this be the milch cow of your desires.'

Bhagavad Gita 3.10

The capacity to sacrifice is the birthday present given to humanity. It is the ability to renounce the world. Having achieved human existence in the evolution of our soul, we are blessed with this capacity as the antidote to the desires which are the only thing now standing between us and God.

It is the 'milch cow of your desires' because, like the mythical cow, it will grant us all our wishes whether they be for the material or the Divine. Give it up and we will have it although we will no longer *desire* it.

This is not a moral theory, it is a law. People who give without thought of repayment are never wanting. The world always gives to them. But those who hoard their possessions, their love, their knowledge are given nothing. They are left clutching treasures that crumble to dust.

What we cling to we lose. What we give away we gain. We see this law operating even in nature. When the seven colours which make up sunlight are absorbed by an object, that object takes on the colour it gives away. A red rose absorbs all colours but gives away red.

The ultimate sacrifice is the Self. If you give the self you gain the Self and the world because they are one and the same. That is what sacrifice ultimately can give you. Every act performed in a spirit of renunciation and service dissolves vasanas (inherent desires), taking you closer and closer to the Divine Self within you.[1]

278.

With this [sacrifice] may you nourish the gods and may the gods nourish you. Thus you shall attain the highest perfection.

Bhagavad Gita 3.11

1. Parth.

Krishna's advice to Arjuna to nourish the gods with sacrifice so that they might nourish him is not an instruction to Arjuna to rush out in search of firewood and ghee even as the enemy is lining up on the battlefield. Ritual sacrifice is a *symbolic* act performed as inspiration for all our actions. But there is not time for Arjuna to help himself along with ritual. Krishna is telling him to go straight to the point and act in the spirit of renunciation and service which makes every act a sacrifice. In Arjuna's case, the immediate act at hand is to fight on the battlefield.

Now the Gita is not advocating war any more or less than any other act. The fundamental theme of the Gita – that we must make our life an act of sacrifice – is all the more powerful because Arjuna is not a sannyasi (one who has renounced) or even a social worker. His occupation is not obviously self-sacrificing. It could easily be one of self-aggrandizement and hatred. It is the right attitude that will make it one of self-sacrifice and love. It's not what we do but how we do it.

We must nourish the gods. In Hinduism there is a god and a ritual sacrifice for every aspect of life to remind us of the Divinity which powers all activities and to which our ego must surrender if the activity is to be well discharged. By embarking on all endeavours in submission to the Divine power, that power is more potently expressed because the ego is not blocking it. We will work smoothly and efficiently. It's the difference between putting petrol into a car in which the fuel pipe is clogged and a car in which the pipe is clear: same petrol, but a very different result.

The gods will nourish us. By acting without egocentric desires we dissolve our vasanas (unmanifested desires), moving ever closer to the state of perfection, the state of Divinity.[1]

279.

Living beings grow from food. Food is produced from rain. Rain arises from sacrifice and sacrifice is born of action.

Action arises from Brahma who manifests from the imperish-

1. Parth.

able Brahman. Therefore the All-pervading rests eternally in
sacrifice.

Bhagavad Gita 3.14–15

Krishna maps out the basic cosmological laws. The fulcrum is
sacrifice.

Out of the Absolute Reality, Brahman, comes the creative
principle, Lord Brahma. He is the first god, the grandfather god,
because he is the first principle of material existence. This
creative principle expresses itself as action. Pure action is
unsullied by desire. It is sacrifice (yagna). When action is free of
the obstructive and divisive ego, the power of Brahman flows
smoothly, producing a bountiful harvest for the benefit of all. At
the relative level this benefit is material well-being. At the
Absolute level it is the individual Self's return to the Eternal Self,
Brahman.

The law of sacrifice is obvious at all levels of existence from the
ecological to the social. The earth and its beings give up their
water which comes back as rain so that the earth flourishes. The
organization whose members give up their egos for the sake of
mutual cooperation reap abundantly, whatever their endeavour.
The whole is greater than the sum of its parts.[1]

280.

I am the Vedic ritual, I am the yagna [sacrifice], I am the
ancestral offering, I am the healing herb, I am the mantra, I am
the ghee, I am the fire, I am the oblation.

Bhagavad Gita 9.16

The Vedic ritual is worship in which the Brahmin (priest) pours
ghee onto the fire as an offering to the ancestors. In the yagna all
participants make an offering to the fire so it glows and blesses
the people. Traditionally, the fire was kindled by friction
between two pieces of wood. This is a wonderful combination
of fire and fuel in the one entity, like the infinite and the finite,

1. Parth.

spirit and matter, in us. By rubbing and rubbing, thought against thought, we bring out the fire of knowledge which burns the matter in us.

But Krishna is warning us when we make a sacrifice; the Brahman, to whom all sacrifices ultimately go, is not a Lord God sitting above. It is all aspects of the ritual as It is all aspects of life. So perform the ritual, understand its significance, but don't get caught up in it. It is all part of the dream of the Brahman from which we must awaken.[1]

281.

... Of all cows, I am Kamadhuk...

Bhagavad Gita 10.28

The cow and bull are the great nurturers, providing milk, dung and tireless effort, tilling 80 per cent of Indian agricultural land even today. They provide the livelihood of a nation and receive a few handfuls of dry grass in return. This is the basis of Hindu worship of the cow and bull. They are symbols of service and sacrifice. Their actions are performed without any expectation of the right to enjoy the fruits – maximum effort, minimum profit. That spirit of self-sacrifice is the spirit of karma-yoga, leading to Eternal Life.

Kamadhuk is a mythical cow said to abide in heaven and grant all wishes. It is the apotheosis of the cow's giving nature because it gives anything and everything without any expectation of repayment. It is Absolute sacrifice, Absolute giving, which begins in a human when his intellect overrules his ego to love others as the Self.[2]

1. Parth.
2. Parth.

282.

He [a Self-realized] person has no interest in doing or not doing, nor does he depend on any being or any object.

Bhagavad Gita 3.18

The Self-realized person has no vested interest in acting one way or another because he does not assign value to the objects and beings of this world. Value is comparative. For a thing to have value, there must be something else which is worth more or less than it. But to the Self-realized person all have become One. Therefore there is no comparison, no value.

It is like the dreamer who awakens. He and the dream world become one in the waker. All are one and the same, so the food he was eating, the tiger he was fleeing, the poor he was helping are instantly without value, although he loves them all as his own self. Similarly, the person who has reached the fourth plane of Consciousness (see p. 35) loves the world as himself, but he does not act according to an evaluation of it. By the same token he does not depend on anything or anyone, any more than the waker depends on the food in his dream to feed him or the job in his dream to provide his livelihood.[1]

283.

Therefore, O Arjuna, those who surrender all actions to Me, with full knowledge of Me, with no attachment and free from lethargy, fight.

Bhagavad Gita 3.30

This is the quintessence of karma-yoga.

'Surrender all actions to Me' means the Infinite Self, the Lord in the Absolute sense (see p. 94), but, as with the rest of the Gita, it is applicable on the relative level as well. You must surrender totally to an ideal, whatever it is, to achieve that ideal. Constant

1. Parth.

dedication is the only means of success, whether you are cooking a meal, training for the Olympics or studying the scriptures.

In all human activities anxieties for the fruits of action are the channels that siphon off productivity. Your yourself know that worries about how you will perform in an exam must not be taken into the exam room. Your concentration will be scattered, to the detriment of your work. Once you know your goal, whether it is finishing a university degree or realizing the Atman (Eternal Self), you have to programme that goal and focus on the task itself.

Contrary to popular misconception, the path to realization is one of constant activity. We have to act to reach that state of perfect non-action and absolute power. Body, mind and intellect are the means given to us to move ourselves there. The more we act the more energy we have. We can see this at the purely physical level. Who has more energy than an Olympic athlete whose body is on the go all day long? As we progress toward Self-realization our activities move from the physical to the emotional to the intellectual. We shed one form of desire for subtler and subtler forms until at last all desire dissolves.[1]

284.

Those who constantly practise this teaching of mine, full of faith, without dissent, are freed from the bondage of action with desire.

Those who denigrate this teaching of mine and do not practise it are deluded of all knowledge. These individuals are confused and devoid of discrimination. Know them to be ruined.

Bhagavad Gita 3.31–32

The technique of action to purify oneself has been given (see p. 212). If all actions are performed for the greater good and with sraddha (faith), the great edifice of desires will collapse like a house of cards, taking with it the wheel of karma which ties us to this world. Sraddha is the sincerity and persistence which turn theory into practice, knowledge into wisdom.

Krishna's playmates, the gopis (milkmaids), had total

1. Parth.

sraddha, working hard all day but with their minds on Krishna. They worked without desire for the fruits of their action, thinking only of the higher Reality. That is karma-yoga.

There are many tales and many eyebrows raised over Krishna and the 1600 gopis. As with all stories of Krishna's life, there is a mystical symbolism which we need to grasp. In the pictures we see of Krishna and the gopis he is in the centre playing the flute as they dance around him. The flute is the body empty of desire which produces the enchanting music of Self-realization. The gopis are the 1600 thoughts of a human being. Krishna plays with them but he is detached from them as they dance to his tune. He is the Atman (Eternal Self) that plays with the world, enjoys the world, entertains the world, but is always detached from it.

Krishna warns in these verses of the fate of those who surrender to their own desires. Such people lose the capacity to learn, to understand, to discriminate. Disorientated, they act on the dictates of desire – the very thing that will ruin all actions and fruits and only create more of itself like bacteria rotting everything in its path.[1]

285.

Whatever you do, whatever you eat, whatever you offer in sacrifice, whatever you give away, whatever austerity you practise, O Kaunteya, do it as an offering to Me.

In this way you will be freed from all reactions to good and bad deeds and by the principle of renunciation you will be liberated and come unto Me.

Bhagavad Gita 9.27–28

The Gita does not preach an ascetic way of life. In fact, it exhorts us to action in the world because it says true renunciation of action consists of action performed without any expectation of reward. Lord Krishna says that people have a right to action but not to the fruits of that action. Nor should we become attached to the action itself through the egotism of 'I am the doer.' We act as

1. Parth.

mere instruments of God's will. If all work is dedicated to God it does not prove binding. It will lead to the highest Bliss.

This principle was totally upheld by King Janaka, ruler of Mithila. He attended fully to the duties of the kingdom but was completely detached from the consequences. Once, while he was engaged in worship of the Lord, his capital city caught fire, but he did not move an inch. He believed that all duties of the state were on behalf of the Lord and put his trust in the Lord.[1]

286.

You will be nearer to heaven through football than through a study of the Gita. You will understand the Gita better with your biceps, your muscles, a little stronger. You will understand the mighty genius and the mighty strength of Krishna better with a little strong blood in you. You will understand the Upanishads better and the glory of the Atman when your body stands firm upon your feet and you feel yourselves as men.

Swami Vivekananda

The Gita preaches action as the law of existence and right action as the law of purity and strength. Reading the Gita will do you no good if you do not make those Truths your own through constant effort. To purify yourself, to discover the infinite power that is your true being, you must act. Play football, play anything, as Krishna played with the gopis, but do so with without desire or fear dissipating your energy. The more concentrated something is, the purer it is, the stronger it is. The power of the Atman will flow through you as a river running fast and clear to the ocean.

287.

Even the least work done for others awakens the power within; even thinking of the least good of others gradually instils into the heart the strength of a lion.

Swami Vivekananda

1. Panch.

We can recharge our batteries by sitting and communicating with God through meditation and chanting. But through selfless action the dynamo is charged, enabling us to progress on our path.

Be free from the egotistical feelings of 'I' and 'my'. Earn your living but do so that others are not burdened by you. Work in search of your soul, not money.[1]

288.

I love you all ever so much but I would wish you all to die working for others – I should be rather glad to see you do that.

Swami Vivekananda

1. Bhav.

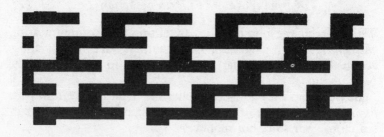

20   Bhakti-Yoga – The Path of Devotion

289.

Tat savitur vareniam bhargo devasya dhmahi dhiyo yo nah pracodayat.

[*We meditate upon the divine radiance of Savita. Let Him inspire our intellect.*]

Gayatri mantra (Vedas)

The famous Gayatri mantra is the sacrifice which all Hindus have been offering daily to God for over 3000 years. By constant chanting of the divine name we purify ourselves. Chanting has a universal power, requiring neither wealth nor strenuous effort. It is a psychological fact that a mind which is saturated with a single, resplendent thought loses its capacity to dwell on evil.

The sun symbolizes the Divinity which illumines the world. By chanting to it, we meditate upon the radiance of God which sustains and protects the whole Universe. The all-pervading power of God permeates everything as the energy of the sun permeates every atom.

The Gayatri mantra makes no request for wealth or material gain but, rather, acknowledges God as the master who has granted us a human body. We ask only for a righteous intellect so that we can progress on the spiritual path. Intellect is the power to discriminate between right and wrong. If our intellect becomes divinely inspired we achieve God.[1]

1. Panch.

290.

What is bhakti-yoga? It is to keep the mind on God by chanting his name and glories . . . Bhakti-yoga is prescribed for this age. By following this path one comes to God more easily than by following the others. One can undoubtedly reach God by following the paths of jnana (knowledge) and karma (action) but they are very difficult paths.

Sri Ramakrishna

It is very difficult for us, limited by our human faculties, to comprehend a God who renders the objective world redundant by being the subject of everything, not least the one we know as 'me'. Therefore, people *like* the religious approach of a personal God outside themselves who can be the focus of their devotion. It is a very natural, familiar way to communicate with God, in keeping with our experience of the dualistic world in which there is always a subject and an object. This preference has increased in India since Vedic times for historical reasons as well. Since the arrival of the Portuguese in the fifteenth and sixteenth centuries the Western Church has given impetus to the devotional (bhakti) path. Certainly, it is a path which helps us elevate ourselves spiritually so that we can realize that the source of Light and Love is within.[1]

291.

O Lord, you are the embodiment of infinite energy. Fill me with energy. You are the embodiment of infinite virility. Endow me with virility. You are the embodiment of infinite strength. Bestow strength upon me. You are the embodiment of infinite power. Grant me power. You are the embodiment of infinite courage. Inspire me with courage. You are the embodiment of infinite fortitude. Steel me with fortitude.

Shukleveda 19.9

1. Bhav.

Human existence is full of limitations and difficulties so we turn to God for strength, energy and courage. This verse is addressed to the ultimate Reality in the form of the god Rudra, ruler of the organs of the senses and action.

In our prayers we petition a personal God but, in reality, we are calling upon this power in ourselves. We cannot comprehend the Unknown so we invest It with a name and form appropriate for the qualities we desire to develop, and then pray to Him. In doing so we are educating ourselves in these projected virtues.[1]

292.

Bounteous One, you are our Father. And you have been our Mother. So we pray for your Grace.

Rig Veda VIII.98.11

Lord Agni, [fire god], I deem my father, my kin, my brother. Deem Him my friend for ever.

Rig Veda X.7.3

The devotee feels a complete humility towards his beloved God, accepting all he achieves as the achievement of God. He is only the tool and is honoured to be chosen so by God. He feels safe and secure to be totally dependent on Him. God is the dearest family member and dearest friend. He is the trustworthy One in whom all relationships culminate.[2]

293.

Mother [Kali], Thou art the operator and I am the machine. Thou art the Householder and I am the house. Thou art the Charioteer, I am the chariot. I move as Thou movest me. I do as Thou makest me do. I speak as Thou makest me speak. Not I; not I, but Thou, but Thou.

Sri Ramakrishna

1. Bhav.
2. Choud.

The nineteenth-century saint, Sri Ramakrishna (see pp. xxxvi–xxxvii), was a priest of the Kali Temple at Dakshineswar. He taught the Divinity of humanity, expressed in his own life as devotion to God and humanity. He declared, 'There is no difference between the Impersonal God (Brahman) on the one hand and the Personal God (Kali) on the other. It is one and the same Reality. When we think of It as inactive, that is to say, not engaged in the acts of creation, preservation and destruction, then we call It Brahman. But when it engages in these activities, then we give it a personal name such as Kali or Shakti.'[1]

294.

O my beloved [Krishna], you might wish to tear all ties but I cannot do that.
How can I just break away the ties of your love and cling to someone else?
You are the tree and I am the nesting bird,
You are the pond, I am the fish living in it,
You are the moon, I am the chakora [nocturnal bird, lover of the moon],
You are the pearl, I am the thread to make the rosary of your name.
You are my Lord and I am your maid Mira.

Mirabai, Bhajan

Mirabai was a saint of the sixteenth century and queen of Chitor in Rajasthan. She left her life of comfort and prestige and took up the life of a devotional minstrel. She was a devotee of Lord Krishna and dedicated her life to singing and spreading God's glory, despite persecution from her family and society at large. She became famous for her bhajans (devotional songs) which touched people's hearts with their simplicity and sincerity of devotion. Her songs are still widely sung in the streets and homes of India.[2]

1. Choud.
2. Choud.

295.

O My Follower, where dost thou seek Me?
Lo! I am beside thee.
I am not in pilgrimages, nor in idols,
Neither in temples, nor in mosques,
I am neither in Kaaba, nor in Kailas,
I am beside thee.
Neither am I in rites and austerities,
Nor in yoga and renunciation.
If thou seek truly, thou shalt find Me at once, in a moment's
search.
Says Kabir, 'O Holy men, I am in your faith and devotion.'

Saint Kabir, Bhajan

Kabir was a weaver and saint of the late fourteenth and early fifteenth centuries who believed that bhajan (devotional worship), along with sincerity and kindness, would lead to God who was the same to the Hindus and Muslims. He is believed to have been a disciple of the famous Vaishnava (Vishnu-devotee) saint, Ramananda, although he was brought up in a Muslim family and was deeply influenced by the Muslim Sufi saints and poets. Kabir did not believe in the efficacy of rituals or external formalities, common in both Hinduism and Islam. He preached a religion of love which would promote unity amongst all classes and creeds.[1]

296.

There are nine characteristic features of devotion to God:
Shravanam, Kirtan, Smarana, Pada-sevana, Archana,
Vandana, Dasya, Sakhya, and Atmanivedanam.

Bhagavatam VII.5.23

Devotion is performed in nine ways – known as *navadha bhaleti.*

1. Choud.

1. Shravanam – the study of God's glory through reading or listening.
2. Kirtan – reciting the name of God.
3. Smarana – remembering and meditating on God and His Divine actions.
4. Pada-sevana – service to God or one of His incarnations.
5. Archana – worshipping the image of God.
6. Vandana – prostration and prayer.
7. Dasya – serving as the most obedient servant of God.
8. Sakhya – loving God as our personal friend (as Arjuna loved Lord Krishna).
9. Atmanivedanam – complete surrender of an individual self with all our belongings to the lotus feet of God.

We can express our love to the Lord through any of these methods. To love Him for His own sake and to act according to His wishes without desiring rewards from Him is very easy.[1]

297.

Whoever offers me, with devotion, a leaf, a flower, a fruit or water, I accept that, the pious offering of the pure in heart.
                                                    Bhagavad Gita 9.26

The Lord is satisfied with whatever little object is available for worship. In truth we only need sincere devotion to gain access to the Lord. He accepts the offerings of His devotees as symbols of love and devotion. We may wonder why the Lord, who is self-sufficient, craves for anything. When a farmer sows seeds in his field he, not the field, reaps a thousandfold. God accepts a devotee's offering out of love and mercy for him and the devotee is blessed a thousandfold by Divine Bliss.[2]

1. Panch.
2. Panch.

298.

Even if the greatest sinner worships Me with total devotion, he must be considered a saint because of his righteous resolve.

Bhagavad Gita 9.30

Lord Krishna has given an assurance to all human beings that no devotee of His would be allowed to suffer eternally. He takes up the responsibility of correcting him, guiding him, protecting him and purifying him. Who has not sinned in this life? Therefore everybody needs this assurance. Lord Krishna gives this assurance only on one condition: 'Those who love me with deep love, I will protect them and see to it that they gain immortality.'

In Hinduism nobody is damned for ever. God is very compassionate. When any sinner repents and surrenders himself to God or one of His beloved saints, he will himself be transformed into a divine personality. Genuine love, but not punishment, changes even a wicked person. The divine Narada transformed a robber into the sage Valmiki who wrote the great epic, the Ramayana.[1]

299.

To those who worship Me with unswerving devotion, who are ever seeking union with Me, I grant yoga and Bliss.

Bhagavad Gita 9.22

From the day we are born we have been taking, taking, taking, through the eyes, ears, nose, mouth, skin, heart, head. We devour, we acquire, we hoard, for ever aggrandizing ourselves. We never think what we can do to repay this debt.

What we have taken is invaluable. How much is all the air we have breathed worth? If we are denied air for thirty seconds, what is its value? Ten pounds? After sixty seconds, how much would we give for some air? Within minutes we would be offering everything we have in the world for just one breath of

1. Panch.

air. And yet we take breath upon breath of this air every day without thinking twice about this precious gift.

The moment we want to repay this debt, we have adopted an attitude of love. We cannot give enough to the world. That devotional love is bhakti-yoga. It is also karma-yoga because we give without desire for personal benefit. It is also jnana-yoga because we give with the awareness of the all-pervading Divinity.

This verse at the geometrical centre of the Gita is one of its most celebrated verses. When Krishna says 'Me' he means the One Self that contains all this world. If we constantly remember that Eternal Self, in and through all physical, emotional and intellectual activities, if we constantly give back to that Self, Krishna promises that It will keep the process going until we reach our final destination which is the Bliss of Self-realization.[1]

300.

By seeing the Self in all beings and all beings in the Self one reaches the Supreme Brahman, not by any other means.

Kaivalyopanishad 10

The importance of this verse is apparent from how often it is repeated in the Gita and other Upanishads. It provides a foolproof test by which to measure your own development. If you are at the most undeveloped stage you identify yourself as your body. Everyone outside your body is not you and therefore their experience of pleasure is not yours. Their money, their colour TV, their delicious food are sources of agitation to you because their body, not yours, is enjoying them. Thus the state of body-identification is the state of greatest friction between you and the world.

The next stage up is identification with your mind and its emotions. Here the breadth of identity expands to family, community and, in certain circumstances, culture. There is a relative blending of personality so that you can watch your

1. Parth.

daughter enjoying a sweet and derive pleasure from her pleasure rather than craving that sweet for your body. Thus, the friction with the world is less. There is a circle of 'mine', an extended 'me', with which you are not competing although, at some point, the circle boundary is drawn.

Further up in development is intellectual identification in which you broaden your base of 'me-ness' through understanding the unity of humanity and all living beings. You are devoted to them all as the Self.

This leads to the fourth and final stage when you realize your true identity as the Atman (Supreme Self) and therefore *are* the Self in all beings, just as the person who identifies with his body is the Self in all parts of his body.[1]

Hare Krishna

301.

> *This individual soul is unbreakable and insoluble and can be neither burned nor dried. He is everlasting, present everywhere, unchangeable, immovable and eternally the same.*
>
> Bhagavad Gita 2.25

The soul is a tiny, tiny spiritual spark which is so powerful it pervades the whole body as consciousness. It is the basic principle of our body just as the Consciousness of the Supreme One is the basic principle of the cosmos.

In the material condition we limit the spirit to the confines of our body but, in truth, our spirit has enormous ability. When the soul is free from the bondage of the body it realizes this potential. The first stage towards this freedom is the simple knowledge of our spiritual identity as part and parcel of Krishna. All the billions of souls are, to Krishna, as the molecules of the sun are to that life-giving star. The rays have enormous energy of their own, yet it is the sun itself which is the ultimate source of their existence.

But, although we are all part and parcel of the Lord, we are

1. Parth.

insoluble. We will never merge with other souls for we are
eternally individual.[1]

302.

*A person in full Consciousness of Me, knowing Me to be the
ultimate beneficiary of all sacrifices and austerities, the Supreme
Lord of all planets and demigods, and the benefactor and well-
wisher of all living entities, attains peace from the pangs of
material miseries.*

Bhagavad Gita 5.29

The cause of our misery is our tendency to exploit the material
world. The more we try to exploit it, the more we suffer. The
reason is that nothing in the material world belongs to us. By
nature, we are not the enjoyer. If we try to enjoy something that
doesn't belong to us we are like the thief who steals but cannot
really enjoy what is not his.

Now God is the supreme proprietor so he is the real enjoyer.
He is the dear friend of all of us. We cannot really understand
how dear a friend he is – more than any friends we can have on
the material plane. God never leaves us, he is always with us. It is
he, not the material world, to whom we must turn for peace.[2]

303.

*For one who sees Me everywhere and sees everything in Me, I am
never lost nor is he ever lost to Me.*

Bhagavad Gita 6.30

When we develop spiritual understanding then we see
everything as spiritual; we do not see anything as material
because the material is only the covering, the external dress.
Behind that material covering there is the Self and that Self is
part and parcel of Krishna.

1. Char./ Das.
2. Char./ Das.

The spiritual person doesn't see anything as separate. Such a person never fails to see the Lord. He is never lost. Everything reminds him of Krishna, like the mother whose son is away from home. If she sees her son's shoes then she immediately remembers her son. Whenever we see anything, we see Krishna. In that sense the devotee is never alone.[1]

304.

And of all yogis, the one with great faith who always abides in Me, thinks of Me within himself, and renders transcendental loving service to Me – he is the most intimately united with Me in yoga and is the highest of all. That is My opinion.

Bhagavad Gita 6.47

In the preceding verses Krishna has described the process of yoga, the path by which we can be linked with the Lord, and now he is saying that the one who renders service in love and devotion is the most intimately connected. He is the greatest of all the yogis because he has directly established his relationship and the process is complete.[2]

305.

O conqueror of wealth, there is no truth superior to Me. Everything rests upon Me as pearls are strung on a thread.

Bhagavad Gita 7.7

Everything depends for its existence on Krishna. If Krishna were not to maintain anything even for a second, it would be destroyed. We take it for granted that everything goes on automatically but, in fact, even in our experience nothing happens like that. For example, in our house with its various arrangements – heating, lighting, keeping it clean, providing

1. Char./ Das.
2. Char./ Das.

food and clothes – somebody has to do all those things; they don't just happen automatically. So there is no reason to assume this is not the case with the Universe. Krishna gives us the analogy of pearls on a thread. The thread passes through every single pearl on the thread and pulls them all together. Similarly, Krishna is present everywhere and in everything and pulls it all together. The devotee never loses sight of that.[1]

306.

This divine energy of Mine, consisting of the three modes of material nature, is difficult to overcome. But those who have surrendered unto Me can easily cross beyond it.

Those miscreants who are grossly foolish, who are lowest among mankind, whose knowledge is stolen by illusion and who partake of the atheistic nature of demons, do not surrender unto Me.

Bhagavad Gita 7.14–15

There are four kinds of mentality amongst those who will not surrender to Krishna. The first is the *mudhas*, meaning donkey, who works very hard to gain the fruits of his work in this world so he has no time for God. He doesn't realize how easily his real enjoyment could be attained. He does not know that action (karma) is meant for sacrifice (yagna). Like a beast of burden he carries a heavy load all day long and suffers being beaten by a stick for a handful of hay.

The second kind of miscreant is *naradhama*, or the lowest of mankind. This is the individual who has the appearance of sophistication – who is socially and politically civilized – but who lacks spiritual principles. In other words he lacks the essence of civilization which is God-Consciousness.

The third kind of miscreant is the *mayayapahrta-jnanah*, one whose knowledge has been stolen by illusion. He may be an extremely intelligent philosopher with a very inquiring mind, and may even express religious beliefs, but out of pride he cannot surrender. He has the knowledge but his knowledge has been

1. Char./ Das.

stolen. The illusory energy of the Lord has stolen the knowledge because that person has not truly surrendered.

The fourth kind of miscreant is the *asuram bhavam asritah,* one who has openly taken shelter in demonic, atheistic principles. He proudly professes his ungodliness.[1]

307.

But those who worship Me, giving up all their activities unto Me and being devoted to Me without deviation, engaged in devotional service and always meditating upon Me, having fixed their minds upon Me, O son of Partha – for them I am the swift deliverer from the ocean of birth and death.

Bhagavad Gita 12.6–7

The material world is like an ocean of birth and death and if we are in the midst of the ocean, no matter how powerful a swimmer we may be, it is hopeless, there is nothing we can do. We are just tossed about by the waves of the ocean. The only hope is that someone may come and rescue us and Krishna does that for us. If we put all our faith and trust in Him, He will come and rescue the living being from the ocean of the material world.[2]

308.

The living entities in this conditioned world are My eternal fragmental parts. Due to conditioned life, they are struggling very hard with the six senses, which include the mind.

Bhagavad Gita 15.7

The living entity is compared to a spark from the fire. The fire is compared to the Supreme Mind. This spark possesses all the qualities of the fire but only in minute quantities. If the spark is separated from the fire, then it can lose the qualities of the fire and be easily extinguished. If it remains with the fire it will retain

1. Char./ Das.
2. Char./ Das.

those qualities. In this conditioned life we are a part of the Lord but we are some distance from Him by virtue of the material conditions we live in, so we are like the spark that is on the edge of the fire and struggling to remain alight.[1]

309.

I am seated in everyone's heart and from Me come remembrance, knowledge and forgetfulness. By all the Vedas, I am to be known. Indeed, I am the compiler of Vedanta, and I am the knower of the Vedas.

Bhagavad Gita 15.15

In the form of the Supersoul Krishna dwells in the heart of every living being and accompanies that tiny being throughout his sojourn in the material world. He is there rewarding and punishing us according to our actions but this is secondary to his main purpose which is to help us to return to Him when we are ready to do so.

Each individual's memory, knowledge and intelligence comes from the Source. The living entity cannot act independently. It is only to the extent that things are revealed to us by the Lord that we have knowledge. It is the Supersoul, the Lord residing in our heart, who gives us remembrance or covers us with ignorance. If we want to forget God then he will allow us to forget Him. Whatever we desire, He will fulfil our desire. As soon as we wish to turn our face to Him, then immediately He helps us to do so.[2]

310.

That which in the beginning may be just like poison but at the end is just like nectar and which awakens one to Self-realization is said to be happiness in the mode of goodness.

1. Char./ Das.
2. Char./ Das.

That happiness which is derived from contact of the senses with their objects and which appears like nectar at first but poison at the end is said to be of the nature of passion.

Bhagavad Gita 18.37-38

Those who are in the mode (guna) of goodness are not impatient immediately to get results. Instead they see everything they do in terms of the long-term benefit and are prepared to perform austerities in the present for future benefit. A person in ignorance wants immediate pleasure, but later he will have to pay the price, he will suffer in the future. Here Krishna says that the highest happiness which eventually leads to Self-realization may be difficult in the beginning, it may feel like poison, but, just as when we are suffering from a disease we may have to take a medicine that tastes bitter, we take it because it will eventually make us better. We see this, for instance, when a person takes up the spiritual life and gives up smoking and drinking and changes his or her diet. At first he may suffer severe withdrawal, but later on it isn't difficult because the taste for those things dissipates as the person moves into a higher mode.

Similarly, if people continue to pursue instant satisfaction this turns sour. Inevitably the result is social disorder. At a personal level it leads to physical and mental degeneration. In the wider context it leads to war.[1]

311.

The one who explains the Supreme secret to the devotee – devotional service – in the end he will come back to Me.

There is no servant in this world more dear to Me than he, nor will there ever be one more dear.

Bhagavad Gita 18.68-69

When one has surrendered himself to Krishna, naturally the question is, 'What is the best way that I can serve Krishna?' Here Krishna says that if we are able to take up the responsibility of

1. Char./ Das.

teaching the science of devotional service, of bringing others to Him, then that person is a most dear friend. This is why Krishna's devotees so often try to surrender their lives to teaching his words.[1]

1. Char./ Das.

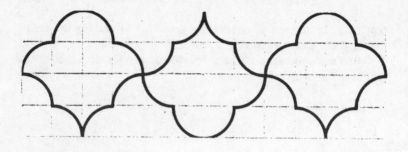

21 Jnana-Yoga – The Path of Knowledge

312.

The eye cannot go there, nor speech, nor mind. We do not know It. We do not know how to teach It.

Kenopanishad 1.3

God (Brahman) cannot be captured by sense perception, action, thought or feeling, for God is the very subject of all experience, not an object of experience. So the equipment of material existence – your body, mind and intellect – are of no avail in trying to find It. You cannot see God any more than you can see your own eye. At most you can see the reflection of God which is this material world.

This verse is spoken by a God-realized person, yet he says, 'We do not know It. We do not know how to teach It,' because God cannot be grasped with the intellect or communicated from one intellect to another. It is untold and will always be untold. God-realization is an experience of consciousness beyond the body, mind and intellect.

The moment we think our intellect has understood God, we defile God.[1]

1. Parth.

314.

. . . Of the knowers I am Knowledge.

Bhagavad Gita 10.38

All knowledge, whether of history or love or your neighbours' eccentricities, is pure Knowledge reflected. We can never intellectually know that pure Knowledge. We can only know its reflection upon something, whether that reflector be an inanimate object, a being or an idea.

Pure Knowledge is like light. You see this book, but if you turn off the light, you can't see the book. So what you were seeing before was the book plus light. If you had seen the book alone you would still see it whether there was light or not. So you only see the book because of the light and you only see the light because of the book, the table, the room, etc. You don't see the light on its own. Light on its own is darkness (see p. 9). You always see light conditioned by an object. Similarly, you always know Knowledge conditioned by an object. The pure Knowledge that enables you to know is ignorance to you. You can only know that Knowledge by becoming it. By being that Knower.[1]

315.

[Krishna said:] I will declare this knowledge and wisdom entirely, which knowing, nothing more remains to be known.

Bhagavad Gita 7.2

Krishna is the Brahman personified. That Eternal Self alone is the source of all knowledge and wisdom.

A teacher can pass on knowledge but he can't pass on wisdom. Knowledge is tuition, wisdom is intuition. There is an interim period between knowledge and wisdom. That's the frustration we go through. We may know certain things but we are none the wiser for this knowledge. The smoker knows he shouldn't smoke. His friends, family and doctor tell him again and again that he is

1. Parth.

damaging his health and risking his life. He knows but he won't think about it. Then one day he has a minor stroke and the doctor tells him, for the hundredth time, 'These cigarettes will be the death of you.' He never smokes again. He is wiser. He had the knowledge before but now he has the wisdom. He has digested the information into his own being. The object becomes the subject.

But this is the problem. We don't want to think about 'it', whatever 'it' is, unless circumstances force us to. Today the cry has gone up, 'Knowledge is power,' so everyone is busy accumulating knowledge – how to programme computers, mend cars, influence people, discover God – but no one has time to stop and think about this knowledge. Opportunities at the material, as well as the spiritual, level are lost because we have lost the art of contemplation.[1]

316.

Aum.
May He protect us both.
May He cause us both to enjoy.
May we both exert together.
May our study illumine us.
May we not hate each other.
Aum. Peace, peace, peace.

Kenopanishad: Invocation

This invocation of the Kenopanishad is a typical opening to an Upanishad, recited by the teacher and his student(s) before they begin their study so that they may work together with conviction and sincerity. It is a prayer to the Brahman, the all-pervading Self.

The invocation asks for Brahman to protect and help student and teacher in their studies. With pragmatic wisdom it also acknowledges the dangers of ego conflicts and prays that this may not arise for this would be the death of learning.

The teachings by the great rishis (sages) of the Upanishads are

1. Parth.

the pinnacle of knowledge. They are all that can be said about ultimate Reality, but they are not a description, they are indicators to the Unknown on the basis of what is known. Reality is beyond the intellect, beyond description. Knowledge points the way, it is the last signpost after action and devotion.

This is beautifully explained by the 'moon-branch analogy', known in Sanskrit as *chandra-sakha-nyaya*. On a clear summer's day you suddenly see the white crescent of the moon in the sky. You say to your friend, 'Look, the moon,' but he cannot see it. So you begin with a point of reference close at hand. 'See the meadow.' 'Yes.' 'Now see the tree in the meadow.' 'Yes.' 'Now follow up the trunk to the branch on the farthest right.' 'Yes.' 'Now, keeping right, follow to the highest tip on that side.' 'Yes.' 'Straight up from there.' 'Oh, yes, I see.' You have taken your friend to the moon, using the meadow, the tree, the trunk, the branch, all of which have nothing to do with the moon. It is far, far beyond them but he would never have spotted it without them. Vedanta (the end of knowledge taught in the Upanishads) is that tree. It takes us from what we know to the very tip of our world so that we can make that final leap of vision when we let go of the intellect. That is the ultimate peace of non-thought. We become pure Knowledge.[1]

317.

Liberation is not possible without knowledge.
                              Hiranyakeshiya Shakra Shruti

The path of knowledge (jnana-yoga) is discipline of the intellect, training it to take any piece of knowledge and contemplate upon it deeply. It is original reflection on Reality, not rote learning, not cramming in information without a second thought. The process of jnana-yoga is summed up in the phrase: *'Nitya anitya viveka vichaara'* (literally, 'eternal non-eternal discrimination reflection'). It is the process of reflecting on the distinction between the permanent and the impermanent aspects of life. It is seeing beyond the names and forms to the substratum that supports

1. Parth.

them. It is seeing beyond your own changing body and personality, which have been baby, child, youth and so on, to that which supports all these changes. It is seeing beyond the tree which is then a pile of logs, a plank, a table, to that which supports all these changes. The search for knowledge is the search for that absolute 'is-ness' which is constant.[1]

318.

The practice of knowledge thoroughly purifies the ignorance-stained Self and the knowledge itself disappears as kataka-nut powder in water.

Atmabodha (Sankara) 5

The practice of knowledge involves negating what we are not – we are not the body, mind and intellect – and asserting what we are – the Divine Self. The simile of the kataka-nut explains how 'I am the Atman', the final focus, becomes the means by which the mind is purified of thought. Kataka-nut powder is sprinkled on the surface of impure water and forms a slimy film. The impurities suspended in the water accumulate on this film until, by its own weight, it sinks to the bottom, taking the rest of the impurities with it. The pure water is then decanted. Similarly, that one thought, 'I am the Atman,' pulls in all other thoughts. That thought then sinks, taking with it all material debris, so that the pure Self is left and can be removed from thought.[2]

319.

Having negated all limiting equipment with the declaration of 'not this, not this', one should realize the oneness of the individual Atman and the supreme Brahman through the mahavakyas [Vedic aphorisms].

Atmabodha (Sankara) 30

1. Parth.
2. Parth.

The first point to make to yourself is that you are not your gross physical body made up of organs of action and perception. You are not the subtle body made up of mind and intellect and you are not your causal body made up of vasanas (unmanifest desires). The declarations of the Vedas which you should use to affirm yourself are: Consciousness is Brahman; That thou art; The Self (Atman) is Brahman; I am Brahman.

These aphorisms are known, respectively, as the statements of definition, advice, practice and experience. They use the unavoidable dualistic structure of language to explain there is no dualism. The Atman and the Brahman, individual consciousness and total Consciousness, the microcosm and the macrocosm, are one and the same.[1]

320.

Making the individual Self the lower firestick and the Aum [Supreme Self] the upper piece of wood and by repeated kindling of the flame of knowledge, the wise man burns the bond of ignorance.

Kaivalyopanishad 11

When we rub wood it generates fire which burns the wood. The wood turns into fire to destroy itself. This beautifully illustrates how our material nature can be used to destroy itself so our eternal Self may be released like the energy from the wood. The Atman is kindled in our material nature through meditation on the Supreme Self. We have to rub our minds with the message of Aum: 'I am the Atman [Supreme Self], I am not the body, I am not the mind, I am not the intellect,' so it ignites and burns at all times as the flame of knowledge. If we are fighting with our spouse, threatening our neighbours, competing with our colleagues, let this knowledge burn away our desires and agitations. In this way the unmanifested Consciousness will be made manifest.[2]

1. Parth.
2. Parth.

321.

> . . . *Of serpents, I am Vasuki.*
>
> Bhagavad Gita 10.28

Vasuki is the serpent in the story of the gods and demons churning the milky ocean (Vishnu Puranas – see p. xxvii). Vasuki is used as the churning rope attached to the mountain Meru, the churning stick. The serpent is the symbol of the ego. Vasuki is the best of egos because he is used in conjunction with the mountain of karma (actions) to churn the milky ocean of the mind until the deadly poison of desire is vomited out. Vasuki is the ego which employs the intellect to think and reflect. From this churning came wonderful objects, creatures and gods, representing material wealth, and finally there came the nectar of Self-realization. Vasuki is the ego used to realize the Self rather than to disguise it.[1]

322.

> . . . *Among the flowing rivers, I am the Ganges.*
>
> Bhagavad Gita 10.31

To Hindus the Ganges is the most sacred of all rivers because it represents spiritual knowledge. Pilgrims to the Ganges immerse themselves and their children in it three times. This symbolizes the submersion of the body, mind and intellect in the ultimate Truth.

In the Puranas is the story of how the Ganges came to earth. The great king and sage, Bhageratha, prayed to the goddess Ganga to descend from heaven and bless the world with her waters which are the source of all well-being.

Ganga answered that she was willing but the force of her waters flowing from such a great height would bore a hole right through the earth and destroy it. At her suggestion Bhageratha prayed to Lord Shiva to act as a bridge between heaven and earth

1. Parth.

so the fall of the water would be broken. Shiva agreed to this and so Ganga poured down onto Shiva's head where she wandered amongst the long tresses of his hair for a time until at last she trickled down to earth.

This story tells the story of realization. If people were suddenly exposed to the full force of ultimate Truth it would simply go right through them and out the other side, having done nothing but damage. They need a bridge between them and Knowledge in order to receive Truth in trickles which they can assimilate. The bridge is the God-realized man, a guru, symbolized by Shiva who is the god of meditation and austerities (tapas). As Knowledge is assimilated it becomes a mighty flow within the individual, nourishing him as the Ganges river nourishes the earth.[1]

323.

. . . *Of arguments I am logic.*

Bhagavad Gita 10.32

The essence of argument is to discredit falsehood and discover the Truth. That is logic. That is the Eternal Self.

There are three types of argument: 1. assertion of one's own opinion against another's opinion ('No, you're wrong'); 2. destructive criticism ('You'd be a much better lily if you behaved like an oak'); 3. logic ('If a lily adopted all aspects of the oak, it wouldn't be a lily, let alone a better one'). Logic follows the irrefutable law (dharma) of the Universe. It is the only form of argument which does not involve the ego. It is the only one actually committed to knowledge; therefore, it is the only one which can lead us to the Truth. However, we must only approach logic having banished our ego, or we risk confusing our own ego-distorted arguments with logic.

1. Parth.

324.

*Of all the letters I am the letter A, and among compound words I
am the dvandvah compound . . .*

Bhagavad Gita 10.33

This pluralistic world is created through thought organizing the
One into names and forms. The Atman is that which gives rise to
all names and is, therefore, equated with 'A', the first syllable a
child utters.

Dvandvah is a compound word in which the accent is on both
syllables. Therefore, it symbolizes the Atman (Eternal Self)
which is in each and every one of us to the same degree. It is a
reminder from Krishna that, although we might select this idol
or that idol as a symbol of the Atman on which to meditate, we
should not make the blunder of thinking it has any more or less
Divinity than anything else. The Atman is Infinite, so its
emphasis is Infinite. We can know it equally well as the
Himalayas or a banana skin.[1]

325.

*The right and also study and teaching; the true and also study and
teaching; austerities and also study and teaching; self-control and
also study and teaching; the fire of sacrifice and also study and
teaching; the sacrifice and also study and teaching; guests and also
study and teaching; humanity and also study and teaching;
offspring and also study and teaching; procreation and also study
and teaching; propagation of the race and also study and
teaching.*

Taittiryopanishad I.9.1

There must be 'after sales' service of your knowledge. This is the
most important aspect.

There is a type of person who buys a brand-new car and within
six months it is as shabby as a ten-year-old car. Such people have
the knack of destroying the beauty of a car by providing no

1. Parth.

upkeep. When they're fed up with the car and its poor condition they buy a new one and so it goes on. But another type of person might only be able to afford a ten-year-old car but has such dedication to the car that he brings it up to showroom condition. So it's not the buying of a car that gives you the benefits of a comfortable new car. It's the follow-up servicing.

Similarly, merely acquiring some new knowledge is not going to benefit you. If there is follow-up on existing knowledge, frankly you don't need this new knowledge. Proper use of the old knowledge will take you to the same place as proper use of the new knowledge.[1]

326.

Better indeed is knowledge than practice . . .
Bhagavad Gita 12.12

Most of us follow rituals without knowing their significance. We remove our shoes before going into the temple, we prostrate ourselves in the mosque, or we cross ourselves before the crucifix because everybody else is doing so. It is knowledge of a ritual's meaning which gives it a religious dimension. Without this knowledge we become attached to the material trappings of the ritual. It becomes mere superstition obstructing our reunion with the Divine Self.[2]

327.

. . . better than knowledge is meditation; better than meditation is renunciation of the fruit of action; peace immediately follows renunciation.
Bhagavad Gita 12.12

After we have attained knowledge we can rise to the stage of meditation. Meditation is absorption in the spiritual Truth. The

1. Parth.
2. Parth.

mind ceases to flit helter-skelter from desire to desire. Thus meditation is the application of knowledge. There is no point in acquiring knowledge if we then pay no heed to its application.

Renunciation follows from meditation. If the mind has divested itself of its desires through meditation then, by definition, it does not seek after the fruits of its actions. Contrary to the belief of many people, unless we renounce the fruit we can't achieve anything. Take, for example, the batsman who bats beautifully up to ninety. When he reaches ninety his mind shifts from the action of hitting the ball to the desired fruit – scoring a century. It is then that he misses the ball and is bowled out because his action is disturbed by the thought of its result. He has not meditated – concentrated with single-pointed thought – on that ball.

Most of us are in a constant state of disturbed action. We are worried about the future fruits we might achieve or those in the past that we did not. Our minds are never on the single point of the present. We are never at peace.[1]

328.

A prudent man is like a pin; his head prevents him from gong too far.

Rama Tirtha

1. Parth.

22 Dhyana-Yoga – The Path of Meditation

329.

But those who worship Me, surrendering all actions to Me, regarding Me as the supreme goal, meditating on Me with single-pointed yoga,
Those whose minds are set on Me, O Partha, I rescue before long from the ocean of death-bound existence.
Fix your mind on Me alone, place your intellect in Me, then you shall, no doubt, live in Me alone.

Bhagavad Gita 12.6–8

When Krishna tells Arjuna to 'meditate on Me' He is telling Arjuna to meditate on the eternal 'Me', the Atman in each one of us. God is in Arjuna as he is in every human being. We are all, each one of us, God plus desires, so by a simple subtraction of our desires we come to God. That is our supreme goal.

But how do we subtract our desires in this equation?

Desires arise out of body, mind and intellect. These three material components make up our shell, beyond which lies the true Self, the Atman or God. But we are confused by our shell, we identify our Self with it, turning to the sensations of our body, the feelings and desires of our mind or the thoughts of the intellect. As we think so we become. This is the principle of action. If we turn to the body we become the body. What affects it affects us. We say, 'I am cold,' rather than 'My body is cold.' Similarly, we say, 'I feel sad,' rather than 'My mind feels sad,' or 'I am quick-witted,' rather than 'My intellect is quick-witted.'

But if we turn to our true Self, instead of attaching ourselves to our body, mind and intellect, we will not be dragged again and

again into the cycle of birth and death in this world. We will come
to God.

The intellect itself can be used in the process of detachment.
By fixing it on a single point of thought, the Supreme Self, we
stretch the thoughts and desires which bind us to our material
shell thinner and thinner until the last thought itself snaps and
we become the Supreme Self.[1]

330.

*Practising meditation they realized that Being who is the self-
luminous god without a second; who presides over all the causes
beginning with time and ending with the individual soul; and who
had been incomprehensible because of the limitations of their own
intellect.*

Shvetashvataropanishad 1.3

The mind is a continuous stream of thoughts which come
between us and the ultimate Reality. The strategy of meditation
is to channel the mind to a single thought and, ultimately, to
crush that thought.

In meditation the rate at which the thoughts and agitations
besiege the mind is slowed, like slowing the speed at which film
images are run across the cinema screen. At a certain point the
experience of a seamless stream of thought breaks, as when the
film images slow to less than sixteen frames per second and the
illusion of unbroken movement falters. Those images can be
stopped completely at one unmoving image in the same way as
we can stop our thoughts at one single point. Once we have
stopped the flickering thoughts they cease to hypnotize us. We
become more conscious of their projected nature, of the
unmoving Atman which is their source. We become detached
from them as we do from a film that has stopped at one image.
We identify less with the thoughts, becoming more conscious of
ourselves as observers. When that last thought is removed we

1. Parth.

wake up to Reality as we wake up to this world when the last celluloid image has gone and the ray of light from the projector is replaced by the cinema lights.[1]

331.

Indeed, he attains immortality who knows It through every state of consciousness. Through the Atman [Divine Self] true strength is obtained and, through knowledge, immortality.

Kenopanishad 2.4

Immortality results from constant awareness of the Atman (Divine Self) at all times. There are three states of consciousness in the material world: waking, dreaming and deep sleep (see pp. 33–6).

In the waking and dreaming states thoughts come and go in constant waves but supporting these waves, as it supports the thoughtlessness of deep sleep, is the pure Consciousness of the Atman. Every thought is enlivened by this Consciousness as the bulb is enlivened by electricity or the car by petrol.

Meditation is the practice of focusing on the light of pure Consciousness rather than on the bustle of thoughts. The mind can continue to have thoughts but we observe them passing, we do not go with them. As a consequence we not only move closer to the Truth but become more powerful in worldly actions because our mind is not constantly agitated by change.

Using this open-eye meditation we can move towards realization in every moment of our life. We can experience the Atman which is in everything and everyone. Everywhere we go, whether to New York or Jerusalem, the roar of the market-place is a beautiful expression of Divinity. If we are able to understand this we will never be lost anywhere.[2]

1. Parth.
2. Parth.

332.

. . . By sound alone is the non-sound revealed. Now here the sound is Aum. Moving upward along it one rises to the non-sound. So this is the way, this is immortality, this is total union and peace. Just as the spider moving upward by the thread reaches unbound space, certainly the meditator moving upward by the syllable Aum reaches self-sufficiency . . . Therefore it has been said there are two Brahmans to be known, the sound Brahman and what is higher. Those who know the sound Brahman get to the higher Brahman.

Maitryopanishad VI.22

In theory, all this reading and contemplating could just as easily be replaced by sitting in the dark and chanting Aum . . . Aum . . . Aum . . . Ten times you might repeat it. Aum . . . Aum . . . That fellow owes me twenty pounds . . . He said he'd pay me on Sunday . . . Aum. The mind will slip. You can't chant. It's not possible. People try for ten, fifteen years and still the mind slips because they haven't done anything to reduce their desires. Meditation must be understood as the point at which all spiritual paths meet (not where they start). Success in meditation is directly related to purity of mind. You have to renounce cravings and attachments so that your mind is free to grasp that which is higher. This is the greatest challenge and price you must pay for reaching God.

To this end constant meditation on Aum – the Supreme Self – in and through all your thoughts and actions is more important than a concentrated 'quick-hit' meditation followed by a day of desire-ridden activity. That is akin to dressing and balming a wound in the morning which you then spend the rest of the day scratching.[1]

333.

With the mind resting on me, with the senses absorbed in Me, constantly discussing this Truth, constantly speaking of Me.

Bhagavad Gita 10.9

1. Parth.

A classical musician has the sruti (that which is 'heard') of the tampura playing the same tune over and over again as he goes through beautiful variations of the ragas and talas (melodies). He is able to perform these superbly because he is constantly attuned to the tampura melody. But an untrained musician asked to sing would agree, 'on one condition: you make that fellow at the back stop all the racket'. The tampura is a distraction to him. He can't sing with it but he can't sing without it either. Similarly, if we are to live classically we must learn to live with that sruti which tells us who we are, where we have come from, where we are going: 'I am the Atman.'

When you turn your thoughts towards the Atman you will receive greater peace and happiness and greater capacity to meditate. If you perform all your yogas – karma (action), bhakti (devotion) and jnana (knowledge) – as meditation you will build towards a state of desirelessness out of which meditation arises of its own accord.[1]

334.

... Of all sacrifices I am the japa [chanting] ...
Bhagavad Gita 10.25

Japa is the chanting of a word-symbol of the Absolute Reality. Aum is the ultimate sound (see p. 3) and therefore considered the most powerful of all chants, but we can choose any sound we like. The point is to use the sound to control the mind. The sound becomes the anchor to pull the mind back every time it starts to wander. When the mind has been stabilized and elevated above the whispers of desire that call it, the chant is gradually slowed and softened to a mental murmur until it fades into silence. The mind and intellect which are totally focused on this chant fade away with it. There is only pure silence and pure Consciousness.[2]

1. Parth.
2. Parth.

335.

In a solitary place, seated in an easy posture, clean, with neck, head and body erect, remaining in the highest order of life, controlling all senses, saluting with devotion one's own guru.

Kaivalyopanishad 5

This verse gives practical advice on how to attain perfect Bliss. You are attempting to reach the state which is devoid of thought or desire. For that you must be in a 'solitary place', in other words, a place where you will be undisturbed. Such a place is a state of mind. You must be free of attachments to the objects and beings of the world which agitate the mind.

You must be 'seated in an easy posture, clean' so that your body does not disturb you with thoughts of its welfare; 'neck, head and body erect' so that the spine and collarbones form a cross on which to crucify the body – to destroy its grip on the Self. This posture is the most suitable one for being comfortable enough to lose all awareness of the body. The body's centre of gravity falls in the centre of the base created by crossing the legs. It may well feel uncomfortable at first but that will be due to habitual bad posture.

'The highest order of life', as all Hindus know, is the fourth and last ashrama (stage of personal development). After the stages of celibate, householder, retirement, the final stage is as a mendicant (sannyasi) when all worldly claims have been renounced. This is the stage you must enter before you can meditate to any effect. Sit with total control of your senses so they cannot venture out into the world. Mentally prostrate yourself to your guru whether it is a person or a book; it doesn't matter which because it is the ultimate Knowledge in them that you are revering.[1]

336.

Meditating on the lotus of your heart, in the centre is the

1. Parth.

untainted, the exquisitely pure, clear and sorrowless, the inconceivable, the unmanifest, of infinite form, blissful, tranquil, immortal, the womb of Brahma.

Kaivalyopanishad 6

The lotus has long been a symbol of the Infinite Reality in Hindu iconography. That Reality we meditate on, in the centre so there is no other point to distract us.

It is inconceivable because It is beyond the intellect, being the power which enables the intellect to conceive.

It is 'the unmanifest, of infinite form' because its unmanifest state gives rise to all manifest forms, just as the post in the dark can become the ghost, the policeman, the burglar, whatever the see-er sees, without the post actually manifesting any of these forms.

It is 'blissful, tranquil, immortal' because it is unchanging. It is the 'womb of Brahma' because it precedes the first creative principle, Lord Brahma. It is beyond Creation, beyond thought.[1]

337.

Let peace reign on the earth, in mid-air and in the sky. Peace be in oceans and all waters. Let herbs be in peace and let there be peace in all forests and plant life. Let there be peace among gods of the Universe and let gods bestow peace on us.

Aum, shanti [peace], shanti, shanti.

Atharvaveda XIX.9.14

The concept of peace, as fostered by Indian rishis (sages), was comprehensive and all-embracing. It is a state of equilibrium and steadiness. Peace is absolutely essential for any kind of physical, intellectual, emotional, moral or spiritual growth. All the world seeks peace. The Indian sages were so conscious of the necessity of peace for healthy and meaningful activity that they prayed for peace, not only for human beings but for all the world,

1. Parth.

including mountains. But in the world today, men and women as well as innocent animals and plants are all deprived of peace.

We cannot lead peaceful lives unless we think peacefully. The ancient sages taught us that peace lies in truth and that must be sought in solitude. Daily practice of short meditation is far superior to all the medicines and tonics in the world. A quiet and tranquil mind cannot be achieved in a day. Like character, it is attained through years of discipline, of detachment from the ephemeral pleasures of the world. Peace is the quality and gift of the enlightened.[1]

338.

As a lamp in a windless place does not waver so the transcendentalist, whose mind is controlled, remains always steady in his meditation on the transcendent Self.

Bhagavad Gita 6.19

The mind's business is to focus the Consciousness. When the mind projects our Consciousness onto material objects, it perceives them as objects for enjoyment, so it becomes very fickle. It is constantly looking at objects and either accepting or rejecting them. In this way the mind is always agitated, always wavering. But the one who has projected his Consciousness onto the Lord has a fixed and single focus so his mind does not waver.[2]

339.

He thought, 'How can this [human] form survive without me?' He pondered, 'By what route should I enter the body?' He reflected, 'If utterance is by speech; if respiration is by breath; if vision is by sight; if hearing is by the ears; if touch is by the skin and thought is by the mind; if metabolism is by digestion and if emission is by the organ of generation, then what function shall I fix for myself?'

1. Panch.
2. Char./Das.

> *Having precisely cleaved the structure of the skull he entered the*
> *body by that access. This entrance is widely known as the portal*
> *and as the place of joy.*
>
> Aitareyopanishad I.3

The head is considered as the summit of the human body but not
merely because, physically, it is the topmost point during the
sixteen or so hours per day that humans spend in the upright
position. The sutures of the skull have great significance especially where they converge at the crown.

When meditation arouses the energy latent in the body it rises
upwards along the spine, being amplified and concentrated in
the spinal centres (*chakras*), until, in the advanced stages, it
surges into the head and culminates in a pervasive feeling of
serenity and limitless Bliss (*samadhi*) in the sahasrara chakra at
the crown of the head.

This reading indicates that God in His universal manifestation
as the cosmic soul (*paramatman*) becomes localized as an
individual soul (*jivatman*), entering the body through the crown
of the head. Conversely, the soul is thought to leave the dead
body by the same route and is symbolically assisted in its
departure by the puncture which is sometimes made in the
crown of the head at the cremation ceremony.[1]

340.

> *God within the body is reached by truth, religious austerity, real*
> *knowledge and continence practised constantly. Then, indeed, do*
> *earnest seekers of God discover Him as a shining light within that*
> *very body.*
>
> Mundakopanishad III.1.5

In humans the presence of God within the body becomes
concealed by the massive sensory input pouring into the brain
from the score or more of known types of sensory receptors. The
concealment is reinforced by the individual's response to this

1. Chand.

input, modified by his hereditary traits, education, culture, perceived worldly interests, etc. Emotional and other attachments develop and preoccupy the attention and consciousness.

By stilling the mind, detaching consciousness from sensory inputs through mental techniques such as meditation (reinforced by dance, sounds, diagrams, asceticism, fasting or prayer), the presence of God within is revealed. Dimly at first, but later more sharply and clearly, this awareness develops so that an aspirant becomes more constantly aware of this internal personal presence of God, and uses it to guide his or her daily progress through life.[1]

341.

[God within] cannot be apprehended by the eyes, by words, by any of the senses, by mortification of the flesh or by rituals. When the understanding becomes clear and the essential character becomes purified, then in meditation one realizes Him, the one and only God.

Mundakopanishad III.1.8

This verse tells of the futility of trying to reach God by sermons, ceremonies or rituals, all of which have their ardent advocates. Penances, which are considered by many to provide a sure way to salvation, are also disparaged here.

Attachment to pleasures and stimulation of the senses distract from the realization of God within. On the other hand, detachment from external events and environmental stimuli, and later from stimuli arising in the viscera inside the body, leads to a balanced mind which can then explore the inward path to God. Meditation is one way to take this internal route to God within. Patanjali's eight limbs of yoga in the Yoga Sutras are designed to lead the follower away from mental entrapment in the external world to the more rewarding inner awareness which the practitioner is taught to adjust and maximize.

Progress is aided by stretching postures, breathing techniques and the mind-training exercise which precedes meditation.

1. Chand.

These all purify the mind and body so that the seeker may proceed with some chance of success to intensive meditation which could lead to the realization of God within and then, in time, to God in the Universe.[1]

342.

As oil in sesame seeds, as butter in curdled milk, as spring water in underground streams, as fire in the stick used for tinder, so is God immanent in the individual soul. He who by truth and religious austerity perceives again and again within himself the Divine Being, all pervasive like butter contained in milk, and who is realized by awareness of His presence within and by meditation, such a person becomes one with God the Universal Power, the provider of spiritual knowledge.

Shvetashvataropanishad I.15–16

God pervades the Universe and has many manifestations, one of which is His presence in each individual soul. This aspect of God is, however, not often immediately perceptible to individuals because of the many distractions furnished by the senses which divert attention and foster concentration on external objects and attachments.

When, however, the individual becomes aware (through a teacher or external events forcing introspection) of the presence of the personal aspect of God within the self, he or she may wish to use techniques such as meditation and asceticism to strengthen and sharpen this realization and to reinforce the initially tenuous contact with God. This contact inspires further spiritual development and closer links with the Divine presence within, until consciousness of a separate identity is obliterated and the individual consciousness becomes one with God, intermittently during meditation or constantly during daily life.

At death such an enlightened person will break away from the cycle of rebirths to higher or lower levels of existence, depending on the laws of karma (action and reaction – see pp. 32–4), and his soul will become one with God for ever.

1. Chand.

Truth is one of the five main yamas (ethical prescriptions) regulating relationships with neighbours and colleagues. Observance of the yamas is necessary for proper and effective meditation (see below).[1]

343.

Regulating activities in this world, deliberately controlling the senses, one should breathe out through the nostrils as the vital activities become quieter. Then, as though with reins curbing rebellious horses, the knowledgeable person should control his mind without allowing distraction.

Shvetashvataropanishad II.9

The preparations for effective meditation form the initial four limbs of Patanjali's eight limbs of yoga set out in his Yoga Sutras some 2000 years ago. The first four limbs are yamas, niyamas, asanas, pranayama, followed by four further limbs, pratyahara, dharana, dhyana, samadhi, which are progressively advanced stages of meditation.

Here the start of the verse refers to three of the first four limbs. The yamas involve observance of prescribed ethical principles in relationships with people and things in the environment. Amongst other principles they proscribe violence, stealing, sexual licence and telling lies; they also discourage the acceptance of gifts.

Niyamas refer, among other things, to the regulation of personal conduct, prescribing purity, contentment, religious austerity, scriptural studies and devotion to God.

Pranayama involves breathing in and out, usually through the nose, with resistance imposed by closure of a nostril or partial closure of the vocal cords. This practice gradually calms the mind so that its control, without distraction, becomes easier at the next stage. Such control is essential for focusing attention inwardly and concentrating on, and developing contact with, God, located within the body of the individual soul.[2]

1. Chand.
2. Chand.

23 Agni, Vayu, Indra, Uma, Brahman – The Story of Realization

344.

It is said that Brahman won a victory for the gods [over the demons]. After that victory of Brahman's the gods became elated. They thought: this victory is ours, the glory is ours.

Kenopanishad 3.1

This verse is the beginning of a story which symbolically explains the nature of Reality. In every myth there is always a deep truth embedded. It is not given to us on a plate – we have to think it out for ourselves and, in so doing, make the Truth our own. We can appreciate the educational prowess of the great rishis (sages) who realized that a story is more memorable than a theoretical explanation. Even if students do not understand the story's symbolism immediately, it will stay with them, and the meaning may be revealed when they have travelled further along the spiritual path.

The scene begins after a battle between the gods and demons which the gods won with the help of the Supreme Being, Brahman. The gods and demons represent the good and evil forces operating in material existence. They are respectively the virtuous and vicious tendencies within us. The vicious tendencies agitate the mind with desires, dragging us into the vicious circle of rebirth. The virtuous tendencies calm the mind so it may progress along the spiritual path to Self-realization.

So when the gods are said to have triumphed over the demons the spiritual tendencies may be said to have triumphed over base material desires. That victory is, by definition, the victory of the

Supreme Spirit, Brahman. Brahman is the all-pervading Self. It
is the true nature of each one of us and of the Universe. It is the
ultimate goal of spiritual seeking.

But the virtuous forces within have only won a battle over the
vicious. They have not, so to speak, won the war – they have not
realized the Self. Therefore they think the victory is due to the
goodness of their personality rather than to the Ultimate Self
(Brahman) which is the powerhouse of personality.[1]

345.

*Brahman knew that the gods were vainglorious and appeared
before them. They did not know that venerable spirit.*

Kenopanishad 3.2

Brahman, the Self, knew that the virtuous personality was
celebrating its virtues as the cause of its spiritual progress.
Brahman made Itself visible to the individual. This symbolizes
the point in a person's spiritual journey at which he has got the
better of his desires and catches a glimmer of the Supreme Self
but only at a distance as something separate and unfamiliar.
'What is that?' the individual asks.[2]

346.

*The gods said to Agni [fire god], 'O Jatavedas [all-knower], find
out who that venerable spirit is.' He agreed.*

*Agni hastened to the spirit. The spirit asked him, 'Who are
you?' and Agni replied, 'I am Agni. I am omniscient.'*

Kenopanishad 3.3–4

The battle over desire has been won, the mind is tranquil, so the
virtuous personality (the gods) has seen an inkling of the
Supreme Self (the venerable spirit).

1. Parth.
2. Parth.

Agni, the fire god, is equated with ritual worship. He is the means by which offerings are made. He is also equated with speech – the illuminator and inflamer of human existence. Speech is one of the five organs of action and is often used in the Upanishads as shorthand for all the organs of action. The simplest and lowest form of worship is through the organs of action. It is the performance of ritual. This is the natural first approach to God: lighting candles, pilgrimage, offerings, etc.

So, in this story, the gods (the virtuous personality) start the quest to know the Spirit (Supreme Self) by delegating Agni (ritual worship) for the task. Agni is able to approach the Supreme Self who then asks him who he is and what he does. Now Agni is the god of all fire, so to stand next to Agni is a million times worse than standing next to a blazing furnace. We would know if we were standing next to Agni, yet this venerable spirit is oblivious to Agni's prowess.[1]

347.

'What power resides in you?' asked the spirit. 'Why, I can burn up everything. Whatever there is on this earth I can burn,' replied Agni.

The spirit put down a straw before him and said, 'Burn it.' Agni dashed at it but was unable to burn it. So Agni returned to the gods and said, 'I could not find out who that venerable spirit is.'

Kenopanishad 3.5–6

Unimpressed by Agni's self-introduction (see above), the spirit asks what he does and then challenges this unimaginable inferno to burn a straw. Agni cannot do this.

Why?

We can best understand this encounter if we imagine a floodlight meeting electricity. The electricity enquires into the floodlight's profession and is told, 'Why, I light up this entire stadium.'

'Well, just light up this corner here,' says the electricity.

1. Parth.

Try as the floodlight might, the corner remains in darkness. The electricity has cut itself off. The floodlight's unrecognized source of power is not delivering the goods. This is why Agni cannot burn the straw. Brahman, his source of power, has cut itself off. Nor was the 'venerable spirit' burned to a frazzle by the presence of Agni, any more than electricity could be blinded by the light of a floodlight.

Agni returns to the gods without realizing the true identity of the venerable spirit. If we commit our organs of action to spiritual activities they can lead us towards the Truth but they cannot realize it.[1]

348.

Then the gods said to Vayu [wind god], 'Vayu, find out who that venerable spirit is.' He agreed.

Vayu hastened to the spirit. The spirit asked him, 'Who are you?' Vayu replied, 'I am Vayu, Lord of the Wind.'

'What power resides in you?' asked the spirit. 'Why I can blow away everything in this world,' replied Vayu.

The spirit put a straw down before him and said, 'Blow it away.' Vayu dashed at it but was unable to blow it away, so he returned from there and said to the gods, 'I could not find out who that venerable spirit is.'

Kenopanishad 3.7–10

The organs of actions represented by Agni have failed to uncover the identity of the spirit (Brahman), so now the gods (the personality) turn to the wind god, Vayu. Vayu is lord of the vital breath (prana) which is associated with the five senses. So when Vayu is sent off to find out the identity of the spirit, the five senses are also being asked to find God. This is the second level of spiritual seeking, above mere action. We know it well. We surround ourselves with visual representations of God – statues, paintings, churches, temples and so. We try to hear Him through

1. Parth.

hymns. We try to smell Him through incense or taste Him with communion bread.

But just as the organs of action cannot catch God, the organs of perception cannot see, hear, touch, smell or taste God. But neither can they operate without God because he is the power that lies behind them, their first cause. So Vayu, Lord of the Wind, cannot blow away the straw any more than Agni could burn it.[1]

349.

Then the gods said to Indra [chief of gods], 'O Maghavan [bountiful], find out who this venerable spirit is.' He agreed and hastened to the spirit but it disappeared from him.

Kenopanishad 3.11

Neither the organs of action nor the organs of perception could find God, so now they send their ruler, Indra. Indra is the mind and intellect.

Indra approaches the unknown spirit but it disappears because we cannot capture Brahman with emotions or knowledge. We can feel religious ecstasy, we can know objectively the theory of the Absolute, but that is not *knowing* Brahman because Brahman is not an object. It is the subject. It is the experiencer, not the experienced, the knower, not the known.[2]

350.

In that very spot where the spirit was he beheld a wondrously beautiful woman, Uma, daughter of the Himalayas. Indra asked her, 'Who was that venerable spirit I saw just now?'

Kenopanishad 3.12

Having approached and lost sight of the spirit (Brahman), Indra

1. Parth.
2. Parth.

(the mind and intellect) encounters Uma, the daughter of the Himalayas, who is, of course, also a symbol. The great rishis (sages) retreated to the Himalayas to realize Brahman. Out of their realization was born the teachings of the Upanishads, so the daughter of the Himalayas is the Upanishads. The scriptures are always personified as women, as is the goddess of learning, Saraswati, because they nurture us with the patience of a mother. They forgive endlessly our mistakes and still continue to help us to grow.

We see that the mind and intellect (Indra), having approached and lost sight of the Supreme Spirit, does not go away but persists in its quest. It asks the Upanishads (Uma) to explain that spirit. The third section of the Kenopanishad ends here on the unanswered question, so students may reflect. It takes times for knowledge to dawn. The structure of the Kenopanishad imitates the structure of the realization process.[1]

351.

'Brahman,' she exclaimed. 'Indeed, through Brahman's victory you attained greatness.' Then he understood that spirit was Brahman.

Therefore, in truth, these gods – Agni, Vayu and Indra – excel the other gods for they came closest to the spirit and were the first to know It was Brahman.

Therefore, Indra indeed excels all other gods because he came closest to the spirit and was the first to know It was Brahman.

Kenopanishad 4.1–3

It is the mind and intellect (Indra) which discover the identity of Brahman, the Supreme Self, not through direct experience but through the Upanishads ... So our mind and intellect cannot, of themselves, feel or know Brahman but we can use them as the ultimate vehicle on the spiritual path. They can carry us through study of the scriptures until we are pushed beyond actions, perceptions and thought to realization.

1. Parth.

Agni, Vayu and Indra excel the other gods because they represent the three forms of worship which help us approach Brahman – ritual worship through the organs of action (chanting, pilgrimage, etc.), receptive worship through the organs of perception (perceiving God in a temple, a hymn, etc.) and devotional, thoughtful worship through the mind and intellect (study, meditation).

Indra (the mind and intellect) excels all the gods (senses) because it is Indra who can come closest to Brahman and, ultimately, lead the Self to realization.[1]

1. Parth.

24 Siddha – The Man of Perfection

352.

He who hates no creature, who is friendly and compassionate...
Bhagavad Gita 12.13

What is a spiritual person? This verse begins the list of thirty-five qualities which Krishna reveals to Arjuna as the qualities of a devotee. A person who possesses these qualities in full is, by definition, God(Self)-realized. To dedicate yourself to developing these qualities is to be a devotee.

1. 'He who hates no creature'. Now most of us will say we are well disposed towards the rest of the world. But can we say, without qualification, that there is no one single being we hate, or is there a 'but...' to our good feelings – a boss, a neighbour, a relative, a nation, a race that we cannot abide? The strength of a chain is in its weakest link. It is not how many people we love which counts, but how many we hate. If we hate even one person, that is our spiritual strength. The strength of the other links becomes irrelevant for, when the chain is used to haul us from the ocean of material existence, that weak link will snap.

It is knowledge that dispels hatred for then we understand that to hate another is to hate our self. The Atman (Eternal Self) within us is in all beings.

2. The second quality, that of friendliness, is the positive aspect of non-hatred. Not only does the spiritual person not hate, but he is friendly to all. Such friendliness is not based on expected reciprocation. Just as we care for our own body, so should we care for others. We do not turn against our body because it becomes sick or grows old and less beautiful or causes

us to feel pain. We respond with care and concern for it, however it acts.

3. We are all in a superior position to someone else. We may have more money or greater knowledge or better health or a happier family life. Whatever benefits we have, we should be ready to help another. It is not an act of pity, for it is to understand that a person's misfortune is a result of karmic action. He suffers as he has made another suffer. But we have all sinned and we have all suffered for it in accordance with the law of karma. Our compassion for others is that which we feel for our own mistakes and suffering.[1]

353.

. . . free from attachment and egotism . . .

Bhagavad Gita 12.13

4. The fourth quality of the spiritual person is non-possessiveness. He or she does not indulge in my-ness – my wife, my husband, my car, my house, my child – because such a person knows there is nothing that he can claim that is his. Anything that we do, anything we have, anything that we achieve, is the result of innumerable factors.

A million things happen – for which we can claim no credit – to make it possible for us to have a child. We can look at our own parents and their parents and so on, or at the rain and sun and soil which produce the food which feeds our digestive system which provides the raw materials for the production of a man's sperm and a woman's ovum. No matter where we start, the contributory factors for any event or achievement radiate out into infinity so it becomes absurd to announce that anything is 'mine'.

5. Freedom from egotism is a natural companion to freedom from attachment. Freedom from 'my-ness' is freedom from 'I-ness'. By understanding that whatever we do or have is a result of countless other beings' contribution, we understand that we are a spoke in the wheel. If we design a new model of a car it is a result

1. Parth.

of all the designs that have preceded it and of all the workers who built the cars so that the models could be tested and a market for cars created.[1]

354.

. . . balanced in pleasure and pain and forgiving.

Bhagavad Gita 12.13

6. To be 'balanced in pleasure and pain' is the state of detachment from the vicissitudes of life. It does not mean that we cease to feel joy and sorrow, simply that we should not be affected by them. They should not buffet us from our course of action. If we don't feel joy and sorrow, we are a plant. If we do feel them and are affected, we are an animal. If we feel them but are unaffected, we are a human being. The attitude is that everything in this material existence passes away so why cling to it?

7. Forgiveness is based on the simple understanding that the difference between the best of souls and the worst of sinners is the difference between the shining brass pot and the tarnished brass pot. The tarnished one is suffering from overexposure to the air. All it needs is a little Brasso and a polish and it will shine like the other pot. Where did the brilliance come from? Not from the Brasso. It is inherent in the brass. Similarly, the wicked man is suffering from overexposure to this world. All he needs is a little knowledge to polish his soul and his inherent divinity will shine as brilliantly as ever. We forgive the wicked deeds and personalities when we understand that they are impermanent. There is no point in clinging in anger to a mask, however offensive, covering that which is true and good.[2]

355.

Ever content, always a yogi . . .

Bhagavad Gita 12.14

1. Parth.
2. Parth.

8. The mind's nature is to desire endlessly. It is up to the intellect to realize there is no limit to desire even though our mind tells us, 'If only I could double my profits, then I would be happy,' or 'If only my daughter were married, then I'd be happy.' The mind does not see beyond the immediate desires to the next and the next and the next. The man in the wheelchair wants legs, the man with legs wants a scooter, the man with a scooter wants a car, the man with a car wants a Mercedes, the man with a Mercedes wants to avoid income tax and so it goes on. To be ever content is a mental state, not a licence to give up work and personal development.

9. The ninth quality, 'always a yogi', may also be translated 'always religious', for the roots of both words mean the same: to rejoin, to return to the origin. Every moment of a spiritual person's life is spent getting back to his original Self. If an activity does not faciliate this, it is not worth doing. Again, this must not be misinterpreted as necessitating a withdrawal from worldly activities. You may play sport to ensure your body and mind are fit for learning. You may earn a living so you can afford to study and grow in knowledge.[1]

356.

> ... *self-controlled, of firm resolve, with mind and intellect dedicated to Me, he, my devotee, is dear to Me.*
>
> Bhagavad Gita 12.14

Krishna continues his description of the person who is 'dear to Me' - in other words, he who has returned to the true Self.

10. The quality of self-control is often misconstrued as self-denial, but self-denial for its own sake is pointless. Self-control refers to unswerving effort towards Self-realization. Any action taking us away from that goal is a violation of self-control, but as long as an activity does not interfere with this, there is no reason not to do it.

11. 'Firm resolve' to finish what we start is the active principle which gives strength to self-control, driving us towards the ultimate goal or the completion of any task we set ourselves.

1. Parth.

12. 'Mind and intellect dedicated to Me' is a blend of mind and intellect – heart and head – focused on the Self; this action will take us back to that Self. We must understand what we feel and feel what we understand, otherwise neither knowledge nor feelings are ours and we remain far from our true Self.[1]

357.

He by whom the world is not agitated and who is not agitated by the world, who is free from joy, envy, fear and anxiety, he is dear to Me.

Bhagavad Gita 12.15

13. Today you are agitated by someone, you resent them, you are made anxious by them because they have desires which infringe upon yours. It may be that they want something directly from you – money or emotional support – or it may be that they want something you also want – they compete with you for business or popularity or love. No doubt the feelings of agitation are mutual.

If we consider those who are free of egocentric desires we see that there is nothing they want from another being; nor do they compete with another being. Such people do not agitate the world, rather, they are greatly loved for they are givers not takers. Their attitude is not 'What can you do for me?' but 'What can I do for you?'

14. Similarly, the spiritual person is not agitated by the world for denying him the fulfilment of some desire. He is independent of the ups and downs of life because he is independent of his own feelings, thoughts and perceptions. Even the wealthy man who is not self-sufficient in this way is a prisoner of his own desires. The bars may be made of gold but they are still bars.

15. Joy, envy, fear and anxiety are the products of material bondage. Those who revel in blessed self-sufficiency have no need to envy others for having more than they, nor to fear losing what they have, nor to be anxious that they may not get what they

1. Parth.

desire. Such people are 'dear to Me' because they are close to the Supreme Self (Atman).[1]

358.

He who is free from expectations . . .

Bhagavad Gita 12.16

16. There is a story in the Puranas of Lord Shiva and his consort, Parvati, visiting a devotee of Shiva. Parvati had insisted they did so after observing how poor and tattered the devotee looked. Shiva had assured her that the man wanted for nothing and would ask for nothing but, on Parvati's insistence, he finally agreed to go down to the man and offer him a boon. As Shiva predicted, the devotee, who was sitting mending his clothes, thanked the Lord but said with surprise, 'What is there that you have not already given me?' Urged on by Parvati, Shiva insisted that the devotee choose a boon. The devotee's eyes fell on his hands as they sewed his clothes and he said, 'I ask that when I stitch my clothes, the thread will follow the needle.'

The devotee asked for what he had already because the Self-realized person wants for nothing. He or she has no expectations of more. Such people are like the ocean. All the rivers of the world can run into the ocean and it makes no difference for the ocean is already full.[2]

359.

. . . pure, expert, unconcerned, untroubled, renouncing all under-takings – he, my devotee, is dear to Me.

Bhagavad Gita 12.16

17. The Self-realized person is pure. His body, mind and

1. Parth.
2. Parth.

intellect are cleansed of their respective material sediments so the eternal light of the Self shines clearly.

18. A Self-realized person is skilful in all things. He is expert, clever, alert, prompt and attentive because his actions are not disturbed by regrets of the past or desire for future benefits. He is perfectly concentrated on each action as it is performed.

19. He is unconcerned with happenings of the world because he is focused on something higher.

20. He is untroubled because he has no expectations to be frustrated.

21. He renounces all undertakings because he understands that everything done is part of a totality. To claim responsibility for something he has done or made is like taking a bucket of water from the Ganges and pouring it back in, announcing, 'I inaugurate the Ganges.'[1]

360.

He who neither rejoices nor hates, neither grieves nor desires, renouncing good and evil, full of devotion, he is dear to Me.
                                                    Bhagavad Gita 12.17

22. We are replete with likes and dislikes from our early childhood which determine our present activities. They take us towards what we like and away from what we dislike, rejoicing in the former, hating the latter. But our likes and dislikes are not the right criteria for determining action that is in our best interests. They are not based on an understanding of the material nature we have acquired in this life and so will not help us realize our true Self. They are a conglomeration of irrationally collected desires. Just as a diabetic may crave sweets despite the fact that they are the worst thing for him, so we may have a taste for the means of our own undoing. The Self cannot be realized with these likes and dislikes cluttering our inner vision.

23. The Self-realized person does not grieve for what was done or not done in the past, thinking, 'If only I had done this or that I would be happy now.'

1. Parth.

24. By the same token he does not harbour desires which he believes will bring future happiness. Happiness does not depend on certain arrangements of the material world in our favour but on our spiritual state. If we rely on the material world we find there is always one more thing we desire before we can be happy.

25. A devotee renounces good and evil in the sense that he is unaffected by them. The nature of the material world is dualistic. Good has no meaning without evil, tall has no meaning without short, pleasant is defined by unpleasant and so on. It is in accord with our material nature to enjoy the variety of the dualistic world, but we should enjoy without being affected. Only then can we be 'full of devotion' – devoted to the ultimate Truth.[1]

361.

Alike to friend and foe and also in honour and dishonour, alike to heat and cold, in pleasure and pain, free from attachment.

Bhagavad Gita 12.18

26. The attitude of the spiritual person should be egalitarian towards all beings. We should look upon a cobra with the same pleasant feelings as we look upon a small kitten. Both are beautiful in their own right. This does not mean we should deal with them in the same way. Obviously, you pick up a little kitten but not a cobra and, in the same manner, you treat a person with a gentle nature differently from someone with a harmful nature. The key is to understand the nature of a being, accept him as such and treat him wisely but with love. So many difficulties arise from the attitude which asks, 'Why isn't the lily like an oak?'

27. This equanimity should follow through in our response to the world's approach to us. The fickle swings in public opinion from acclaim to disdain should have no effect on our view of our self or the world. These are the fluctuations of the mind, just as heat and cold, pleasure and pain are fluctuations of the body.

28. Free from attachment we participate in life without becoming embroiled in it. Left to its own devices our material shell will attach itself to whatever it can – wife, family, business,

1. Parth.

money, power or a swami. With attachment comes unhappiness because we immediately begin to fear loss or harm to the object of attachment. For instance, we are ever anxious that our car will be bumped or scratched. In a hired car we drive in peace because we have no attachment to the car. Thus we should behave to all our possessions as though they were hired objects in which we have no stake. We can enjoy them without them becoming an extension of the material body, binding us ever more tightly to the material sphere.[1]

362.

To whom censure and praise are equal, silent...

Bhagavad Gita 12.19

29. This verse deals with fluctuations in the intellectual dimension of life as the previous verse dealt with swings of perception by mind and body. The principle remains the same, that we stay balanced in our self much as a lighthouse shining in the darkness, whether a stormy sea lashes it or its light is reflected in a tranquil sea.

30. To be silent means to understand the horrors and usurious nature of the world without having to comment. Although this is taken by some to advocate literal silence, it is a state of mind that Krishna is advising. We should behave as an actor on stage. The actor speaks as is required of his character but adds no comments of his own because he understands that, in truth, he is separate from the events on the stage.[2]

363.

... content with anything, homeless, steady-minded, full of devotion – that man is dear to me.

Bhagavad Gita 12.19

1. Parth.
2. Parth.

31. A person is 'content with anything' when he has fulfilled the ultimate purpose of life – Self-realization. It is a state of extreme contentment, complementing the state mentioned earlier (see pp. 276–7) which refers to contentment with material circumstances.

32. To be homeless is an attitude rather than a physical requirement. It is not necessary to sell your home tomorrow to be homeless. Your home should be as a hotel to you – a place where you stay and which is kept clean and tidy. You appreciate it and pay attention to its state but it does not become an extra material coating for you. Similarly, your family, which is the heart of your home, should receive your care and concern without being draped over your personality.

33. A steady mind is a natural consequence of cleaning away desires and fixing the mind and intellect on higher knowledge. With the mind steadied in this manner, you will not speak or act impulsively or on the basis of selfish fancies.[1]

364.

They, indeed, who follow this set of eternal principles as declared, worship Me with faith, regarding Me as the Supreme – those devotees are exceedingly dear to Me.

Bhagavad Gita 12.20

34. The word sraddha (faith) carries a meaning easily misunderstood. To worship with sraddha is the capacity to take ideas, reflect upon them until we have assimilated them as our own and then to be transformed by the learning.

35. The final attribute, 'regarding Me as the Supreme', is to know that the Atman in each of us is Supreme. This is the fourth and highest stage of Consciousness when we have fully awakened from the dream of material existence. Then are we exceedingly dear to Krishna because we are one with him. We have returned to our Self.

Between them, these thirty-five attributes define a *bhakta*

1. Parth.

The Essential Teachings of Hinduism

(devotee) who has become Self-realized. The degree to which we develop these qualities is the degree to which we have developed toward Self-realization, the degree to which we are 'dear' to that Self.

The definition of a bhakta has been divided into qualities for our understanding but, in truth, they are all aspects of the one state. If you take one or two of these qualities to practise in your life you will find that the other qualities develop accordingly, just as water poured into the river at any point will raise the level at all points.[1]

365.

... Of all secrets I am silence ...

Bhagavad Gita 10.38

Aum   Aum   Aum

---

1. Parth.

Bibliography

Direct Sources

Parthasarathy, A., *The Vedanta Treatise*, Vedanta Life Institute: la Landsend, Malabar Hill, Bombay 400006, 1984 (2nd edn).

Parthasarathy, A., *Atmabodha (Commentary)*, Vedanta Life Institute, 1971.

Parthasarathy, A., *The Symbolism of Hindu Gods and Rituals*, Vedanta Life Institute, 1983.

Parthasarathy, A., *Lectures on the Bhagavad Gita*, taped recordings, Vedanta Life Institute.

Parthasarathy, A., *Lectures on the Kenopanishad, Isavasyopanishad and Kaivalyopanishad*, taped recordings, Vedanta Life Institute.

Dayton, Brandt, *Practical Vedanta – Selected Works of Swami Rama Tirtha*, Himalayan International Institute of Yoga Science and Philosophy, Pennsylvania, 1978.

Prabhupada, Swami, *Bhagavad-Gita as It Is*, Bhaktivedanta Book Trust, West Germany, 1983.

Ramyana, with commentaries by Tilaka, Siromani and Bhusana, Gujerati Printing Press, Bombay, 1882.

Suddhasatwananda, Swami, *Thus Spake Ramakrishna*, Sri Ramakrishna Math, Madras, 1972.

Suddhasatwananda, Swami, *Thus Spake Vivekananda*, Sri Ramakrishna Math, Madras, 1975.

Indirect Sources and Background

Bose, A. C., *The Call of the Vedas*, Bhratiya Vidya Bhavan, Bombay, 1970.

Easwaran, Eknath, *Gandhi the Man*, Turnstone Press, Wellingborough, 1983.

Gambhirananda, Swami, *Eight Upanishads*, vols. I and II, Advaita Ashrama, Calcutta, 1958.

Gelberg, Steven J., *Hare Krishna, Hare Krishna*, Grove Press, New York, 1983.

Hinnells, John R., *A Handbook of Living Religions*, Penguin Books, Harmondsworth, 1984.

Ling, Trevor, *A History of Religion East and West*, Macmillan, London, 1968.

Madhavananda, Swami (trans.), *Brhadaranyaka Upanishad*, Advaita Ashrama, Himalayas, 1950.

Prabhupada, Swami, *Srimad Bhagavatam*, Bhaktivedanta Book Trust, California, 1977.

Radhakrishnan, Sir Sarvepalli, *The Thirteen Principal Upanishads* (ed. R. E. Hume), Oxford University Press, 1921.

Stutley, Margaret and James, *A Dictionary of Hinduism*, Routledge & Kegan Paul, London, 1977.

Vireswarananda and Adidevananda, Swamis, *Brahma-Sutras According to Sri Ramanuja*, Advaita Ashrama, Calcutta, 1978.

Zaehner, R. C., *Hinduism*, Oxford University Press, 1962.

Zaehner, R. C., *Hindu Scriptures*, Everyman Library, London, 1967.

Some Other Rider Titles

Autobiography of a Yogi

Paramahansa Yogananda

Paramahansa Yogananda was the first great master of India to live in the West for a long period (over thirty years). In this book he explains with scientific clarity the subtle but definite laws by which yogis perform miracles and attain self-mastery. A graduate of Calcutta University, Yogananda writes with unforgettable sincerity and incisive wit.

'There has been nothing before, written in English or in any other European language, like this presentation of Yoga.'

Columbia University Press

'A fascinating and clearly annotated study.'

Newsweek

'I met Paramahansa Yogananda in Calcutta in 1935. I have been following the accounts of his activities in America ever since. As a bright light shining in the midst of darkness, so was Yogananda's presence in this world. Such a great soul comes on earth only rarely, when there is a real need among men.'

His Holiness the Shankaracharya of Kanchipuram, revered spiritual leader of millions in South India.

£5.95 Paperback
0 7126 1424 9

Opening to Inner Light
The Transformation of Human Consciousness

Ralph Metzner, Ph.D.

Written by one of the foremost figures of the Californian human potential movement and author of the well-known book *Maps of Consciousness, Opening to Inner Light* is a study of how the various and variegated spiritual traditions of mankind have sought to achieve 'enlightenment' and how the use of symbols and images reveal a common understanding of the human condition and the processes of transcendence.

£5.95 Paperback
0 7126 1558 X

The Hidden Teaching Beyond Yoga

Paul Brunton

One of the late Dr Paul Brunton's last books in which he suggests that there is a mystic teaching underlying all forms of yoga, and far more profound than any of them. The author explains that there has been in existence in Asia, for many thousands of years, a hidden doctrine which was originally intended for an intellectual elite but for which the world is now ready.

In this book Dr Brunton begins the process of revealing this teaching which harmonizes the mysticism of yoga with the deepest insights of modern science.

'The fruits of rich experience and a rare and sympathetic insight into the hitherto obscure wisdom of the Orient.'

Illustrated Weekly of India

'He argues his thesis with the least possible ambiguity in untechnical language.'

The Times Literary Supplement

£7.95 Paperback
0 7126 1550 4

The Inner Reality

Paul Brunton

In these linked essays Dr Brunton deals with a wide range of topics from *What is God?* to *The Gospel of St John*, from *Practical Help in Yoga*, to *The Mystery of Jesus*.

Underlying all his writing is a profound simplicity, a refusal to blur his ideas to conform to conventional doctrine, and a deep understanding of the inner meaning of Yoga. *Inner Reality* reveals Brunton at his best.

'Paul Brunton has a profound knowledge of metaphysics and the ability to express in understandable language much of its deeper aspects'.

Psychic News

£6.95 Paperback
0 7126 1577 6

'Miracles Are My Visiting Cards'
An Investigative Report on the Psychic Phenomena
Associated With Sathya Sai Baba

Erlendur Haraldsson

To millions of Indians, Sathya Sai Baba is an *avatar*, a
messenger of God. For decades he has taught and
healed and performed – or appears to have performed –
extraordinary miracles.

Professor Erlendur Haraldsson has been investigating
Sai Baba's 'miracles' for many years and now publishes
his assessment in full.

£6.95 Paperback
0 7126 1514 8

The Complete Yoga Book

James Hewitt

The Complete Yoga Book is an encyclopedia of yoga practice and practical yoga as well as of the philosophy and background of yoga. It is divided into three sections.

The first of these is concerned with raising the levels of health and energy through breathing. The second section constitutes one of the most important guides ever published of the *Asanas,* or postures of yoga. Clear, easy to follow instructions and drawings accompany Hewitt's descriptions of over 400 postures. The author includes warm-ups and many modifications of basic postures for beginners or those with specific problems. The third section deals with the history and philosophy of yoga and surveys in depth the various meditative methods including transcendental meditation. He discusses the possession of psychic powers and the potentialities of bio-feedback and relates all these developments to the classic techniques of meditation and yoga.

'Hewitt's book... is well organized and a marvel of description in Western English... excellent as a reference book...

Choice

£9.95 Paperback
0 7126 1143 6

The Complete Relaxation Book

James Hewitt

Stress is a major cause of disease today. This book is a manual of instruction in the art of relaxation. Based on thirty years of study and experience, it is a unique synthesis of the techniques of Western therapies and Eastern mysticism.

James Hewitt starts with a survey of those empirical, Western relaxation techniques which yield physical and emotional benefits: progressive relaxation, self-hypnosis, authogenic training, biofeedbck, and posture and breathing exercises. These exercises relax tense minds as well as tense muscles, and open up the possibility of 'peak experiences'. Carried over into everyday life, the deep psycho-physical relaxation they induce leads to enhanced, 'poised', living and integrated well-being.

He then turns to an examination of Oriental techniques such as Yoga, Zen and other Buddhist methods. The reader can then find the technique most suited to his temperament and situation. (*Previously published as 'Relaxation East and West'*)

£6.95 Paperback
0 7126 1423 0

Uncommon Wisdom
Conversations with Remarkable People

Fritjof Capra

The famous author of *The Tao of Physics* explores the emerging intellectual and spiritual trends which are changing our relationship to nature and our understanding of health, economic growth, science and spirituality. In his discussions with some of the wisest teachers and scientists of our time – such as J. Krishnamurti, Werner Heisenberg, R.D. Laing, E.F. Schumacher, Carl Simonton, Hazel Henderson, Gregory Bateson and others – Capra makes clear the overall shape of a new world view. This is a stimulating and rewarding book, highly readable yet profound.

£12.95 Hardback
0 7126 1634 9